Behavior Science
Translation

Phrayā Rajathon

Phya Anuman Rajadhon

Life and Ritual in Old Siam

Three Studies of Thai Life and Customs

Translated and Edited by

WILLIAM J. GEDNEY

HRAF PRESS NEW HAVEN

Library of Congress Catalog Card Number: 61-13465
© Copyright 1961
Human Relations Area Files
New Haven, Conn.
All Rights Reserved

Two of the three studies in this volume have appeared in the original Thai. "Life of the Farmer" was published in 1948 by Luang Arthaprichachanu-pakarn as an act of merit-making at the cremation of his mother, Mme. Phiw Chatinanthana, and "Customs Connected with Birth and the Rearing of Children" was published in 1949 in similar circumstances (see preface on page 101). The translations were begun in 1952 by William J. Gedney for the Human Relations Area Files and submitted to Phya Anuman for comment (his amplifying remarks have been incorporated in the footnotes). In 1955, the Yale University Southeast Asia Studies with the permission of HRAF mim-eographed a limited number of copies of "Life of the Farmer" for inclusion in its translation series. "Customs Connected with Birth and the Rearing of Chil-dren" is published here for the first time in English.

The history of "Popular Buddhism in Thailand" is somewhat different in that it was written by Phya Anuman in English. The manuscript came to the attention of Robert B. Textor, Research Associate in Anthropology and South-east Asia Studies at Yale University, who urged that it be given to Dr. Gedney for editing and published with the other two studies in this volume.

The contribution of Dr. Gedney to this volume is second only to that of the author himself. Having finished the original translations several years ago, Dr. Gedney submitted the manuscripts to a most painstaking scrutiny and re-editing. Dr. Gedney, who is presently Professor of English and Southeast Asian Languages at the University of Michigan, brings to his work as a Thai scholar a background which few Americans can equal including six and a half years residence in Thailand and a total of eighteen years devoted to the study of the Thai language.

In addition to guiding us to the manuscript of "Popular Buddhism in Thailand," Dr. Textor offered us the use of the many photographs he had taken in the village of Bang Chan in central Thailand (see the photographic section following page 98) and gave generously of his time both to advise us on our selection and to write the captions.

The drawings of farm implements appended to "Life of the Farmer" were made for HRAF by Gary Vescelius from sketches supplied by Phya Anuman with some additional details from photographs and from consultation with per-sons familiar with Thai farm implements.

The photograph on the cover, of the Wat Rajabophit Monastery in Bangkok, originally appeared in Cultures of Thailand by Phya Anuman Rajadhon (Thailand Culture Series, National Culture Institute, Bangkok, 1953) and is used here by permission.

Publication of this volume was made possible in part through the finan-cial assistance of the Asia Society, whose aid is gratefully acknowledged.

v

Preface

Phya Anuman Rajadhon occupies, or rather has created for himself, a position in the field of Thai letters and scholarship which is unique and paradoxical. Though he is not an academician by training, his scholarly attainments have placed all younger teachers and students at his feet and made him one of Thailand's most highly respected university professors. Though he is not a trained anthropologist, no one has made so great a contribution as he to the study of traditional Thai culture. Though he is not primarily a student of language and literature, no one can proceed very far in Thai philological or literary studies before he has to seek enlightenment from the contributions which Phya Anuman has made in these fields. Though he is not a product of Western education, hardly anyone has done more than he to introduce and popularize Western learning among the Thai. Though he is much more than a popular author, one could hardly find a professional writer in Thailand who can match the grace and wit of his prose style. Most astonishing of all, though he is not a Thai by ancestry, no student of Thai culture, history, literature, and language has displayed greater devotion to these fields.

The translator of any of Phya Anuman's prolific writings is faced with two conflicting aims. On the one hand, he wants to render the content as accurately as possible, since foreign readers are likely to be most interested in the factual material that he presents; on the other, he would like to preserve as much as possible of the delightful flavor of the author's prose style, which has all the vigor and pungency of the best conversational language. In the translations presented here it is to be feared that the latter desideratum has had to suffer at the expense of the former.

Thai terms are transcribed in the phonemic system devised by Professor Mary Haas as revised by her in Thai Reader (American Council of Learned Societies, Washington, D.C., 1954).

William J. Gedney

Ann Arbor, Michigan
May 1961

Table of Contents

Drawings (following page 58)

Water Wheels and Water Scoops
Plows and Yokes
Smaller Farm Implements
Threshing, Pounding, Milling, Winnowing, and
    Measuring Implements

Photographs (following page 98)

A Village Wedding: Informal Merrymaking on the Side
Merit-making: Never Too Young
Merit-making: Never Too Old
Procession to the Ordination
Ordination: Supreme Moment
Pilgrimage: Memorable Period in the Annual Cycle
Topknot Cutting

THE LIFE OF THE FARMER

Introduction

I will tell about farming, which everyone knows and can tell about. It seems at first glance that farming is a simple matter; everyone knows about it, just as everyone knows how to cook rice, the daily duty of the housewife. If anyone wants to know about it, he can ask questions himself; it is not necessary to explain it. Therefore no one has written a book on this subject, since no one would want it. It is true that there are books on auspices, or textbooks on modern agriculture and its superiority to old farming methods. But these do not help us to understand the life of the farmer, and so I have written a book about farmers as they were in the old times.

I feel that no story is so hard to tell as the story of farming. If one were to make comparison, it is like telling the story of oxen and buffaloes; if you make an error, even children know you are wrong. Moreover it is a simple, unexciting subject, which everyone knows. It is much better to tell about lions or nymphs, because if you make a mistake, no one knows it, for these exist only in legends and no one would dare say you were wrong. Or if you tell about camels or seals it is still better than telling about oxen and buffaloes, because these animals do not exist in our country. Even if we have never seen them, we have books written by others, and it is easy to write from them without being afraid of making a mistake. Also people prefer to listen, because it is unusual, whereas the subject of oxen and buffaloes is like "grass at the gate of the pen"; it is easy and yet it is difficult.

But let us try. We will tell the story of farming from the point of view of the observer, not from the point of view of one who knows or one who performs. Those of you who were once farmers, but have long ago abandoned farming to seek your fortune in the city, when you hear the story of farming which I, who have never been a farmer, am telling here, it may remind you of the past and refresh your memory to some extent. Also, you will undoubtedly know where my account is deficient or mistaken. I beg that you be so kind as to inform me; I will be very grateful. This is the situation. One might say that it is as if I who have never given birth to a child, and am one who will absolutely never have an opportunity to, were to be so bold as to tell women about childbirth. It feels rather odd, and so I must make my excuses in advance.

For the story of farming, Phrá Thewa Phinimmit (Chaaj Theewaaphínimmíd) has kindly noted down his memories of farming among the people of Nakhon Ratchasima. I have used these notes as data for relating the story of farming, together with the verbal accounts of many other friends who have seen farming and have been kind enough to explain farming to me. I wish to thank all of these people at this time.

Fine Arts Department
Bangkok, Thailand
11 February, 1948

Phya Anuman Rajadhon

Table of Contents

THE LIFE OF THE FARMER

The City and the Country

Not too far out from the city, one sees great vacant space as far as the eye can reach; clumps of trees rise at irregular intervals. In the extreme distance one sees the treetops looking as if placed in orderly rows. The sky is clear to the distant horizon. The scene is quiet and lonely, with only the sound of crows and the sound of the wind blowing from time to time. At long intervals one sees a few people in the distance. The air one breathes feels pure and fresh. This is the condition of the meadows and fields outside of town; their characteristics are just the opposite of those of the city. In the city there are many people; whatever places are gathering points for people are crowded with thronging humans. There is a deafening din of people and of cars almost all the time. One cannot see anything at a distance, for buildings and shops and houses intervene almost everywhere. The atmosphere is hot and oppressive and impure; one breathes with difficulty. Foul and rotten odors assail the nose frequently. Some places are disgustingly dirty and cluttered. Life in the city and life in the country offer sharp contrasts. One is close to nature; the other is remote from nature. One is the source of food and health; the other is a place where people gather to share their food, and disease germs. To say only this much makes it appear that in the city there is only evil, not to be compared with the country. Actually if one were to speak of the good points, the city has many advantages over the country, because the center of progress is in the city. If this progress spreads to the country in appropriate proportions, one can say that the nation, both city and country, achieves prosperity. If the city is selfish to too great a degree -- seeking only to accumulate wealth to provide entertainment and comfort for itself, becoming remote from nature and never glancing toward the country -- the progress of the city will be like a light that flares up only for a moment and then goes out for lack of fuel, that is to say, food. The country has the function of producing food to feed the city. Therefore the city has to depend upon the country for sustenance. To speak of the country, people living too close to nature will have the living conditions of nature. Whatever life is like, it continues so, with no progress upward and forward, because the country must depend upon the wealth, intelligence, and power of the city for maintenance and improvement in order that the country may advance and grow toward prosperity. World civilization and progress in the history of various nations depend upon both city and country. Each depends upon the other, and neither is better or worse than the other. If there are tools but no rice, or rice but no tools, there is hardship. Therefore in Thai it is said that nation and possessions [the expression for "possessions" is literally

"rice and things"] go hand in hand; if separated, neither nation nor possessions exist fully.

City people call people outside the city "countryfolk." When one
speaks the word "country" he thinks at once of backwardness both in wealth
and in knowledge, but if city people did not have country people to help
them, they could not live, for they would have no rice to eat, and would
have no riches or happiness. For this reason we should share our knowledge
and our wealth with the country people; thus we help the nation and help ourselves at one and the same time, for the people together form the nation.
If one divides them broadly as I do, there are only two groups, the city people and the country people. I will use the term country people [literally,
people of rural areas] instead of the term countryfolk [literally, people of
outside areas] to avoid unpleasant connotations in the story that I will tell,
namely, the story of the life of farmers and country people, who are the majority of the population of the country and who are the part of the population
that renders the country prosperous in food by farming, the oldest and most
widespread industry of mankind.

If you spread out a map of the country and look at it, cities are located
at points where they draw little circles. The big cities are big circles, and
small cities are small circles. Outside these circles is an area outside the
cities; the area is great. If you take the cities, where a great many people
live, put them together, and compare them with the area which is not city,
anyone can see at once that the area which is city is many times less than the
area which is not city. These non-city areas, aside from forests, mountains,
streams, and lakes, are orchards and gardens and farms, made by the country
people to plant crops and sustain themselves, from ancient times down to the
present. Because of the fact that the country people settle in broad areas,
since they must use much land in making a living, people live in clusters far
apart from each other, causing one to feel that the number of country people
is less than the number of city people. Actually if all country people were
assembled together, they would outnumber city people by nine or ten times.
They are the majority of the population of the country.

When we say that the country people constitute the largest part of the
population of the country or, as they say, the backbone of the country, this
is usually an end of the matter. No one is interested in knowing about country people, except to have them farm much and produce much rice, to feed
the centers of population, namely, the cities. As for the life of country people and the difference between their conditions and beliefs and amusements
and those of city people, no one seems much interested, for it is a question of
country people, who could not possibly have anything better than city people.
Whatever the country people think or believe is old-fashioned, unchanged
with the times. This is true, but the majority of country people live in small
groups, not large groups like city people, because none of them has an

opportunity to become acquainted with other people to open his ears and eyes, surrounding circumstances limiting him. Whatever country people have done and believed in the past with satisfactory results, they continue to do and believe, not changing readily. It is as if we had always used our own tools until we are handy with them; if we replace them suddenly with new tools it is like an about-face; we have not sufficient time to adapt ourselves. Such change causes confusion among the country people, for the old familiar tools are destroyed before use of the new tools has been learned; this amounts to destroying good things without providing anything better, so that the only door is broken. For this reason the country people advance slowly. Alone, they do not dare change the old for the new because they are unsure, differing from the city people who have seen things of various kinds and so advance quickly; but sometimes they misstep, because of advancing too fast. Therefore it is said, "Knowledge of the life of mankind, from the remote past down to the present, besides helping us to predict the future, shows us our duty toward the world, which each of us finally must leave more beautiful than when we first found it."[1]

Preparing the Fields

In telling about farming, I will speak first of the characteristics of the rice fields. A field is a flat piece of land with a ridge of earth all around it for holding water to nourish the rice plants. Each field so marked off by ridges is called ꞇan naa, or kàbîŋ naa or tàbîŋ naa. The classifier for fields used in old books, such as Chronicles of the City of Nakhon Sithammarat (version of Village Headman Naaj Khǎaw), is tàbîŋ. Each field is usually rectangular in shape, sometimes large and sometimes small depending upon the area divided up. If the field is very big, it is necessary to work many days in plowing it. The lower end of the field is not always rectangular, because of adjoining hills, trees, marshes, or canals. This area is left over, but cannot be allowed to go to waste; a ridge is made around it according to the shape of the area. If a field has a long slender shape like a flag it is called naa sîaw. If one side is long and straight but the other side is curved, the long straight side is called wɛɛŋ and the curved side is called rúŋ, while the other two sides are called kwâaŋ as in normal fields; this sort of field is called naa rúŋ naa wɛɛŋ, but at present the word rúŋ has come to refer to the side or kwâaŋ. There are also fields with ridges of small size; these are usually sowing fields, in low places. In the wet season they are flooded for a long time, and it is not necessary to make strong water barriers, but only to divide the fields to keep separate various sorts of rice that are sown, and to serve as paths for walking. In the hot season, during the fourth and fifth lunar months, the fields are dry, and not a drop of water is to be found. In the fields one sees nothing but rice stubble everywhere, and some places are burned over in black strips, sometimes still burning. They set fire to the rice stubble in the fields to burn the rice straw and turn it to ashes to provide fertilizer for the fields again, for these fields are rainwater fields, incapable of receiving sediment from the river water which overflows its banks and provides fertilizer.

Implements used in farming are the plow and the harrow, which everyone has seen. In the farming season one sees oxen or buffaloes drawing the plow through the fields, with a person holding the plow and following along behind. You have no doubt already seen such a plow. It is a curved piece of wood waist-high. One part is called the khan jaam; the end which the plowman holds is called hǎaŋ jaam. There is another part with a hole in it to fasten it to the lower part of the khan jaam, curving forward to join the ʔɛ̀ɛg nɔ́ɔj, which has two ropes tied to it. Beyond this is the ox or buffalo that draws the plow. This curved wood is called the khan of the plow, and the rope tied to the ʔɛ̀ɛg nɔ́ɔj is called the khlâw rope. The bottom part of the plow appears from time to time in the water and earth; at the time of plowing lumps of earth form along the forward edge, which is a thick piece of wood about one-half meter long, the front of which curves up like a shoe and is called the "pighead." The upper part is a high projecting piece for cutting the earth, called the pighead blade. At the end of the pighead there is a piece of iron, triangular in shape and a little larger than the palm of the hand, fitted over the end of the wood, for jabbing the earth and breaking it apart so that it can be easily turned up. This iron is called the phǎan of the plow, or in some localities the pàkhǎaŋ. The plow as well as the harrow are made by the farmers for their own use, except for the phǎan iron which must be bought. These are bought from traders having oxcarts loaded with various sorts of iron, including phǎan, knives, hoes (cɔ̀ɔb), spades (sǐam), 2 etc. They come from provinces where there are people who mine iron ore and do blacksmithing for a living, such as the province of Loei. In the dry season during the third lunar month, merchants bring iron articles in oxcarts to sell among the villages, coming in groups of nine or ten carts. When they arrive at a village they stop and sell there. Whatever kind of iron implement the peasant needs, he buys at the oxcart parking lot, which is called the "oxcart dock." In every province there are regular places for this. When the traders have finished selling at one village, they move on to another. When they are sold out, if they see anything that strikes their fancy, they buy it and take it away either to sell or to use. What I have described is the story of people's trading in former times. Trading was originally like this, whether the transport was oxcart or beast of burden or carrying pole, or boats along waterways. Upon arriving in a village, a trader would stop and sell for many days, moving on to other places as the situation demanded until sold out. There was no trader serving as middleman to purchase goods wholesale for resale later as nowadays.

Farming may be said to begin at the waxing phase of the fourth lunar month, for beginning at that time the farmers prepare their farming equipment such as plows and harrows to await the auspicious day to conduct the first plowing ceremony. This is a day in the fourth lunar month, and they seem to choose even-numbered rather than odd-numbered days. They find the day in a textbook. [3] If they have no textbook, they borrow one and memorize it or copy it out, or ask those who know. This textbook is apparently obtained from monks learned in astrology and is therefore most likely to be found in monasteries. Anyone who can read and write goes and copies it out in a Thai folding book, and it is then copied again and again. It is a book in the same category as textbooks of medicines and textbooks on methods of worshiping spirits. Textbooks of this sort are found everywhere and are called household textbooks. If the villagers have a government calendar, they usually accept the first plowing day given in the calendar. As for the time, in bygone days when the textbook gave the time in hours and minutes it was not convenient, for the old-time farmers had no clocks to watch the time. Therefore they used the Indian method of telling time in stages of sunshine; that is, they measured the length of their own shadows by the number of consecutive footlengths. The number of times one had to set his foot down to equal the length of the shadow was the number of stages of sunshine. In the morning when the sun had just risen, the shadow in the open sunlight would be longer than in the late morning. They measured their own shadows with their feet, and the number of footlengths gave so many stages of sunshine.

Before the auspicious hour they built a temporary shrine to the guardian spirit of the field, called an eye-level shrine, in a place near the field appointed as the place of the first plowing. They had to prepare both objects of worship and offerings. This eye-level shrine was built only firmly enough to serve temporarily as a shrine. They used six bamboos planted as pillars, as high as eye-level, with crosspieces tied with creepers. The shrine had the form of a high rectangular platform of no very great size, only sufficient to lay the objects of worship and the offerings. The floor of the shrine was made of bamboos laid in a row, or they might be split and flattened. If it was not firm and steady they used creepers or strips of bamboo to tie it; one need not speak of nails, for they had none. What has been described was the usual method of building. If they could not find bamboo, they could use other wood; it was a question of using whatever they had, without limitations. The same was true of offerings; whatever they had to eat, they offered, as chance might afford, or as the popular phrase is, "prawn salad or fish salad." There had to be an offering of rice; this could not be omitted. They were required always to use the top rice of the pot. These offerings were arranged in a flat basket, or at the very least laid on flat banana leaves. As vessels to contain offerings they used only flat baskets or banana leaves;

even in making offerings to the gods the same was the case. This custom probably comes from India, where some groups of Indians of high caste like to eat rice from banana leaves, regarding them as cleaner and purer than other containers, which might be polluted because of having been used by others. To use a vessel that has already been used by a person of low class, such as a śudra or a caṇḍāla, is considered a sin, the stain accruing to the person using the vessel afterward; however clean one might wash the vessel, the stain is not removed, according to the belief. Banana leaves are better, both clean and convenient. After use they can be thrown away. We ourselves also like them, because they are convenient. Their only disadvantage is that we like to throw used banana leaves away everywhere, cluttering the place, disregarding the locality in a barbarous way. As to objects of worship, there were flowers, incense sticks, and candles. There was some difficulty with respect to incense sticks; in those times they did not know how to make these themselves, and it was not easy to buy them, for there was no place that sold them. The people had to depend upon monks, asking them for one or two sticks according to their needs. The candles used for worship were not hard to procure; the peasants made these themselves. Beeswax is not hard to obtain in the country; in the forests there are lots of bee's nests and beehives. Usually these are mîm bees, with small bodies; if one heats the honeycomb with fire he obtains wax. These objects of worship depended upon what one had or could procure. If one had nothing it did not matter, depending on chance. If they simply worshiped and made offerings without any marker for the place of the spirit of the land, and had a feeling of emptiness, they picked up a lump of earth and laid it on the shrine, pretending that the lump of earth was the place of the spirit. At the time of worshiping and making offerings, they would make a speech asking that their farms this year be fruitful, that their rice produce fine grain, that there be no dangers such as biting crabs or nibbling worms. When they finished worshiping and making offerings they set to work plowing a field, for which the auspicious hour had been set, to serve as a ceremony of first plowing. The work of first plowing took about one hour; when they had finished, they might return home, and need do nothing further. They left the shrine of the land spirit as it was; there would be one more ceremony of making offerings and worshiping when they began to transplant rice. In the northeast they call the spirit of the land phĭi taa hêεg or phĭi taa rêεg. There is a ceremony of making an offering of a chicken and making a wish, as described elsewhere (in my work, Belief in Spirits). In some places, for example in the district of Ayutthaya, so far as it has been possible to investigate, they make four triangular flags, of white or any color, and set these up at one of the north corners of their fields. They set them up in a rectangle and then sit down and address the Rice Goddess, the Earth Goddess, and the Spirit of the Place, asking that harmful creatures such as aphis and crabs not damage the rice which they are about to sow.

In olden times people who depended upon crops as their major source of sustenance had knowledge and experience in planting. They knew which sorts of earth were suited to which sorts of crops, what should be done at the time of planting to get good results, what to do to provide fertilizer for the earth. But even if they had knowledge and experience in these matters, and were as diligent as they could be, the people in former times were helpless in matters of weather and crop enemies. When they thus found themselves helpless, it was natural for them to turn to magic things for aid, with doctrines and conduct handed down traditionally, to ensure fruitfulness for their farming. For this reason people formerly feared dangers which might befall their farming, because nothing was such a source of disaster as failure of crops. Because of this fear they had to have ceremonies of making offerings to spirits and gods, and rites connected with every step of farming until their crops were harvested and put away, before their worries were over. For the same reason various nationalities, even those which have progressed, still have various rites and ceremonies connected with farming which have been handed down to the present time. These serve as evidence as to original beliefs, behavior, and conduct. But even if the beliefs have now faded out because famines do not occur often as formerly, and there is not much worshiping and begging of spirits of the place as described above, nevertheless the selection of auspicious hours has not been given up at the time of the first plowing, because this is regarded as important. In extreme cases, some people, even if they do not select their own auspicious hour, watch to see when others, such as the village headman or the important man in the village, begin the first plowing, and then begin their own. Those who are still cautious and fearful take flowers, incense sticks, and candles and lay them at the head of the field ridge, and make vows to the shrine, speaking to it in traditional ways. There are still people who do this; it is deep in their bones, and they must perform one thing or another to be happy. People who believe in auspices and who are learned make sure the first plowing is done in an auspicious direction, avoiding inauspicious directions such as the directions of the phǐi lǔaṉ, lǎaw lèg, thágkàthin, and yommǎkhǎn, which are given in textbooks of astrology. In the first plowing they plow only three circuits to serve as ceremony. Probably they plow three circuits because three is a number regarded as magic. In some places they have a textbook for beginning first plowing according to the age of the farmer; for example, if he was born in the year of the rat, he begins to plow on Sunday, and if born in the year of the ox, he begins to plow on Wednesday, etc. [4]

When they have finished the first plowing they leave the field as it is. When it rains and the earth is wet enough to begin plowing, they set to work plowing the field of the first plowing before the other fields. While they are waiting for the rain, they have to plow for sowing, that is, plow the field in which they will raise seedlings for transplanting. In plowing for sowing, if they are superstitious, it seems that they select an auspicious day, avoiding days when rats will bite or birds will carry off the rice; these things are told in the textbooks. Fields for sowing rice for transplanting may be made in many places, one plot for sowing "heavy rice," which is rice that forms grain slowly, taking about four months to ripen and be ready for harvesting, also called "four-month rice"; and another plot for sowing "light rice," which is rice that forms grain quickly, taking about three months to ripen and be ready for harvesting, also called "three-month rice." There are other plots for sowing black glutinous rice and white glutinous rice, etc.[5] It is also possible to sow them together in a single plot, dividing it into sections by digging ditches. For a place to sow rice for transplanting, they select a spot near enough to water that they can scoop up water to nourish the seedlings easily. The rice that they sow for seedlings is rice that they select and keep aside from the year before; they take the rice of the Rice Goddess, which they summon forth from the field at the time of the previous year's harvest and tie up in the form of a small human doll and keep in the barn, and mix this with the rice to be planted. There are only a few heads of this Rice Goddess rice which they mix in for ceremonial purposes to cause the seed rice to have life and heart (see my work on the Rice Goddess).

The method of sowing rice is to put the rice in a flat basket and soak it in water in order that the light-weight paddy grains and empty grains will float to the top; these they pick out and throw away. Then they pour the paddy into another flat basket which is lined with straw or grass, and water it constantly, not letting it get dry, until the rice germinates. This is called in the province of Nakhon Ratchasima khâaw tɛ̀ɛg càab. Then they take it and sow it in the seedling plots, which have been plowed and formed into ridges and ditches in advance. The ridges, formed of mud and made smooth and flat on top, are separated by ditches. Besides dividing the plot according to kinds of rice as described above, these ditches are also used as paths for walking while sowing, so that they need not tread on rice grains already sown; the ditches also serve as water channels. Before sowing the rice they speak a simple invocation to the Rice Goddess, informing her that they are about to plant her rice to make future crops, and asking that the rice plants flourish and be fruitful. Then they sow the rice; this is called thɔ̂ɔd klâa or tòg klâa. After sowing they must keep watch. If it rains hard during this time the seedlings are in danger, for their roots have not yet taken hold of the earth and even the distribution of the sowing will be destroyed, the seedlings being thrown together in crowded clusters; if this happens they will not grow well; the plants will be of unequal size, some small and some large.

Plowing the Fields

After sowing, if there is no rain for two or three nights, the roots of the seedlings take hold of the earth. After this even if it rains hard it does not matter, but it is necessary to watch and scoop up water, although not in excessive amounts. The farmers watch over the seedlings until they are about half a meter or more in height, when they are fit to be transplanted. If the seedlings are too long, they do not do very well when transplanted because they lose strength and the rice plants do not flourish. Rice seedlings which are oversize are called khâaw klâa kὲε tὲεg khɔ̌ɔ nɔ̂ɔ kàj [literally, "old seedlings jointed like a chicken's legs"] ; they turn into plants similar to those of broadcast sown fields, which are less productive than those in transplanted fields. Seedlings, if they have good earth with plenty of fertilizer and water, will grow to a size to be pulled up and transplanted in about fifty to sixty days. If they are left long for lack of opportunity to transplant them, they may grow old and produce grain, but the crop is small. The greatest enemies of rice seedlings are water birds; they like to eat rice seedlings and will come down in flocks. As soon as the rice grains burst into green leaf and are about to become plants, these birds like to descend and peck at them. In only a moment the seedlings lie flat and ruined. These wretched birds come down and eat at night, and there is no way to keep one's eyes open and watch for them; if they come to eat during the day it would be possible to give some protection. They are dreadful. The duty of watching and protecting rice seedlings includes scooping water and letting it flow onto or off the seedling plots, in order to let the young rice seedlings receive new water to nourish them constantly. This is the job of the women, because the men are busy with plowing and harrowing. You have no doubt seen rice seedlings in the fields. They are visible as patches in the fields, fresh light green in color, attractive and refreshing to the eye. When they have grown to a height of a quarter meter or more, in the fresh morning air the breeze blows in gusts and the tips of the seedlings flutter and wave back and forth in rhythm, graceful as dancers welcoming the sun at dawn. If there is also a fine shower falling, the picture is all the more refreshing and pleasing. Those of you who have been farmers but are so no longer, have you ever felt and seen this in the past? Whatever your reason for abandoning the fields and coming to live in the city, have you ever seen this sort of natural scene in the city?

During the time that the seedlings have not yet grown to the size to be transplanted, the men rise in the early morning. If the fields are distant, they must leave the house as early as 4 A.M., carrying the yokes, plows, knives, hoes, and spades on their shoulders and leading the oxen or buffaloes out to plow. If they do not carry these things themselves, they may have the oxen or buffaloes carry them instead. They set to work to plow the field where they had the first plowing before the other fields. For the plowing at this time there is no auspicious time. They do dàʔ plowing [the Thai term is retained here because no exact English equivalent is known; dàʔ is a verb meaning to plow an entire area the first time] in a circle along the boundary of the ŋaan that they have marked off in the field. If the particular field is divided into two parts, or two ŋaan, they do the plowing in two time periods. They plow one ŋaan in the morning; when it is finished, they continue to plow the second ŋaan in the afternoon. If it is a large field, they may divide it into as many as four ŋaan. They usually ask one another, "How many ŋaan (shifts) of plowing will finish this field?" The answer is, "It will probably take four ŋaan (shifts)." This shows that the field in question is very large, that it requires four shifts of plowing. At the first plowing they plow straight from the head of the field ridge in one corner to another corner. If they plow with their right side toward the field ridge, the ridge of earth plowed up falls to the left the whole length of the furrow. When they are near the end they raise the plow to help the buffaloes, and have them turn to the left along the end of the field. This is called "blaŋ hǎaŋ thǎj, líaw hǔa ŋaan," and means that they have finished plowing one row. Then they continue plowing till they have traversed the end of the ŋaan, and turn the plow and plow straight along the other side. Then they plow across the end and come back to the starting point. They have finished the outer margin of the ŋaan, and now plow new rows inside the first row which are gradually smaller until they reach the center. Then the ŋaan is finished and they stop to rest, and begin the second ŋaan at another time period. When both ŋaan are finished, and one field is completed, they must plow two or three more circuits around the part next to the field ridge, keeping it to the left, because when they plowed the first time they kept the field ridge to the right. The head of the plowshare which fits over the pighead turns to the left and bites more earth to the left than to the right; thus they must plow with the field ridge to the left in order to have the plow bite the earth to the left, next to the field ridge, completely. In terminology for areas, one râj is four ŋaan; this probably comes from the ŋaan or shift in the work of plowing fields. During the plowing, when the earth is broken and turned up in sheets by the plow, there are many small red earthworms turned up also. Earthworms of this kind are called field earthworms. One will see Thai mynah birds (Acridotheres siamensis) descending in flocks to eat the earthworms. These birds are tame, because people do them no harm, their flesh being unpleasant to eat and the birds being regarded as dirty; for this reason they are spared danger.

They begin to plow in the early morning. About 10 A.M. or later, that is at nɔ́ɔŋ pheen (they have no watches to look at, and depend upon watching the sun's shadow and noticing their own hungry stomachs), they stop to rest, releasing the oxen or buffaloes from the yokes to rest and eat grass and straw. The men eat their rice; this may be called eating morning rice or, in the ancient term, eating ŋaaj, because ever since rising in the morning, when they rinsed their mouths and washed their faces, they have eaten nothing at all, except to smoke a cigarette, and, if they are betel chewers, to chew a wad of betel. They cannot be without a tobacco box, which is usually made of the inner shell of the ripe sugarpalm fruit, and a flint and iron; these are always kept on the person. If they chew betel, their wives prepare betel and areca and put them in a box for them. They wrap these in their phaa khǎaw mǎa, and tie them around the waist, or else tie on a triangular cloth bag into which they stuff betel box, tobacco box, and other things. In some places they plow in the morning and stop to eat in the late morning; then they continue plowing till pheen [11 A.M.] and stop. Thus as a rule farmers eat their morning rice or eat phraw ŋaaj in the late morning. There is therefore no midday meal; when they eat again it is the evening meal. It is the duty of those at home to prepare food and send it to the fields. Sometimes if they have the opportunity they also catch raw fish and eat them with pepper sauce. They squat and eat at the head of the field ridge or wherever convenient, selecting a big tree to furnish shade from the heat of the sun. For this reason if there are big trees they do not cut them down as in the city, where they are not tolerated because they are in the way; they usually preserve them as a place to rest and eat, sweeping the area flat and smooth for sitting and lying down. At the bases of big trees with cool shade like this, if in midday the heat of the sun is so intense as to be visible, and the wind sighs from time to time, and otherwise it is so quiet that one hears no noise at all, one feels lonely and is tempted to spread a mat and stretch out comfortably. It is precisely this which gives rise to the Thai idiom, "shade of trees, eaves of roofs," but for the farmers, even if they have endured the sun and are weary, there is no opportunity to rest comfortably like this, because there is much other work which they must do. When they have finished eating, they put the pots in the basket and hang them up on a tree branch at the head of the field. Then they go out and inspect the land. If they see grass growing thick anywhere in the fields, they cut it. If weeds have grown up obstructing the field ridges, they cut them. At points where the field ridges are broken or sunken, they plug them or raise them with earth. They keep watch to preserve and improve the land. In some places the fields are open, and it is impossible or inconvenient to find big trees nearby to provide shade for rest; they build a temporary hut for shelter, or they may build a field shed. Originally a field shed of this sort was called in Thai thǐaŋ naa, or by corruption chǐaŋ naa. Sometimes field sheds are built with elevated floors and open spaces beneath, of permanent construction. They are probably used as farming quarters throughout the season, that they are built in this way.

As for the oxen and buffaloes that are turned loose to rest and eat grass and straw, they are not turned loose to eat alone. If they are turned loose thus, to follow their noses and eat grass farther and farther away, they might easily be stolen. It is necessary to take great care with respect to oxen and buffaloes, because they are the important source of power in farming, and so there are always evildoers waiting to steal them. When they turn oxen and buffaloes loose to eat grass, there must be a person to tend them. This duty falls to the children. They tend them together in groups of many households; sometimes a group numbers many tens of individuals. They are called oxherds and buffaloherds, and everyone knows full well what sort of youngsters they are. They are hopelessly naughty, and go to extremes in their play. If there are trees they climb and clamber up all of them. Sometimes they play at fighting crickets, and sometimes at pitchpenny. What do they use for pennies to pitch? They use the closing lids of large snails which occur plentifully in the fields; these are the pennies that they pitch. Worse yet, during the farming season when there are large snails, they roast them and eat them. It is unnecessary to speak of quarrels and fights; they occur constantly. As for crickets, which city children have a very hard time finding one at a time, or must buy from others for many sàtaaŋ apiece, in the fields in the cricket season there are plenty, and they are easily found; it is only necessary to part the dry grass to find nine or ten at a time. Buffaloherds being so naughty and inclined thus to play more than to keep watch, how can they be much trusted in the matter of tending buffaloes? To trust them is to associate with children in building houses [a Thai proverbial expression for trusting youngsters in serious matters]. Therefore usually four or five adults, when they have free time, go and take charge. Actually oxherds and buffaloherds are just like monastery boys or any other group of boys, whether of low class or high class; when they get together in a group and are turned loose to play by themselves they are all alike, instinctively naughty, because boys will be boys, and not adults.

When afternoon comes and the sun starts its descent, about 2 o'clock, the boys drive the buffaloes back and plowing the second ŋaan is begun. (If they use oxen to plow, they plow only in the morning; in the afternoon they turn them loose and do not use them to plow, for oxen do not have endurance.) They plow until the sun is very low, about 4 P.M., and then unhitch the plows to give the buffaloes another period of rest. This time of day is called bàaj khwaaj [literally, "buffalo afternoon"]. The buffaloes know well that their work is finished for the day; they head straight for their wallows and soak themselves happily, for they have been in the hot sun. When they come up from the wallow they eat grass, eating and walking at the same time as they gradually shift along. In the evening they turn their heads toward home. They have an excellent memory for their own homes; even if they go far astray, unless someone ties them up they know their way home. When they arrive they enter their pens themselves; no one needs to herd them in. The reason for turning oxen and buffaloes loose to rest like this is necessity; otherwise the animals cannot stand the work, and become chronically listless, weak, and thin; they are no good the rest of their lives. At this time when the buffaloes are turned loose to eat grass, there is some time left before dark; the farmers seek fish, set fishtraps, gather vegetables, and break up firewood, according to what they have. They carry this themselves or load it on the backs of buffaloes to take it home. In the evening when the sun is low, in order to rest they ride the buffaloes and let them walk idly through the fields, trudging straight toward home. There is a breeze from time to time, refreshing the spirit. One's weariness disappears completely, and one's heart feels as unobstructed and clear as the vacant fields stretching to the horizon. They ride the buffaloes along singing quietly the whole way. The happiness and content of the farmers at no other time can equal this evening time. This is related from the past of a man who once was a farmer. The true life, when one forgets troubles and sorrows and worries and has happiness and contentment for a moment, is at the time when the arduous daily work is done and one rides a buffalo and sings quietly as described. The meadows and fields, forests and mountains, playing a flute while riding a buffalo, these things it is that the Chinese regard as the ideal of happiness, peace, and contentment which mankind should seek. The farmers have too much of this and so like to come to town, where there is naught but gaiety and comfort, but happiness and peace are hard to find.

The first plowing as described above is called daʔ plowing; it consists of turning up the earth in ridges. After plowing it is left for many days in order to let the grass rot and become fertilizer. They plow each field and then leave it in this way, and then return to plow it again; this is called prɛɛ [literally, "turning"] plowing, and consists of plowing the overturned ridges back rightside up again. This is tantamount to loosening up the soil. For both daʔ plowing and prɛɛ plowing, it is not desired that there be too much water in the field. If there is a great deal of water, they do not see the furrow and may replow an old furrow or diverge from the straight line of the first straight furrow. In this case some of the earth will be cut by the plow blade and some not, rendering harrowing and transplanting difficult. What has been described is what happens when they have enough time to plow twice. If they are unable to finish in time, they simply do daʔ plowing and then harrow, omitting the prɛɛ or second plowing, but the transplanted rice is not fully productive because the grass is still fresh, not having had time to ferment and rot and become fertilizer. If the field is a sown field, not a transplanted field, there is no previous plowing; they simply sow the rice on the field and then plow it under, doing only the first daʔ plowing. But if there is much grass in the field, they must first do daʔ plowing just the same; they plow to pull up all the grass, and then sow and plow again to turn the seeds under. If sown fields are plowed under only once, there are usually grass and weeds growing up with the rice plants. These are chiefly Triumfetta bartramia, Cyperus rotundus, and soŋ kàthiam. If these grow among the rice to any extent it is necessary to keep watch and pull them up often.

It is sometimes said that if we changed our plows and used iron plows like those of western countries, we would get better and quicker results than with our old plows which have been used for a long time and have never been altered or improved in any way. The explanation is given that western plows are very heavy; oxen and buffaloes can scarcely draw them, and they dig too deep into the earth. Also, they are more expensive than local plows;[6] the farmers usually do not have enough money to buy them to use. This is fact, but there is also another fact, namely, that in the case of anything that has been done in the past and has produced visible results, and has long since become custom, not normally manifesting any defects or disadvantages, it is usual among farmers not to want to change, for they do not trust new things, being uncertain that if they change they will receive the expected benefits. If their expectations are not fulfilled, they are in trouble, and so they prefer to do as they have done in the past rather than venture to change to unaccustomed things, unless someone first acts to serve as an example proving that good results are obtained, in which case they consent to change. Their ideas stopping at this point, it is impossible that there should be any thought of change or improvement to fit circumstances, unless someone acts as leader to set an example. At present it is learned that there is a new style of plow, an improvement on the old style, but this is a question of modern farming and has nothing to do with the farming of the peasants we are describing. Speaking of this reminds us of a plowing story set long ago in Burma. They say that an important European financial commissioner with intelligent ideas and good intentions desired to see the various nationalities living in the north of Burma, who are backward forest and hill people, receive the benefits of progress. He reasoned that the plowing of these people was done with backward, out-of-date plows. If they used western plows, which plow very deep, they would be richer than before. Having made his decision, with good intentions, he invested in the purchase of a modern plow and sent it to the governing committee of a local district with a detailed explanation of the method of use, requesting that they instruct the jungle people regarding the new plow. This plow that he sent for them to try out really plowed deep, so deep that it turned up the hard undersoil as well. When the jungle people saw this they were displeased, because they knew full well that it is impossible to grow anything in the hard undersoil, and so they refused to use the new plow. The welfare of the district officer depended upon his convincing the jungle people; he therefore tried in every way possible to induce the jungle people to use the modern plow. All his explanations and recommendations were useless. Finally he had to use threats, saying that if they did not consent to use the modern plow, the commissioner would be very angry, and if he ever became angry there would be dreadful consequences, because one of the eyes of the commissioner had a flaming fire to burn the stubborn to death. For this reason the commissioner had to wear a monocle to cover this eye so that it would burn no one. Even when thus threatened, the jungle people were still unwilling to use the western iron plow. Finally the commissioner learned of the matter and came himself. He reasoned with the jungle people, explaining the merits of the iron plow, and saying that he felt very sorry that these jungle people were stubborn and unwilling to act in accordance with his good intentions and his hopes for their progress and prosperity. The commissioner was absorbed in his explanation, when by chance his monocle fell out. There was an instantaneous scream, and the jungle people present fled in panic from the flaming eye, fearing that it would burn them to death. From that time on all the jungle people disappeared; searchers could not find them, for they had fled into the jungle. Thereafter they were never seen again. This is a story of breaking a knife handle with the knee or pushing an ox's horns down to force it to eat grass [Thai proverbial expressions for trying to achieve results by force]. It was an attempt to achieve sudden change, without trying to alter things gradually in order that the people may follow step by step, and so it failed.

Harrowing and Transplanting

To return to our story, after the plowing comes the harrowing. A harrow (khrâad) is an implement to comb the grass and weeds out of the earth. It is a piece of wood with teeth in a row which are called lûug khrâad, and it is drawn through the field by buffaloes. The first harrowing must be done in the plot where the ceremonial first plowing was performed. At the time of harrowing they must let water onto or off the field in order to get the proper amount; the water must cover the plowed earth slightly. They harrow back and forth until the plowed earth is broken up in mud and forms a flat smooth area. Wherever there are weeds and plants, they are pulled out and thrown away, to facilitate the transplanting of rice. When they have finished harrowing they leave the field for a night or two for the mud to settle, and then they bring the rice plants and transplant them. At the time of harrowing the youngsters catch snails, crabs, and fish in the plowed and harrowed earth in great fun. Not only the youngsters have fun; the pond herons also enjoy it, for they get a chance to catch fish, and one sees them wading through the water in white flocks.

When they have harrowed the fields and left them to stand, they begin to pull up the rice seedlings and separate them according to variety. This is the work of the women, because the men are busy with plow and harrow. The method of pulling is to stoop over and take the plants in both hands to cause the clay clinging to the roots to fall off. Then they grasp the rice plants at the base and strike them against a wooden panel, which they have prepared, in order to even up the bases of the seedlings. Then they tie the upper part of the plants together with a bamboo strip. Each bunch is called a kam, but in the province of Nakhon Ratchasima it is called a khób. The ends of the seedlings have to be cut short and even. If they are not cut, but are left as they are, when they are transplanted they are long and disorderly and the leaves will grow slowly. When they have finished they tie the bunches together in pairs, which in the province of Nakhon Ratchasima are called puŋ. They insert a bamboo which is flattened at both ends into the puŋ and use this as a carrying pole to take them to the place where they are to be planted.

Before setting to work to plant the seedlings, they again prepare offerings for the spirit of the land at the shrine which was built at the time of the first plowing. They must plant the field of the first plowing before all other fields. This field is divided into two parts. In one part heavy rice is planted and in the other light rice. The rice that is planted in this field is for use as seed rice for planting the following year, because it is regarded as rice which has been properly treated according to auspices and ceremonies in an auspicious field. Other fields are also planted in rows and sections according to varieties, without mixing. The method of planting is by stooping over, as everyone has seen. They take hold of the clump of seedlings in the left or right hand, whichever is convenient, and turn the base of the seedlings away from the body. The free left or right hand takes hold of the base of the seedlings and picks off six or seven plants, and then plunges them into the mud with the thumb. Before withdrawing the hand from the rice plant, they press the mud with two fingers to bury the base of the rice plants firmly and to smooth the mud around them. Using the thumb to press a hole in the earth, particularly if the earth is rather hard and they work at it for long hours for many days, makes the thumb very sore. For this reason in some localities they have to use a stick to poke a hole first. This method is certainly slower than usual, but if necessary it must be used. This stick is called in the province of Nakhon Pathom hŭa jôog or taŋôog. They take a piece of bamboo as high as the knee, with a prong projecting from a node to serve as a handle, and whittle the base sharp. They jab this into the ground to make a hole as deep as desired, and then poke the rice plants in and press the mouth of the hole with the fingers. If they do not do this, but use the sore thumbs to press a hole, they cannot bury the rice plants deep, and the plants may come loose and float. Transplanters always keep their backs to the sun in order to keep the sun off the face. For this reason, in farming -- at all stages, whether plowing, harrowing, transplanting, or reaping -- it is necessary always to wear a shirt and keep the back to the sun. On the head, if they are women, they wear ŋôob [farm hats]; if they are men they usually take their phâa khăaw máa, which they always have with them, off the waist and wrap it around the head. If they have betel boxes, cigarette boxes, or pocketbooks, they take them out and lay them down at the head of the field.

When they have finished transplanting and time has passed, the rice plants burst into lush green clumps. When touched by breezes or showers the tips bend gracefully with the wind, chasing each other like waves in the sea. They take up the rainwater, which gives them a fresh green appearance. This is the period between the beginning of Buddhist Lent and the tenth lunar month. When the time arrives for the rice to bloom (in the province of Ayutthaya this time is called khâaw phlôoŋ) the rice forms flowering heads, and clusters of blossoms, light green in color, appear throughout the meadows. The rice always flowers all at the same time, not at different times, because it was all planted at the same time. The farmers rise in the morning, rinse their mouths and wash their faces, and then go out to inspect the rice plants in the fields. When they see the rice plants full of blossoms you may be certain that they are happy, because the fragrance of the rice blossoms in the morning pervades everything. It is a fragrant odor like the odor of the chommánâad flower, but weaker; for this reason the chommánâad flower is called the "new rice flower." When one thinks of the morning air in the fields at the time when the rice is in bloom, one feels refreshed, for one breathes fresh air scented with the fragrance of the rice blossoms drifting down the wind. In the eastern sky one sees the sun as a great red ball just appearing and throwing its light upon the sky, yellow and brilliant as gold. It is quiet and peaceful, and one hears only the humming of the bees which hover about collecting the pollen of the rice blossoms. The farmers do not come out to the fields to admire the beautiful scene or to breathe the fresh cool air, because farmers are familiar with such natural beauty and purity. They come out rather to inspect the rice and fields. If they see that the rice in any section is bent down and about to topple over into the water, they find a bamboo to make a rail to hold it up, for if the rice plants fall into the water the tops will be completely eaten off by the Anabas testudineus and Puntius javanicus fish which abound in the fields. If weeds are growing anywhere, they pull them out. When their work is finished they either stand admiring the scene and the rice plants which are in full bloom, or return home.

When the rice begins to form fruit, short leaves appear around the heads and the stalks begin to swell, with thin leaves enclosing and covering the grain. The rice is said to be pregnant. The farmers in the province of Ayutthaya call it khâaw klàd hǎaŋ plaa thuu. At this time there is a ceremony of invoking the Rice Goddess. In the province of Ayutthaya they always select a Friday for the ceremony, probably being superstitious about the name of the day (sùg), which is homonymous with both the word for happiness and the word for ripe. They select a time for the ceremony in the afternoon, between 3 and 5 o'clock. They go out to perform the ceremony in the fields at the place where they planted flags on the day of first plowing. They prepare offerings, including one orange, one banana, and a banana-leaf cup of sliced sugarcane; the banana is a nắmwắa banana cut up. These things are placed together in one small wicker basket, and there are also powder, perfume, and a comb placed on a stand. They take the basket and the offerings and hang them up on a flagpole, and sprinkle the powder and perfume on the rice leaves and rice plants. They make a gesture of combing the rice leaves with the comb. This is an act of dressing the Rice Goddess. The offering of an orange is said to serve as a remedy for morning sickness in pregnancy. When they have finished they pronounce an invocation, saying that at the present time the rice, or the Rice Goddess, has conceived, and so they have brought offerings to her and things to dress her; may she be happy and well and fruitful; and let no dangers disturb her. Thus the ceremony is finished. At this time they usually set up a square chălěew [magic pentacle figure made of two interlaced bamboo triangles], or a fish basket may be used instead. The setting up of a chălěew is said to be merely to provide a symbol to make it known generally that the rice in this field is "pregnant," and boats or oxen and buffaloes are not to be allowed to enter and damage the rice plants. In reality the chălěew is a protective device connected with spells and charms of the sort which Europeans call "magic," to keep spirits and animals out. It is the same sort of thing as the chălěew placed at the mouth of a medicine pot and the chălěew that they set up in the house when they have taken a corpse out of the house, as is done in the north and the northeast. Originally it was probably a real fence, and then no doubt it was reduced to a rầadchắwắd fence and a chălěew, because it was seen to be rather a matter of warding off spirits or magic spells.

In the south (Chaiya District) they perform an invocation called khôd khầaw when the rice first starts to form fruit. For offerings they use only cakes, such as red boiled cakes, white cakes, bean cakes, sesame cakes; there are also powder and perfume. When they reach the field they select rice which seems to be forming fruit very well, and at this point they set up their offering of cakes. They light incense sticks and candles and pronounce an invocation to the Rice Goddess. Then they smear the powder and perfume on the rice leaves in the manner of anointing them. They do this to three to seven clumps. They lay the offering of cakes down in a suitable place. When they have finished they take the cakes back home, while the powder and perfume are usually put away in the barn.

The farmers in some localities of the province of Ratburi, after returning home from making merit at the monasteries at the time of the sầad festival, take a portion of the sầad cakes and fruit which they keep aside at the time of making merit, and put these in a small bamboo-leaf cup or funnel and lay them on a vessel which is woven in the form of a crude basket with legs. They plant this at the head of the field ridge, in a single place or in many places. This is an act of making an offering to the rice in the field and invoking the Rice Goddess to come and watch over the rice; it is

called sòŋ khâaw bin. This last ceremony seems to be mixed with the
Srăddha ceremonies of the Brahmans, in which they have piṇḍas of rice as
offerings to the dead, and with the Sărada or Sărada ceremony, which is
another ceremony associated with autumn; this will be treated in a separate
study. The first ceremony of making offerings to the rice seems to be the
same as the ceremony of making offerings to the Rice Goddess which is explained in the Old Textbook of Rice Planting (National Library edition published in 1924).

The matter of making offerings to rice and to the Rice Goddess no doubt
comes from the belief that various things have life; whether a human being
or an animal or a plant, everything has something abiding in it which is called
the khwăn. If the khwăn is not constantly present, the living thing dies. Rice
is regarded as having life and a khwăn, and so the khwăn of the rice must be
treated in such a way as to cause it to remain present and not slip away, for
this might cause the rice not to flourish or cause it to die (for the khwăn see
my work on khwăn ceremonies). If the fields are near the edge of a forest,
when the rice has flowered and the grains begin to form, there is usually a
certain danger, namely, from forest animals such as hogs and deer. These
animals like to come and eat rice; they cause great damage to the rice plants.
The owner of the fields must go and sleep there in order to be on hand to
drive away the animals; this is very difficult, because this is the rainy season
and the ground is still wet and muddy, so that it is necessary to build a hut to
serve as a shelter, or to use bamboo pounded flat and laid on the ground in a
high spot, such as beside an ant hill, spread an oxhide on this, and then build
a fire on either side and sleep on the oxhide. If it happens to rain there is
great trouble; the oxhide used for sleeping must be taken up and used as a roof
to keep off the rain, the smouldering fires go out, and there is danger from
wild animals. This is the life of farmers in some localities. If they cannot
endure these hardships they go hungry.

Profit and Loss

In planting rice they leave different intervals depending upon whether
it is a lowland field or an upland field. If it is a lowland field they leave
rather distant intervals, because the rice may form big clumps, with eighteen
to twenty plants in a clump. If it is an upland field they usually plant the
rice at rather close intervals, because the rice does not form very big clumps.
Farming depends upon the ground. If the soil is loamy and black it is regarded
as rather good, because there is sand mixed with the mud. If the soil is too
clayey it is not very good; it is hard to plow and harrow, and the soil binds
the clumps of rice, not allowing them to expand and flourish. But this is still
better than soil which is entirely sand. If it is sandy soil it must be "duck

manure sand," that is, with some admixture of earth; this is usable. If the
soil is white like diatomaceous earth it is not good; although it may be possible to raise crops, the rice will not do well and produces a small crop. In
fields which are newly cleared or have too much fertilizer, the rice usually
grows too well; it grows so much that the plants are tall and big and the
leaves are crowded thick as a kingfisher's nest, clinging together like tousled
hair; the rice usually produces big grains but in small amounts and with little
meat, being all hollow. Also, if the rains are not good, failing to fall when
the time arrives for the rice to produce grain, the young rice grains will wither
and die on the plants throughout the meadow. This is called khǎaw mǎan or
khǎaw taaj phraaj; it is such a calamity to the farmers that they must sit hug-
ging their knees and weeping, because the rice will come to nothing and
their weary labor has been in vain. Worse still, they know they must soon
reach the point of going hungry, because a crop failure is a calamity afflict-
ing the entire community and there is no one to turn to for aid, everyone
being in the same predicament. If the fields are near a river or a canal, it
is possible to bring water and preserve some of the rice plants, but not enough
to cause the rice to produce as good a crop as if there were rain to sprinkle
the plant tops, because the young rice blossoms which are bursting open are
baked all day long every day by the blazing sun, and the water below which
nourishes the rice plants is also hot, combining to cause the rice to spoil.
If this happens to rice seedlings they are said to taaj fɔ̌j.

There are many other sources of damage to farms, such as floods,
biting crabs, and nibbling worms. The crabs mentioned are field crabs.
When they want to do harm, there is no knowing where they come from.
They come in great numbers, as if they were migrating. Where they are
born, where they come from, and where they go later has never been learned
from research. They do not simply come; they also bite off the rice plants
so that they float about everywhere. They are like beasts of fate to the farmer, because after biting off the plants they do not eat them. They simply
bite them off for fun, or so it appears to one who does not know why they
bite. In midday when the sun is hot they can be seen fleeing from the heated
water and climbing up the rice plants; one plant has many of them, up to
nine or ten. Elsewhere they may be seen wriggling and floating in rafts.
Any attempt to destroy them, as by trapping, is impossible; their numbers
are tremendous. The farmers are very much afraid of these wretched animals. In any year that they come, troubles are many. After investing money
and labor to plow and transplant until the rice has grown, the farmer loses
everything because of these dreadful creatures. Fortunately they come only
at long intervals, only once in many years. It is a matter of taking a risk.
You who like to eat crabs no doubt think that since field crabs are so numerous,
the farmers enjoy eating them. Not so, for field crabs do not have a great
deal of meat like saltwater crabs. If they trap them they do not know what

to do with them, for there are too many to eat and they are not delicious. It is possible to make a boiled coconut-cream curry of some of them, but there are very many left over and nothing can be done with them. The only thing is, if there is salt, to stir up live crabs with salt as they do to preserve sàmɛ̌ɛ crabs, to cause them to die of drinking saltwater. Then they pound them with roasted rice and squeeze out their thick juice to use as sauce. But if there is much of this and one eats it often, one gets tired of it.

Another kind of animal that damages the rice plants is the worm. Worms occur in the fields at the time when the rice plants are growing well; if one tried to estimate the numbers it would probably reach millions and tens of millions. They float in the water in rafts so dense that one can hardly see the water, looking so green and crawling that they give one gooseflesh. When the young shoots of the rice plants rise a little above the surface of the water, these worms float up and eat them comfortably. They eat ravenously, skipping nothing. They cannot resist the tops of the rice when they emerge; as soon as they rise above the surface of the water they are all eaten off short. The worms eat not only the rice plants; if there are grass and weeds growing on the field ridges, they eat these as well. They eat all the leaves on a plant, leaving only the stems and branches. The farmers are unable to combat them, because there are so many of them. They can only make vows to the shrines and invoke the spirits of the place as best they know how. The worms descend on a field and live in it like this for about fifteen days, and then disappear completely without leaving a trace. Worms like this appear once in a great many years. It is necessary to take chances just as with crabs, but they are better than crabs in that they bite only the tips of the rice plants, whereas the crabs bite the plants off at the base; the plants are still young and tender; the stems are flat, and not yet rounded out, and are unable to produce new leaves to survive. A great enemy to the farmers at a time when the rice plants have survived flood and drought are these wretched crabs and worms. One might call them a plague descending to eat up the rice plants. They are terrible. There is also the grasshopper, which also damages rice plants. It is likewise a creature which comes in migrations once in many years. They come in great numbers, flying so thick as to darken the sky. Wherever they light, they eat the rice plants for a time, making waste a whole area, but they are not as violent as crabs and worms. One might classify them as a secondary plague to rice. These grasshoppers are probably of the same category as the half-grasshopper, half-cicada which in England is called a locust, because locusts descend and eat grain plants in foreign countries in the same way.

The kind of losses we have been describing only occur once in many years. If a natural disaster comes after the transplanting season, the farmer is distressed to the point of tears, for it is too late to plant rice again, and he must go hungry and poor. If this happens everywhere there is a famine, which is a terrible calamity. There are also gains in farming, and the gains are greater than the losses. Thus in any year that there is plenty of rain, the crop is abundant beyond expectation. Rainfall that is regarded as good is heavy in the beginning of the season, moderate in mid-season, and occasional at the end of the season. If it falls according to this schedule, there is profit in farming. By rainfall that is inappropriate the farmers mean occasional showers at the beginning of the season, little or no rain in mid-season, and heavy rain at the end of the season. If it rains heavily at the end of the season, and there is too much water, or if there is moderate rain at the beginning of the season, light showers in mid-season, and drought at the end of the season, this is called "rain which deceives the farmers." When the farming is done a drought sets in and the rice dies while the grains are forming; thus the entire crop is lost. With rice that produces well it is possible to obtain fifty baskets to one basket of seed rice. It produces fine big heads, equal on all the plants, with heavy, firm grains and a minimum of empty grains, differing from the kind that has unfilled, light-weight, angular grains. If it has much meat it is good rice, with round grains without angles, the base curved and fine.

Transplanting rice is usually begun in the eighth lunar month or, if the farmers have been a little slow, in the ninth lunar month. Light rice transplanted in the eighth month begins to form heads in the waning half of the ninth lunar month. Heavy rice transplanted in the eighth month forms heads in the waning half of the tenth month. The age of rice is counted from the day of sowing the rice seedlings. When they have finished transplanting it, they keep watch over it and pull out weeds and grass and watch the water that nourishes the rice plants. When they are unoccupied, they fish and seek food. At this time the heavy work that they have done is over, and they have no worries for a time. During the farming period from the beginning of the plowing to the end of the transplanting they must leave home early in the morning; when they arrive they set to work until time to stop and rest and eat the morning meal. The working time at this period is at least four hours. The wives and children are at home; if they do not busy themselves with looking after the rice seedlings, they are not idle; they have the duty of cooking food to send out. Boys of the age of nine or ten go to tend the buffaloes. The aged who are unable to do heavy work like the others stay to watch the house and do small jobs, weaving and repairing utensils and baskets, as it is against the nature of old people to remain idle. If any family has only the husband and wife and young children, they have a very hard time; they must shut the door of the house, take up the ladder, and leave the house, carrying their infants along and hanging up a cradle for them in the hut or field shed. They do their cooking on the spot. When there is a great deal of transplanting and farming to do, it is impossible for one person to finish in time. They help each other in bees, but these are not as much fun as harvesting bees; there is only racing to see who transplants faster or slower than the rest.

Going out to farm in the early morning and stopping to rest and eat at 10 A.M. delays the time for eating until very late. They eat nothing to sustain themselves; exercising and working from early morning, they are very hungry by the time they eat. Sometimes when the time arrives they stop and wait for a long time before the people at home send food to them; they no doubt are very hungry and irritable. This sort of thing probably happens often. A story is told that a man went out to plow. When the time arrived to stop and rest, his mother had not yet brought food to him. He watched and waited, restless and irritable from hunger. When his mother brought his food, in his hunger he glanced at it and felt that there was only a little, not enough to eat. He became angry, berated and reviled his mother, and beat her. When he set to work to eat he could not finish it all. He realized his great fault in having been harsh to his mother, and felt very sorry. When this man died he was born as a tiny bird the size of a bulbul, with green body and grey head, which perches in the shrubs in the fields and cries nîid diaw nîid diaw ["only a little, only a little"]. It cries like this all day long. Wherever one goes in the fields, one always hears it crying.

Animals and Plants in the Fields

When the rice forms heads and ripens it looks bright yellow everywhere. The farmers still have to busy themselves guarding the rice, not allowing paddy birds to come down and eat it. The paddy birds come from time to time; if they are chased away they flee for a time, but if one is careless they come back to eat the rice in the fields. They come in flocks numbering thousands, flying so close together as to darken the sky. If one does not take care, they pluck off the heads of rice and carry them off, eating the grains and throwing the husks away everywhere. But the damage resulting from paddy birds, though it occurs every year, is not as violent as that from crabs that bite off the rice plants, for there is all told a great deal of rice, ripe and yellow all over the meadows. The birds eat without fear; when they descend to eat and one chases them away, they fly away to eat rice in the field of someone else. The owner of that field chases them on, and so they proceed by stages. Sometimes they disappear for many days and then return. This shows that they have been eating rice in the fields of others at a distance. It is not easy to keep watch and go out to chase them away often, and so the farmers make wooden rattles and hang them up in various places; a person sits and pulls a cord in the field shed. Sometimes they make windmills for the wind to turn and make a noise. The birds are afraid to alight in the fields. Sometimes the villagers make figures in the form of persons. Wherever the field is low and near to ponds or marshes, there birds of many kinds abound. It is necessary to build a hut to live in while chasing birds.

This duty falls to the women and children. If birds alight they chase them away. One hears a cry of chasing away birds, wàa hə́əw wàa hə́əw, drifting down the wind in the quiet midday air; it is a peculiar, lonely sound. If birds do not come down to eat the rice, they spin cotton and silk in order not to lose time at their work. The cotton that they spin is to be used for weaving monks' robes, in which the villagers compete in craftsmanship on the day of presenting kàthǐn robes, which I have already written about (see my work on the custom of presenting Kàthǐn robes). If the fields are near the forest and there are wild animals, it is necessary to build a platform in the trees or a tower as a place to rest while chasing away birds. When the birds come they use a plummet made of a lump of earth with a long string to swing and throw far out. Children like this work, enjoying the task of throwing these at birds. If a young woman goes to chase away birds she is usually accompanied by a younger brother. This is an opportunity for the young men to come and flirt, or if they are already sweethearts, they chase birds and eat together; this is a story of love in the fields.

If you walk past the market, sometimes you will see them selling little birds the size of sparrows, boiled and yellow in color, tied in bunches of three or four. These are the paddy birds which come down and eat rice in the fields. They make a snare out of a fishnet, with a rod to spring the snare and cause it to fall. Sometimes there is a paddy bird tied up as a decoy under the net. When a flock of paddy birds comes down to eat rice under the snare, the person who is hiding and watching pulls a cord to pull the springpole loose. The fishnet which is spread falls down over the birds. They are able to catch many tens of birds at a time; if there are a lot of paddy birds they may catch as many as a hundred. Another kind of trap is called "tiger sweeping its tail." It is made with a springpole which is simply a broom. This kind of trap catches the birds dead more than alive; any bird that is swept violently by this springpole dies, or if it does not die it is in a very bad state [literally, "has a yellow chin," idiom for being on the point of death]; its legs are all broken. The name of the paddy bird is familiar from childhood; lying in our cradles we are told that it has a yellow head. I have had this lullaby poured into my ears so often that I can remember it:

> O yellow-headed paddy bird,
> You come with two heads of rice from the city fields in your beak;
> You bring them saying you are going to make a royal farm;
> Your cheeks are fat.

Another kind of animal that eats rice in the fields is the guinea pig. It digs holes and lives in the fields. If in the rainy season its hole is flooded, it can make a nest of grass floating on the water. The amount of rice that it eats constitutes no serious damage, because it does not bite off heads and throw them away; it only eats the rice grains one head at a time. If there are many of them, there is considerable loss. These animals can be eaten by human beings. Farmers catch them and roast them like pork; they say that they are very delicious.

Speaking of animals that occur in the fields, one is reminded of field turtles, which are animals of two habitats; they live in marshes and ponds, and in meadows and grass thickets. They do not like to live in fields for they know that there is danger from people who watch to catch them and eat them. The eleventh and twelfth lunar months are their season for laying eggs, but nevertheless they are molested by people who seek their eggs to take and eat. People are not as bad as the flamingo and the mongoose, which are better than people at seeking turtle eggs to eat. In any place where there are flamingoes and mongooses, cobras and other harmful snakes cannot live happily; they are harmed by these two species. This is all a matter of nature seeking a balance; if there are too many or too few of any species, human beings are caused trouble. Look only at field crabs; because there are too many, farmers are caused inconvenience. If there are many cobras, one may take a false step and tread on them and be bitten; but if there are none to eat the mice in the field, there are many mice to damage the rice. If the flamingoes and mongooses should destroy all the snakes, it is not known what damage these two species might then do. They say that in some places in India tigers are very common and do harm to many hundreds and thousands of people every year, to the point that they have to be destroyed. When they destroy all or most of the tigers, the wild pigs which are food for tigers no longer have tigers waiting to kill and eat them, and so they increase and there is insufficient food for all; they come and trample down fields and eat crops that have been planted, causing not a little damage. It takes a long time to put them down and reduce their numbers.

Speaking of animals in the fields, there is still another kind, namely, the field waterbug [Belostoma indica], which occurs frequently in marshes, ponds, meadows, and grass thickets. When there is rain or a storm some of them stray into the fields. People like to eat these waterbugs. It is very strange for they have an unpleasant odor like that of the kàthέε insect, but people of every class, whether commoner or aristocrat, really like to eat them. They tear them apart and pound them up with pepper sauce or pickle them with fish sauce. The body of the creature has no flesh or skin. Its only merit is its unpleasant odor, which is a fascinating smell. This is probably the same sort of thing as the odor of the human body. It appears that not only the Thai like to eat insects and worms; other races like to eat them as well. In the Bible of the Christian religion it is said that Saint John, who was rather like the teacher of Jesus, was observing a fast in a lonely forest, eating grasshoppers dipped in honey. Grasshoppers of this sort are what are called locusts, which Africans also eat as food. If they come in great numbers, darkening the sky and covering the earth, the people catch a great many of them and press them into bars to keep to feed to livestock. The field waterbugs are caught in the morning, when they come up to lay eggs or are clinging to their eggs on the grasstops. People steal up and pounce on them. When the sun is hot and heats up the surface of the water, the waterbugs usually flee from the heat and climb to the tops of the grass, wriggling there, or hide in the water at the base of the grass plants. If any grass plant has waterbug eggs, it is sure that there is a waterbug nearby. If one shakes the grass with his hand, it rushes up out of the water, worried about its eggs and ready to fight to protect them. People pounce upon the waterbugs and take them away to eat. If one is not careful in catching them, they may sting one painfully with the stinger in their mouths. In Bangkok one sees people catching waterbugs at night. They are driven astray by rainstorms, and fly into big electric lights like those of the Plaza of the Equestrian Statue. Both children and adults watch to trap and catch them. When they fly low, people beat at them with cloths to knock them down. Formerly the price for which they were sold was at the cheapest five sàtaaŋ. The upper classes in their automobiles also go to lie in wait, to trap and catch field waterbugs -- or to buy them -- showing that it is not only farmers who like to eat them; city dwellers riding in automobiles also like them.

In the farming season there is floodwater everywhere in the meadows. Wherever there are field ridges, the rice plants are in bright green leaf, attractive to the eye. When the rice heads form, some plants cannot withstand the weight of the heads, and fall over half in the water and half out. This provides bait for the fish in the fields, such as Anabas testudineus and Puntius javanicus, which eat their fill. People like to trap them for food, because they are fish with much meat and oil from having eaten their fill of rice all the time. There is an idiomatic expression, "new rice and oily fish," which probably refers to these kinds of fish. There is a kind of creature which causes annoyance to farmers, namely the leech. The water looks clear and quiet as if there were nothing in it, but if we only disturb the water and make a splash, the leeches swarm in. There are both "needle leeches" and "buffalo leeches." Wherever there are marshes or ponds, leeches abound; when the ponds overflow, they swarm out into the fields. When they are thick, the farmers who are plowing and transplanting rice are attacked by them on the legs, many at a time; it is not easy to pull them off, because they cling tightly, sucking the blood. It is necessary to prepare a cloth ball containing strong tobacco and lime and keep this tucked in the waist. When one feels that a leech has taken hold, he rubs this cloth ball against it; the leech cannot stand it, and falls off voluntarily.

In a field the water looks perfectly transparent, because it is still and the mud settles to the bottom. Fish of the sorts which like to swim near the surface are clearly visible, for example Trichopodus trichopterus and Rasbora argyrotaenia. Also one sees water-loving weeds and edible plants growing lush on the surface of the water and spreading out verdantly and attractively.

These plants include watercress (Jussiae repens), sǎaj tı̆ŋ, Desmos crinitus, Begonia obovoidea, "turtle's liver," Ottelia alismoides, and sǎaràaj. Along the field ridges there are Centella asiatica and Ipomoea aquatica, growing down into the water. The farmers utilize these vegetables, dipping them in pepper sauce and plaa rǎa. They are crisp and tasteless, not particularly delicious. Some species are rather acrid and bitter. One sees the farmers gather these vegetables and pile them up in big heaps, squatting in a circle and dipping the raw vegetables in pepper sauce and chewing them up noisily in big bites as if they enjoyed them. For food to eat with pepper sauce, they catch fish and cover them with mud and put them in the fire. When they are cooked they peel off the earth, the scales and skin coming off also; the pure white flesh of the fish is visible, very appetizing indeed. If the fish that they catch are small, they wrap them in leaves of plants such as Zingiber zerumbet and put them in the fire. If there are many bones they first chop them up fine. This kind of food is called ŋǒb plaa. If people who are not farmers go out to the fields in the wet season or the farming season, they cannot resist gathering the plants in the fields, for they are very lush and appetizing, and make one feel gay and amused. At this season the farmers have an abundance of fresh vegetables to eat, and do not go hungry. The best known vegetable is Ottelia alismoides. It has white flowers and floats on the water, intermittently visible like the head of a snake; the stems which are visible in the perfectly clear water are also curved back and forth like a snake, so that one has long since heard it said that when the Ottelia alismoides plant grows old it turns into a Herpeton tentaculatum snake. Actually one encounters real snakes of the group of fish snakes that watch to catch fish in the water, and so people jump to the conclusion that these are born from the Ottelia alismoides plant. Wherever the water is deep, there are lotuses in full bloom. These lotuses are pulled up and sold. They are called flexible-stemmed lotus; sometimes they are called bitter lotus, because the heads have a bitter flavor. The heads are round and large, two or three inches in diameter. The leaves are circular; the underside of the leaves is pig-blood red and hairy. The edges of the leaves are jagged like saw teeth. The flowers are white, the outer petals tinged with pink. The tips of the petals are blunt or slightly pointed. They bloom at night, and close in the afternoon of the following day. Their name in botany is Nymphaea lotus, var. pubescens. They are lotuses of the same category as the white-flowered sàdtàbùd lotus and the red-flowered sàdtàban lotus, which are domestic lotuses, not growing wild. Besides flexible-stemmed lotuses there are other lotuses which grow thick in the fields in the wet season. If you ride past on the train you will see them often. They have abundant attractive white flowers, only a quarter-inch or more in size, but it is learned that there are also big ones as large as five or six inches in diameter. These lotuses are phyan and phǎn lotuses, which in botany are called Nymphaea stellata. They have round heads about one inch in size. The leaves are oval, purple underneath but not hairy, and the edge of the leaves is smooth, not jagged, or at most the edge is wavy. The petals of the full-blown flower are long and sharp-tipped; they are entirely white, or the tips may be faintly tinged with indigo when they first bloom and then change to pink and purplish pink when they are old. These are day-blooming lotuses; in the evening they close. The species that has entirely white flowers, or faint indigo at the tips of the petals, and does not change color, is called the phỳan lotus, while the species that changes color from indigo to pink is called the phǎn lotus. The phỳan lotus is less fragrant than the phǎn lotus. The lotuses of which they eat the heads or roots are these lotuses, for they are not bitter. The stems can be eaten raw, for example, by dipping them in plaa ráa, but they are not boiled or made into curry like the flexible-stemmed lotus.[7]

> They looked lovable and delicate, sending forth pollen,
> The phỳan lotuses growing lush beside the path,
> Prawn's claws [Begonia obovoidea] in overlapping layers, crowding
>   the sǎaràaj beneath the water;
> Sǎaj tĩŋ alternating with "turtle's liver"
> In clusters seen in rows to left and right;
> Water chestnut, water lettuce, and lotus blossoms full blown,
> Scattered white like glittering stars.

> Oh, if the girls come and see this
> They will descend to play in the meadows;
> Those who have little boats will float and paddle about,
> Pulling stems of phǎn lotuses and sǎntàwaa plants [Ottellia
>   alismoides].

These are lines in admiration of fields in the wet season by Sǔnthɔɔn Phǔu, showing that the fields also have a distracting beauty if one has a poet's eye to see.

We have been absorbed in describing things of nature in the fields in the rainy season to the point of forgetting the frogs and bullfrogs, which come what may, there must be. At night they cry loudly, their voices very deafening, but poets hear them as "like the sound of gongs and drums resounding"; but they are certainly less deafening than the sound of motorcycles and loudspeakers. Actually things of nature, if we speak of their good points, include many lovable and attractive things occurring in the fields; they all appeal to the eye and heart. One sees:

> The rice plants in the field
> Flourish cheeringly;
> The rice is quick to form heads,
> In waving clusters.
> Their tips and leaves soar

In every meadow and field,

...

Producing dropping heads,
Most admirable.

Reaping the Rice

When the rice in the field forms heads which ripen to mature rice grains,
between the twelfth lunar month and the waxing phase of the first lunar
month, they set to work harvesting, in the first and second lunar months;
or sometimes they delay until the waxing phase of the third lunar month.
First they harvest the rice in the field of the first plowing, harvesting and
putting the rice aside in portions to be used as seed rice later. Then they
set to work harvesting the rice in the other fields. In some localities before
harvesting they first lay the rice in order to reap it easily; that is, they use
a pole held at the center by a person who walks through the field, which at
this time is getting dry but is still damp, and presses down the rice plants to
left and right with the pole, so that they lie in flat rows to be reaped easily.
If they do not do this, but leave the rice plants to fall over of themselves as
chance directs, they are tangled and difficult to reap. It is as they say, "To
have a drunkard husband is like reaping rice beaten down by pigs"; that is, it
is tangled as if pigs had gone in and trampled the rice plants. Laying the
rice is done according to the direction. It does not matter whether it is done
lengthwise or crosswise in the field. The only requirement is that it be done
correctly according to direction. For example, sections which it is desired
to harvest in the morning must have the rice laid toward the west; if it is
to be harvested in the afternoon, they must lay the rice to fall toward the
east. All this is in order to be able at the time of reaping to turn the face
away from the sun and the back toward the sun.

Whenever there are bees to help one another in harvesting rice, young
women and young men are glad to come and harvest together, for they will
have an opportunity to mingle merrily, playing while they work, reaping and
singing at the same time, and flirting gaily. At this time there are not yet
likely to be sarcastic repartee songs because it is a time for work. If such
songs are sung at this time, it is only because some young man is in love with
a woman and takes this opportunity to express his feelings by singing wooing
songs. The young woman is aware of this, knowing that if she reaps rice
near to this man she is certain to be wooed; but usually she is perfectly willing, for she will get to sing repartee songs showing off her verbal skill. If
she is not good at singing and has no confidence in herself, she invites intimate girl friends who have verbal skill to reap on either side of her. If the
man sings cuttingly, he is answered at once. The fun is in this. In reaping

rice they reap side by side in a row. When they have gathered the rice plants in the hand and cut one handful, they may tie the handful or not, as convenient. Then they carry it on the arm, or may pile it up at once. Whoever finishes reaping his row and reaches the field ridge stops to rest, waiting for the others who have not yet finished reaping their rows. When everyone has finished reaping, they go to harvest another section. Therefore whoever reaps slowly and arrives late is the victim of teasing. If it is known that someone is awkward and slow at reaping, the others reap in such a way that their own rows veer out, in order that the row of the slow reaper will be widened and he will have to lose even more time in reaping it, while those who have finished reaping their own rows go and sit waiting on the field ridge. Reaping like this is called "reaping around an island." Whoever is a victim of reaping around the island is mocked gaily by his companions, both men and women, who sit laughing at him. As the song has it, "Reach out, sister, reach out; hurry to reach the field ridge and we will be able to chat." In this merry fun the old people hardly concern themselves; they usually reap by themselves, striving only to work more than to play. Even if they play, they do not find it amusing. They let the young have their fun, for the young will be young; it is the natural order of the world, and to act otherwise is to obstruct natural laws. "If anyone complains that he is bored, don't believe him." Therefore there are some who even though old still like to let themselves go; usually these are widowers or men who leave the monkhood when they are old; they join in the fun with the others, furnishing an object of raillery for the young people.

They usually begin harvesting rice early in the morning. When the sun gets hot later in the morning they stop to rest, beginning again in the afternoon, following the same schedule as for plowing and transplanting. Whatever amount anyone reaps is piled up together in stacks. It is the duty of the owner of the rice, when the harvest is over, to tie it up in sheaves to be easily carried. For cord for tying they use bamboo strips; if they have none and it is not convenient to use these, they use rice stalks twisted into ropes for tying, called kh<u>ānèd</u>. For tying it is also necessary to have experience and skill. If the sheaves are not tied well, or not tied tightly, they may come loose.

Let us speak of the old people who stay to watch the houses, and do not come to reap rice with the others. They do the cooking and have the children deliver the food to the fields to feed the workers in rest periods. In the evening when they have stopped reaping rice, they all play harvest singing games. At this time they play in earnest, not merely playing while they work, but playing for play's sake. This is called têên <u>kam</u> <u>ram</u> <u>khiaw</u>; that is, each player holds in one hand a handful (<u>kam</u>) of rice and in the other a sickle (<u>khiaw</u>). As they sing they gesture, dancing in rhythm to the melody that they sing. Please read the article on harvest songs in the book, <u>Thai</u>

Culture: Native Games. One suspects that playing at tên kam ram khiaw was not originally merely playing at harvest singing games for amusement as at the present time. It may be a form of playing and dancing handed down as a custom from olden times, consisting of singing and dancing in connection with harvesting rice according to certain beliefs; but later these beliefs were lost or changed and there remained only the fun, while the original purpose was forgotten. Nothing can be learned from examining the words of the harvest songs, because the words that are sung have changed with the times. There remains a bit of evidence in the name tên kam ram khiaw.

While they are playing at tên kam ram khiaw, the owner of the rice is tying up the handfuls of rice stacked up, making sheaves and assembling these in groups and stacks, while the players play on. When night falls they stop playing and everyone returns home; there is no feast of any sort. The owner of the rice and his assistants hurry to separate the sheaves of rice into groups -- seed rice, light rice, glutinous rice, etc. Then they set to work to carry it to the threshing ground at the house. If the sheaves are very big, a person who has never carried them cannot carry even two of them because they are very heavy. Once they have lifted the rice to the shoulder, they cannot set it down midway for fear that the rice grains will fall off. Carrying the rice from the fields to the threshing ground, if the distance is not great, is not very difficult, but if the distance is great and there is a large amount of rice, they haul it by sledge or oxcart, but this is the case only with people of means. Ordinary people usually carry their rice. If the fields are far from the house, it is not easy to carry it in one trip; they carry it and deposit it at a midpoint where they have a rest hut sufficient for sleeping and guarding the rice. They harvest and carry the rice in this way every day until finished.

During the period preceding the harvest, the old men who remain at home guarding the house prepare a ground for threshing the rice. (Threshing is the process of causing the rice grains to come loose from the straw.) They flatten the space to be used as a threshing ground until it is perfectly smooth and the earth is hard and firm. Then they take fresh ox and buffalo manure and dissolve it in water, mixing in wood bark that contains gum, or this may also be omitted, and smear this all over the threshing ground, covering the earth completely. If they can smear it thick, all the better. Even if a heavy rain falls the ground is not spoiled, because the water does not soak through to the soil; the water stands on the surface, and before long evaporates by itself. Rain that falls at this period is called rain that cleanses the threshing ground. Smearing the threshing ground with ox and buffalo manure is done in order to protect the rice while threshing; the rice does not get mingled with dirt and sand. When the people in the fields carry the rice up to the threshing ground, it is the duty of the old people to arrange a prism of rice on one side, keeping the varieties of rice separate. The prism is made in a

shape like a triangular pillow; the size depends upon the amount of rice.
They say that stacking the rice in this shape protects it from the rain. Even
if it rains hard it does not matter much; only the rice on the outside is wet
by the rain, and the rice inside does not get wet because the rain water runs
off the surface of the triangular stack, which serves as a roof. If the threshing ground is located far from the house, they build a roof over it, and old
people sleep there to guard it. There are both large threshing grounds to be
used collectively by the entire village, and small threshing grounds for threshing rice belonging to one household.

When they have finished harvesting the rice and carrying it to the
threshing ground, in some places they set up a flag on the stack of seed rice.
This flag may be made of cloth or anything else; they generally use white
or red cloth, of a single color or two colors. I have been unable to find out
why they set up this flag. When they have threshed the rice and carried it
up into the barn, they take this flag or a new one and set it up on the stack
of seed rice in the same way. After setting it up, when the work is finished
they throw it away, taking no further interest in it. Why do they set up the
flag? If one were to guess, he would have to say that it is a marker to indicate that the rice in the stack is to be saved for seed; if this is stacked with
other kinds of rice in one place they might forget, and a mixup might occur.
The original use of flags was as markers and indicators, before they came to
be used as decorative banners as well; also, flags were first used in religion,
so that setting up flags has a sacred air, making them better than other things
for markers. 8

After carrying the rice to the threshing ground, they go out to gather
scattered fallen rice heads in the fields. There are not many. They gather
them up, of whatever variety, in sufficient quantity to suffice as a gesture.
This is called inviting the Rice Goddess. When they are going to gather this
rice they speak the words, "O Rice Goddess, come you up into the rice barn.
Do not go astray in the meadows and fields for mice to bite you and birds to
take you in their beaks. Go you to the happy place, to rear your children
and grandchildren in prosperity. Come you! Kǔu!" (On the word "Kǔu"
they draw their voices out long.) If they do not know the invocation, they
speak whatever they can think of that seems appropriate. Then they gather
the rice of all kinds that has fallen and put it in a cloth wrapper or in a basket, and put it away in a suitable place in the threshing space. This rice that
is gleaned is called the rice of the Rice Goddess, which is regarded as the
life or the spirit (khwǎn) of the rice. When they have finished performing the
ceremony of making merit at the threshing ground, they mingle straw with
these heads of rice and tie them together as a figure of the Rice Goddess,
which they put away in the rice barn together with the seed rice, to be used
together with the seed rice for future planting, as described at the beginning.

In the province of Ayutthaya they have a ceremony of invoking the rice khwăn to the threshing ground (according to notes made for me by Naaj Maaniïd Wanliïphoodom). At the time of harvesting the rice and carrying it to the threshing ground, when they have carried in almost all the rice, they prepare to perform a ceremony of inviting the khwăn of rice or the khwăn of the Rice Goddess to the threshing ground and the house. They prepare cere-monial food, including one banana-leaf holder of red boiled cakes, one banana-leaf holder of white boiled cakes, one banana-leaf holder of "ele-phant's ear" cakes (made of glutinous rice flour moulded into a triangular shape, boiled till done, and then rolled in salt and coconut), one bunch of nămwăa bananas, one boiled egg (sliced in sections), one lump of rice from the top of the pot, or this may be put in a banana-leaf funnel, and one new set of clothing, that is, one new stole and one new lower garment, which may be of either cotton or silk. For the day to perform the ceremony they choose Friday in the late afternoon. When they reach the field they unfold the garments and spread them out on the ground; or they may simply unfold them as a gesture. Then they bring out the food and make an offering. When this is finished they tie up rice stubble in the form of a small human figure and hold this up while they speak an invocation to the Rice Goddess, saying, "You have come out and borne the sun and the rain for a long time in the fields. Do you return to the cool shade of the threshing ground and the house." Then they take this figure in to the threshing ground, leaving the offerings in the field, and at that spot they must cast harvested rice, in an appropriate amount, as alms to the birds and crows. When the rice has reached the threshing ground, they must unfold the set of garments and drape them over the stack of rice sheaves which have been harvested and brought together. Then they plant the figure on the cloth, pretending that they are putting new garments on the Rice Goddess, and bring out a new set of offer-ings including the same items as those taken out and offered in the field. They offer these and make various speeches according to whatever they think auspicious for their making a livelihood. Thus the ceremony is finished.

In the province of Ratburi there is a ceremony of making an offering to the threshing ground very similar to what has been described. That is, when they have finished carrying the rice sheaves to the threshing ground, they spread a mat in the middle of the threshing ground, and sometimes spread a white cloth on top of this. They set out a meal of meat foods and sweets as an offering, and lay out farming tools such as sickles, straw hooks, hoes, spades, etc., together with a new set of garments. They light incense sticks and candles to worship and make an offering, and then take a cotton thread dyed with turmeric and tie it around the tools in a khwăn ceremony. As for the large tools which are hard to carry in, such as harrows and plows, as well as the oxen and buffaloes, they need not be brought in; taking the thread out and tying it on them to tham khwăn is enough. To the center pole of

the threshing ground they tie one bunch of nâmwáa bananas and one dried
coconut. When they have finished making an offering to the Rice Goddess,
they put this coconut away in the rice barn together with the rice of the Rice
Goddess. They simply put it away so, not doing anything with it until the
time for making merit; then they bring this coconut out and use it to make
offerings for the monks. As for the ripe nâmwáa bananas, when the ceremony is finished they are left on the center pole of the threshing ground, and
are not taken away and used for anything, but they do not last long, for the
children pull them off and eat them one or two at a time until they are gone.
Sometimes they do not last even overnight.

In the south there is a ceremony of tham khwǎn when the rice is ripe
and ready to be harvested, called "tying the rice." If the rice that is planted
includes both light rice and heavy rice, they must perform the ceremony of
"tying the rice" every time. After this there is a ceremony of tham khwǎn
for the rice which is performed both when they are going to thresh it and when
the rice has been put away in the barn; this is performed occasionally, not
regularly like the ceremonies of tham khwǎn at other times.

This matter of gleaning fallen rice and regarding it as the rice of the
Rice Goddess is strange in that various nations of Europe also have this belief,
but they take the last head of rice that is harvested as the rice of the Rice
Goddess. Whether harvested or picked up from the field, the important
feature is the same, namely, that the last remaining rice is the life or the
spirit (khwǎn) of the rice. If it is not brought in, the rice that is kept for
seed might not grow well, because it lacks the life or the important part of
the rice. (See my article on the Rice Goddess.)

The khwǎn ceremonies for the rice and the threshing ground are performed when all the rice is gathered in from the fields. Usually this occurs
around the end of the third or the beginning of the fourth lunar month. This
is only for sown fields. For transplanted fields the time is earlier, around
the end of the twelfth or the beginning of the first lunar month.

Threshing the Rice

When they have finished inviting the rice of the Rice Goddess to the
threshing ground, they set to work threshing. They thresh the various kinds
of rice separately, always beginning with the rice harvested from the field of
the first plowing. If one is going to thresh his rice at a communal threshing
ground, he threshes this first rice on a special private threshing ground.
There are two methods of threshing. In one method they use two pieces of
wood about a meter long, tied together at the head with a rope. The rope
is long enough to form a loop to go around a sheaf of rice and be caught up
at the far end of the piece of wood. They raise the sheaf of rice and bring

it down sharply on the floor of the threshing ground or on a mat, and the rice grains fall off the straw. This piece of wood is called a "wooden threshing pole." The method of threshing is similar to that used by westerners, who have a threshing implement called a flail. The other method, used when there is too much rice to use the first method easily, employs oxen or buffaloes to tread on the rice. They set up a pillar as high as one's head in the center of the threshing ground, called the center pole (săw kĭad); sometimes this is corrupted to săw cĭad. At the top of the pole they generally tie a branch of thorns; usually this is a branch of Indian jujube. It is not reasonable that it should be for protection against birds and crows lighting. This pole also sometimes has garlands of flowers hung on it. They lay the rice sheaves in order around the center pole, placing the "heads" of the sheaves, that is, the bottoms of the sheaves, upward. The other sheaves placed next outside are laid with the rice heads up, just the opposite. Probably they desire to lay the sheaves with the rice heads up, and so they lay the sheaves nearest the center pole with the "heads" of the sheaves up to serve as a support for the rice sheaves that are laid in rows around the center pole. If there is a great deal of rice, the sheaves are laid profusely around the center pole and extend to a distance. They tie the oxen or buffaloes to the center pole, arranging them in a row extending out from the center. Then they drive the oxen or buffaloes round and round the center pole to tread on the sheaves of rice. The sheaves of rice are broken down and the rice grains fall off the rice heads and straw. Before bringing the oxen or buffaloes in and tying them up, they spread straw on the threshing ground for them to tread on. If they do not spread straw, the threshing floor, which has been properly smeared with ox and buffalo manure, might crack and break from the weight of their hoofs. They usually make baskets to put over the mouths of the oxen and buffaloes used in threshing, so that they will not eat the rice. If buffaloes are being used, they put old ones near the center pole, where the running circuit is small, because old buffaloes have less strength and walk slowly. Also, they are elderly buffaloes and not playful; they can be trusted; while other buffaloes with the strength of virile youth are not placed near the center pole because they will walk too fast, and other buffaloes in the big outer circuits will not be able to keep up. Therefore they put the young male buffaloes at the extreme outer end. If there is a mother buffalo with calf mixed with the others, the calf runs around the circle following its mother. When the buffaloes have made many circuits treading on the rice sheaves, the stacks of rice break down and the rice grains drop off the straw and fall to the bottom. At this time there are people standing in a row, usually young men and women, holding straw hooks (khŏɔ chǎaj) in their hands. These are long bamboo poles with knots in the ends, cut off short enough to serve as hooks. Straw hooks with iron hooks at the end are a modern invention. In some localities they are called mǎj dɔɔŋ hǎaj, which is the same as the term used in the old

laws. The name is also corrupted to mǎj kàdɔɔŋ hǎaj. Actually chǎaj and
hǎaj are the same word, meaning to make smooth (chǎaj = camhǎaj, dɔɔŋ =
long pole like a carrying pole: Cambodian). When they see a rice sheaf
break down, but with the straw still sticking to the sheaf, they pull it up with
the straw hook and then thrust the rice sheaf toward someone else. If he does
not duck in time and is struck squarely, it hurts. The one who thrusts is
usually a woman, and the victim of the thrust is usually a man, but sometimes
the opposite occurs. If there is going to be a game of thrusting rice sheaves
it is necessary to give advance notice to be prepared. When someone makes
a thrust, the other raises his straw hook and receives the thrust, like Chinese
actors fighting. This can also provide fun. In some places they do not thrust
the rice sheaves; they use their sickles to cut away the straw cords and bamboo strips which tie the sheaves, and then spread out the rice. This is called
chǐig ʔòg. When they have spread out the straw, they have the buffaloes
tread on it again, watching to pick up the straw with the straw hooks and shake
it for the rice grains to drop off and fall to the bottom. In some localities
this is called nǔʔ. When they see the rice grains drop off and the straw come
to the top, they pick up the straw and lift it outside. They do this until only
rice grains remain, and then they turn the buffaloes loose and the threshing
is finished.

Threshing is done beginning in the early morning. Later in the morning they stop to rest because the sun is hot, and if the straw is struck by the
sun it turns brittle. There is no threshing in the afternoon for the same reason.
Sometimes they thresh at night. At this time they have fun, and the young
people all gather. As the verses for the buffalo khwǎn ceremony have it,
"I'll tie you up to the stake, and then thread a rope through your nose and
lead you around in a circle, in the presence of all the young men and young
women, until the rice is leveled all over the threshing ground." If it is the
dark of the moon, they build a straw fire to give light. They have refresh-
ments, consisting chiefly of glutinous rice cooked in coconut cream with
"fragrant" bananas. [The "fragrant" banana of the Thai is the familiar
variety sold in the United States.] They have an uproariously gay time
while they sort out the straw from the threshing floor. One can imagine that
this is fun, for it is a simple sort of play mingled with work. This is work that
they gladly and willingly help one another do. It is in the clear open air,
with no unpleasantness to interfere. Formerly at the time for threshing rice
each village usually made a big threshing ground to thresh the rice collectively, taking turns at using the threshing ground for one day or two depending
upon whether the individual had much rice or little. They use what oxen
and buffaloes they have for the threshing, even having ox and buffalo races;
that is, they seek out oxen and buffaloes with speedy feet, and tie them at
the end of the row in descending order to the number of twenty. If the animals at the end of the row are not fast enough they get dragged; if the animals

at the end of the row are very fast they can run and curve the row; for this they are praised as good. This is all great fun. When the rice has been trodden and some of the straw begins to float up, it is picked out. After two or three spells they stop and rip open the sheaves and then pick out the straw again. After two or three spells more it is finished. At this time of picking out straw and ripping open the sheaves, the people all assemble with their straw hooks, picking out straw and shaking it as they sing. For songs sung while picking out straw and shaking it, they use brief, simple verses, like:

> Pick out the straw, sister, pick out the straw; brother has come
> to sit at the edge of the threshing floor and help sister pick out
> the straw.

> Shake out the straw, sister, shake out the straw; O sister with
> joined eyebrows and graceful throat, come and shake out the
> straw.

If there are good songmasters and songmistresses, they sing long repartee songs as at the harvest. But nowadays if you go out to the country you will have difficulty finding a big threshing ground. There are only small threshing grounds using two or three oxen or buffaloes to tread on the rice. Each person has his own, and they do not work together well. The spirit of the farmer has deteriorated seriously, and threshing songs have deteriorated as well. [9]

They thresh the rice until the triangular stacks are all gone; when every triangular stack is finished they ask everyone to help winnow the rice, winnowing and pouring the threshed rice grains. Both men and women help. Women who do this work must wear a crossed stole [the method is to bring a scarf around from the back, cross it on the breast, and tie the two ends at the back of the neck, like a modern "halter"], because they have to stoop over constantly, and if they do not wear crossed stoles like this, they ["they" is a euphemism for the breasts] will swing and flop unattractively, or will be half visible and untidy looking. The winnowers stand in a long row holding wooden shovels with which they scoop up the rice and winnow it. They pour it against the wind, for the bran and rice dust to blow away with the wind. Even this is not enough. There must also be people to shake the mats with their two hands and help to blow away the dust and empty rice husks. In shaking the mats they have dancing gestures, not simply shaking them, for they dance to show off to the women and so must shake gracefully and in rhythm. Therefore shaking the mats becomes the duty of the young men who are strong. They do not feel very tired, for there are people smiling nearby to cheer them. To work like this is good in that one never gets tired. The mats that they shake are panels woven of bamboo, in shape like big monk's fans. In the verses for the khwǎn ceremony for threshing and winnowing rice it is said neatly: "Oh do not take fright when you are put on the threshing and winnowing ground for the buffaloes to tread on. We carefully sweep you up and winnow you to make you clean, and carefully scoop you up for the wind to blow you. Not even a tiny particle of straw will remain mingled with you." When they have finished winnowing every stack of rice, they scoop up the rice in triangular heaps. If there is a large quantity of rice it is slow and difficult to scoop up the rice; generally they use a board to scoop it. This board is called the "rice scooping board." Sometimes they make the rice scooping board with a rope threaded through each end to pull the board with and reduce the labor. If the heap of rice is small they use a small board with a long handle for scooping the rice. This sort of board is called thảdthaa, sometimes corrupted to krảthaa. When they have finished making the triangular stacks, they measure out the rice to be used for seed into portions, counted in basketfuls according to a "dog's tail" account. That is, they break and bend bamboo strips, and each break represents one basketful. When they have made breaks representing many basketfuls, the bamboo strip will curve up like a dog's tail, and hence the name. When they have finished measuring out and heaping up the rice according to variety, they take bran ashes and smear a streak on the heap of rice. This is called "ghost's streak" or "ghost's mark." They say the reason for doing this is to provide protection against thieves; if anyone steals they will know it, but they would probably know only that the rice was short. Perhaps they smear the rice to render it "defective," to deceive spirits into thinking that the rice is spoiled, so that they will not molest it, just as the Indians have a custom of daubing cupboards and vessels in order to show the spirits that the objects are defective. Or perhaps they smear and mark the rice to indicate that this rice is the property of spirits and gods, marked by the spirits; if anyone steals the rice he will offend the spirits. What the explanation is, is not clear, but in any case, when they put the rice away in the barn they measure it again according to the "dog's tail" account. This is a recheck for certainty. When they finish winnowing the rice, they have a traditional feast. As for the straw from which all the rice grains have dropped, they leave it piled up on the threshing ground. Later when they have time they carry it out and heap it up in a triangular stack, for feeding to the oxen and buffaloes when there is a shortage of grass. But while the straw is still stacked up on the threshing ground, they have to be rather careful, for the children are very mischievous and like to play tag and hide-and-seek in the straw. Sometimes they take wood and make a cave, cover it with straw, and crawl in to lie inside, where it is warm and comfortable, this being the cold season. Merely lying there does no harm, but if they play with fire near the straw it is as likely as not that a disaster will occur. The straw catches fire and blazes up quickly, and may roast the children to death. There have been instances of news of this sort in the pages of the newspapers.

Making Merit at the Threshing Floor

Before carrying the rice up into the barn, the time arrives for making merit at the threshing floor. They make a pavilion and set up a place for the Buddha image and seats for monks at the threshing ground. In the evening of the day appointed for making merit at the threshing floor, when the time arrives monks come and perform evening chants at the threshing ground. The host invites relatives and close neighbors to gather and make merit, listen to the chanting, and present food to monks at the threshing ground next morning. The pavilion is usually built of bamboo and roofed with rice straw. Sometimes they tie rice heads on the pavilion as sprays and drooping garlands to decorate the pavilion, and they bring the rice of the Rice Goddess, put it in a vessel, and lay it down as one of the ceremonial items. On the threshing floor they set up parasols made of rice heads, planted on the stacks of threshed rice in the same way that they plant parasols on sand pagodas. The stringing of a sacred cord in the ceremony begins with the Buddha image and goes to the begging bowl. Then it is tied around the center pole of the threshing ground. From the center pole it goes around the area of the threshing ground and then goes back to the starting point. When the monks have finished chanting, one part of the ceremony is completed. If they desire to have entertainment at night, they have any sort of games they choose, enjoying themselves in the traditional manner of the peasants of the area. The following morning they make merit by putting rice in the monks' begging bowls and feeding monks at the threshing ground. Then they feed everyone who has come to help. The monk who presides over the ceremony is usually the abbot of the monastery. He sprinkles the rice of the Rice Goddess and the rice kept aside for seed, the center pole, and the other stacks of rice with holy water. When this is finished the monks return to the monastery. In this matter of making merit at the threshing ground, if their farming has produced an overabundance of rice they make merit gaily and feast joyously. If they get a great deal of rice they are very happy; it is like getting a wishing jewel, for whatever they lack, there will be people to bring it to them in exchange for rice. If they get little rice, they are not happy, and they do not have a big ceremony of making merit, abbreviating it to just enough to preserve the custom. They only offer food to the monks, the crucial part of the merit making. There is nothing strange about this because everyone is in the same condition. In the book of collected khwăn verses there are verses for a khwăn rite for the fields. I have been unable to learn clearly when they perform this. It is probably a custom that is not much performed nowadays, and so no one knows as much about it as in the case of the other khwăn rites.

When the affair described is finished, they carry the rice up into the barn. If there are children living separately they apportion out shares for them. If they can carry the rice up into the barn quickly it is all the better, for the rice is stacked up on the threshing ground, and if their luck is bad there will be a heavy third lunar month threshing ground cleansing shower. They have no advance warning, and the rice may get rained on and spoiled. They must find mats and prepare to cover the rice well whenever rainclouds appear. In carrying the rice they first carry in the rice of the Rice Goddess and the rice to be kept for seed, of every variety, as a ceremonial gesture. Then they carry up all the other rice until finished. It is at this time that they recheck the rice according to the dog's tail account. The different varieties of rice can be mixed in the barn, except glutinous rice, which is kept separate in a krɛ́a or phɔ́ɔm. A phɔ́ɔm is a large basket, swelling at the center and with a wide mouth, but without the finished rim around the mouth found on a regular basket. For a lid, they use a flat basket of the sort used for sunning things. The rice that is kept for seed is put in a phɔ́ɔm or other receptacle and set aside in a part of the barn. Then they take some heads of the rice of the Rice Goddess, mix them with straw, and usually tie them up as a doll with legs and arms, just good enough to be recognizable as the figure of a seated person. Sometimes they dress it in clothes to show that it is a woman. The figure is not very large, usually about half a meter high. When they have finished tying it, they set it up on the stack of seed rice. While "inviting" it, they speak an invocation in the same vein as at the time of gathering the fallen rice in the fields; it is a request to the Rice Goddess to remain and guard the seed rice. In this invocation there is no offering of any kind except flowers, incense sticks, candles, scented powder, and perfumed oil. Why they tie together a figure of the Rice Goddess only when they put the rice away in the barn, unlike the European custom, which is to tie it up and bring it in from the fields when the harvest is finished, and what the purpose is, are not clearly known. There is another belief which is maintained in the province of Ratburi, namely, that once the rice is put away in the barn, they must not open the barn and take rice out often. They may open it only when they sell rice, or when there is necessity for using a great deal of rice for some purpose. When they are going to open the barn they must first light incense sticks and candles and worship the Rice Goddess. What words they speak, my informant cannot remember. No doubt they beg forgiveness of the Rice Goddess for disturbing her and taking her rice out. The reason for forbidding opening the barn frequently is probably fear that the Rice Goddess will become angry and flee away. For this reason before putting the rice away in the barn, they first apportion out enough rice to eat for a long time, so that it will not be necessary to worry about opening the barn unnecessarily.

In the province of Ayutthaya they have a ceremony of closing the barn and a ceremony of opening the barn. They perform the ceremony of closing the barn when they have finished threshing the rice and put the rice all away in the barn properly. They must leave about a bowlful of paddy on the threshing ground for use in the ceremony of closing the barn. For the day of the ceremony they likewise choose Friday. They select a woman or man born in the year of the dragon, regarding this as a zodiacal sign [so the original!] which does not harm crops, to perform the ceremony. They prepare offerings including white boiled cakes, rice from the top of the pot, and an egg, as usual. They have the person born in the year of the dragon make the offering at the threshing ground. Then they use a big spoon to pick up the paddy remaining on the threshing ground and put it in a metal bowl. As they scoop up the rice they speak, asking that the Rice Goddess cause there to be so much rice that they will never finish scooping it up and measuring it. When they have filled the bowl with rice, they take the bowl and empty it in the rice barn, like the seed rice of the Rice Goddess. When they have finished making the offering, the ceremony of closing the barn is completed.

In the south (as noted down for me by Naaj Win Chajjáráq of Chaiya District) there must always be some rice left in the bottom of the barn, called the "khwǎn of the rice of the lord of the place." When the time comes to put new rice in the barn, they scoop up the remaining old rice in the bottom and place it in the center of the barn. Then they set up offerings to the khwǎn of the rice, including three heads of first ripened rice which were brought in from the khwǎn ceremony in the fields. Then they make an offering of cooked rice from the top of the pot and roasted fish. They take a little from the head and the tail and the middle of the body to serve as a ritual representation of a whole fish; they call this "fish with head and tail." This is of the same category as the offering made to spirits and gods in other regions with a whole pig, that is, the head, tail, and four feet. Besides these there is one small stone, one plate for cooked rice, one small cup for water, and one piece of iron. It is not known what the stone and iron are used for or what they mean.

The ceremony of opening the barn to sell rice out of the barn involves superstitions about days; they absolutely refuse to measure out rice to sell on a Friday. On other days they may open it to sell. (In Ratburi they add the Buddhist holy days as days when they refuse to open the barn to sell rice.) The refusal to sell rice on Friday no doubt comes from a superstition about the sound of the word Friday (sùg), fearing that they will sell their happiness [sùg]. The ceremony of opening the barn is to scoop up a bowlful of paddy with a metal bowl used for offering food to monks. At this time it is not necessary to use a big spoon to scoop. Then they speak an invocation to the Rice Goddess, telling her not to be alarmed, and asking her to abide with the home and the fields, giving them rice measuring a hundred cartloads or a thousand cartloads. When they have finished speaking the invocation, it is all right to measure out rice to sell. As for the bowlful of rice that was scooped out, they take it and grind it to white rice, and cook it to put in the begging bowl of a monk to end the matter.

In the south they have superstitions about days in which they may not take rice out of the barn, namely Buddhist holy days, the sàad days, the beginning of Lent, Sŏŋkraan day, and the last days of the year, that is, from the thirteenth day of the waning phase of the fifth lunar month to the beginning of the waxing phase of the sixth lunar month. They regard these as days when the spirit of the Rice Goddess desires to be calm or to meditate, and does not wish to move. Whoever persists in taking rice out is wicked and may be caused to become poor again. The prohibition of taking rice out on these days also applies in other regions: The reason for this is self-evident. When they take rice out to sell they must mention the name of the Rice Goddess every time, asking her pardon for daring to take away her rice. In this affair there is an offering of cooked rice from the top of the pot and fish, as usual. This duty falls to the woman who is mistress of the house.

The barns which they build for storing rice are low buildings, but in the north they elevate the floor higher than the floor of the house in which they live, probably to show respect to the Rice Goddess. There are pillars and scantlings outside the walls. The walls may be of woven bamboo or of real wood, as the builder chooses. In the main, country people hardly use boards for the walls because they are hard to obtain. Usually they make the walls of woven bamboo. In the province of Nakhon Ratchasima they weave them of a kind of grass called tàkhúʔ, which they lay on to make walls for the barn. This kind of grass has round, hard stems as big as a lead pencil and two meters or more in length. They use this kind of grass, believing that termites do not eat it. The inside of the barn walls is smeared with fresh ox or buffalo manure in order to close up any holes that may exist and prevent the rice stored in the barn from leaking out. In some places they use mud to smear. Please do not be hasty to criticize the farmers as terribly uncivilized, to use ox and buffalo manure to smear the floors and walls. If they do not use these things to smear, what will they use? These things they have already or can obtain easily; they need not spend money to buy them, and so they use them. What else can they use? It is a question of living far from modern progress and not having to spend money to buy things. They must depend upon themselves almost entirely. The good and the bad must go together. It is impossible to choose only the good; the bad must also go with it in order that we may know the good and the bad. When we speak the word barn (júŋ), the word chǎaŋ almost always follows it. A chǎaŋ is a large barn, built in a long shape as a place for storing large quantities of rice. They may be seen at railroad stations. They differ only this much. Farmers who have no barns in which to store their rice weave phɔ́ɔm for storing it, or weave big baskets, but with open bottoms, or make round baskets to cover or enclose the rice which is heaped on the ground, smearing the area with ox manure and covering it with mats. If they do not use mats, they spread straw to prevent seepage of water which might make the rice damp. Then

they build a small shed covering this to keep the rain off. They merely
cover the rice. The rice may burst out in the lower part, and so they twist
straw into a cord and loop this around the lower part of the basket. On the
inside they likewise smear fresh ox and buffalo manure. This sort of place
for storing rice is called a tàlɔ̂ɔm for rice, but if they surround it with mats
or weave an extension with bamboo strips, they call it a tǐam, about which
there can be no doubt that it is a word borrowed from Chinese. Even if they
have a barn for storing rice, if they wish to separate varieties of rice -- for
example, nonglutinous rice and glutinous rice -- they may make a tǐam or
tàlɔ̂ɔm as a separate storage place.

Household Tasks and Implements

The farmer's receptacle for measuring out rice is the basket (kràbuŋ),
which there is no need to explain as it is well known. But the baskets which
they use for measuring rice are of two sizes. The small size is called kràbuŋ
lûug sàd; the large size is called kràbuŋ sìb hâa. If we compare the sizes of
these two kinds of baskets in terms of units for measuring paddy, one kràbuŋ
sìb hâa, when ground to white rice, amounts to about one and one-half pails
of white rice. If it is a kràbuŋ lûug sàd, it amounts to about one pail of white
rice. This is only an approximation; it depends on the large and small sàd
measures of various individuals. Forty sàd of rice are one kwian [literally,
cartload], showing that formerly the oxcarts used for transporting were used
as measures of large quantities of rice. Another kind of kràbuŋ is the kràbuŋ
hàab [used for carrying on a pole over the shoulder], short and squat in shape,
with the bottom curved more than that of the kràbuŋ lûug sàd. These have
handles for attaching cords, used for carrying paddy or other things on a shoulder pole. This kind of basket, if woven very tightly and then bathed in oil
or pitch both inside and out, with a handle for carrying or for inserting the
carrying pole, becomes a khrúŋ for carrying water. There is also the kràchəə
which is another kind of basket, with flaring mouth. The flaring mouthed
baskets which we always see the Chinese using to measure rice are also a kind
of kràchəə. The kràchəə is used everywhere as an instrument for measuring
rice, but it is not a standard measure like the kràbuŋ lûug sàd. Another kind
of receptacle used for cooked rice is called the kràbaaj; in shape it is like a
waterbowl. It is woven closely, and there are various sizes. If it is small in
size but flat in shape it is called a kàbaan, and is used in place of dishes and
plates for cooked rice. After eating rice with a kàbaan it need not be washed;
they beat (khɔ̀ɔg) it to shake off the rice still sticking to it; after shaking it
clean they hang it in the sun. Perhaps it is this that is meant by the expression khɔ̀ɔg kàbaan ["to thump the head"], that is, to knock a vessel of this
kind, or really to thump the head, used in both meanings. There is still

another kind of woven receptacle also similar to the kràbuŋ, but with curved
bottom, like a spittoon with bulging middle. They call this a kràthaaj, and
use it to carry things about on the hip, as in the verses for the preaching of
the Chuchok canto [of the Vessantara Jātaka], when they praise Lady Amitda:
"The beauteous Amitda walks along with the old Brahman, holding on her hip
a kràthaaj painted with appliqué figures, looking radiant and lovely." If the
kràthaaj has a flat shallow shape, with very wide mouth, it becomes a kràcàad.
The kràthɔɔ is the name of another kind of woven receptacle, in shape almost the same as the kràthaaj, but round like a lamp chimney, with a lid
and handles for threading cords to hang it up or carry it on a pole. The
kràthɔɔ is usually lacquered and gilded for holding clothing and other things
which should be put aside. The kàlôo is also another kind of woven receptacle, woven closely, with round flattened squat shape like a can fruit and a
wide mouth, for carrying things on the hip. I have formerly seen lady barbers
carry their hair-cutting implements in these on the hip as they went to cut
hair in private homes. There are two kinds of kràdôŋ: the kràdôŋ for sunning
things and for use as a lid for the phɔ́ɔm, whose shape it is not necessary to
describe, since they are still used everywhere; these are mates to the tàkrɛɛŋ
for sunning things, which is woven more coarsely, with large interstices.
The other kind of kràdôŋ is smaller in size than the kràdôŋ for sunning things,
oval in shape like an egg. This is the rice-winnowing kràdôŋ. There are
wooden crosspieces for separating sizes of rice at the time of winnowing.
There is still another kind, the tàkrɛɛŋ, which is shaped like a fishtrap. They
use it for scooping up fish. When the word tàkrɛɛŋ is spoken alone, one does
not know it, and thinks always of the shape of a tàkrɛɛŋ for sunning things.

These receptacles will soon disappear, because they have been replaced
by better receptacles made of other materials, as we have seen new things
substituted for old ones already. But, in any event, to speak of the past, the
farmers did not buy from others, but made these things for their own use.
They studied the method of weaving and making these receptacles from generation to generation. When they had free time from farming, they wove
baskets. How can one accuse farmers of being lazy? They had to spend as
much as eight months of the year farming, performing heavy work at least
from before daylight till evening. As has been described, the remaining
three months they did not remain idle. For one thing they still had to make
gardens, according to their needs. Their greatest amount of free time was
when they had harvested the rice and put it away in the barns, about four
months, but they had other personal and traditional duties, as has been described elsewhere. The time when they were genuinely free and need do
nothing at all was at the time of the Sɔ́ŋkraan festival.

You have no doubt heard the criticism, "They pound white rice and
pour it in the pot only in sufficient quantity to eat." This means that whenever the country people would cook rice, they must pound white rice right

then, pounding only a little, enough to pour into the rice pot and eat. This seems terribly lazy; even rice, which is the daily food, they have no desire to pound, no desire to prepare adequately in advance. If you think thus it is because you do not know the condition of the life of farmers. The reason for not pounding a great deal of rice in advance to eat over a long period is that they cannot eat it fast enough and if it is kept long it does not taste good. It is not like newly pounded rice, which is much more delicious. They pound only enough to eat from day to day. The duty of pounding rice goes with that of carrying water; these are minor household tasks, and fall to the daughters and granddaughters. They usually mention the two tasks in a single phrase. Before pounding the rice they first sun the paddy until perfectly dry. If they do not do this, when they pound it the rice husks will be hard to break open. The first time they pound it, it becomes klɔɔŋ rice; that is, rice that has bran still clinging to it. They must pound it again, called sɔɔm. On the second pounding the bran slips loose, leaving only rice grains. When they have finished pounding the rice, they winnow it for the husks to go in one direction, and the rice grains, broken rice, and rice bran in another. In the language of farmers this broken rice is called kɔ̀g khâaw plaaj khâaw, to be kept and mixed with other things as food for animals. This rice winnowing is strange: it looks easy, but when one tries to do it he fails. He cannot separate a single grain of rice from the broken rice. He gets angry and shakes the rice a little harder and the rice spills. If you don't believe this, try it. As for the mortar for pounding the rice, they also make this themselves. They cut a tree stump and whittle it into shape, and then cut a hole in the center of a size to form an appropriate hollow. This need not be very deep. Then they build a rice bran fire in the hole. The fire burns down into the wood until they see that it is deep and wide enough for use. When they use it for a long time, the rough rice husks will of themselves polish the wood in the hole smooth. The longer it is used, the deeper the hollow of the mortar gets, until the bottom is thin and finally cracked and broken and unusable any longer. Then they replace it. Most mortars are for hand pounding. There are also mortars used for pounding with a big hammer-shaped pestle, but women do not much like them because if one is not skill-ful the work is very heavy. Lever-pestle mortars and rice mills are later innovations. Only some families have them, for pounding rice or milling rice in large quantities for making merit and for feasts.

Carrying water and pounding rice are the duties of the daughters and granddaughters. Besides carrying water and pounding rice, they must also cook rice, spin cotton, and weave cloth. If it is a mother with small children and no one to help, she is very busy and hardly has free time. She must apportion her time for various jobs appropriately. Any time a young un-married woman works, no matter what the work is, there are always young men around. This is the great drama of the world; if there is a heroine but no hero it seems wrong. Therefore at the time of pounding rice there are young men who come to provide amusement, or even volunteer help in pounding. "When night fell I always pounded rice and waited, càgkàlan [sound imitating the lever-pestle mortar]; brother walked down the highroad. I forgot the basket, and brother went straight to take it to his sweetheart." After the rice is pounded, next morning it is the duty of the aged women to sɔ́ɔm it again, because in the morning the young women are busy carrying water. Carrying water is done at two times, namely in the morning and in the evening. In the morning they carry water for the betel vines and other plants, while drinking water is carried in the evening. At this time they usually return home more slowly than in the morning, for young men watch for them to flirt at the landing or well or pool. It is for this reason that they say girls are always willing to carry water, for they will get to see their sweethearts. If the place where they get water is a pool in the monastery, the evening is the time when the monks bathe. If they have a sweetheart in holy orders, they thus have an opportunity to make a reverence to the reverend brother. If convenient they may remind him by asking, "When are you going to leave holy orders? How many more months or years are you going to remain a monk?" The duty of carrying water falls to the woman apparently everywhere; pictures of people carrying water in Europe and India are always of women. They always use pots carried on the head, or carry the water on the shoulder. One notices that the Chinese who draw city water along the streets are more often women than men. All this is because the work of carrying water was daily work of the household in olden times, and fell to the women everywhere, of whatever nationality, and so it has come down to the present.

Now that we have told the story of farming, it will be seen that the gaiety of farmers depends upon farming productively. It is as they say, "rice to spare and salt cheap," or "the fields are full of rice, the water full of fish." This is to be regarded as prime happiness, because there are few other needs. If one has rice he can exchange rice for all other things that he needs. There are traders who bring things to the spot to trade; it is not necessary to seek them out. If one does not have a cotton field, there are people who bring cotton to exchange for rice. When cotton is obtained, the women spin and weave it into cloth for the family's needs. The happiness that comes from not lacking food and clothing belongs not only to the countryfolk. The monks derive benefits, not lacking for food and robes. The important thing for all humans is the desire for happiness, fun, and comfort. To speak only of farmers, if they are not addicted to evil ways, such as gambling, they have not a little happiness, because they have few needs. It is happiness deriving from the surroundings, namely nature. When they have enough to eat and enough to use they are happy. We have only just recently gotten away from making things for our own use and providing our own amusement, and so we do not feel the great value of making things for our own use and providing our own amusement like the farmers. I have told the life of the farmers, which is a simple, smooth life, not adventurous, not progressive, not wealthy, and not powerful. However things are, they go on like that. It appears that farmers would seem to have extreme happiness; not so! Normally a badge on the chest has two sides. One side is beautiful and glittering. There must also be a reverse side, whether it be a big badge or a small badge; there must be a reverse side in suitable proportions.

Before closing my story I wish to ask you a riddle: "What is it that cooked in the earth can be eaten, cooked in wood is good to eat, and cooked three times becomes sweetmeats?"[10]

APPENDIX

FARMING IMPLEMENTS

Key to Drawings of Farm Implements

WATER WHEELS AND WATER SCOOPS

1. water wheel

2. bamboo tube for dipping up water

3. conduit for receiving water, sugar palm tree or bamboo conduits are chiefly used

4. drag-type water wheel made entirely of bamboo and hardwood

5. tripod-suspended dipper

6. tripod

7. handle of tripod-suspended dipper

8. dipper or water scoop

9. half-dipper, woven

PLOWS AND YOKES

10. khan of the plow

11. dâm, or handle, of the plow

12. plowshare, tip is of iron

13. "pighead"

14. ʔɛ̀ɛg nɔ́ɔj

14a. modern plow

15. yoke

16. ꪫꪚꪙ, made of bamboo

17. hitching rope

18. khlâw rope

SMALLER FARM IMPLEMENTS

19. harrow

20. khan of the harrow

21. harrow teeth

22. iron rake, Chinese style

23. iron shovel

24. wooden shovel, old style

25. spade

26. hoe

27. sickle

28. chick-head knife

29. lĭam, a kind of big curved knife with long or short handle

30. bamboo pole for carrying rice seedlings over the shoulder

THRESHING, POUNDING, MILLING, WINNOWING, AND MEASURING IMPLEMENTS

31. straw hook, made of bamboo, used in threshing and picking out straw

32. threshing "chopsticks" of hardwood and bamboo for holding rice sheaves and beating them

33. shovel with groove, made of lightweight hardwood, for tossing rice

34. mats for shaking out rice dust, woven entirely of bamboo including the border

35. board for pushing rice, of the kind having ropes which they vie in pulling ceremonially

36. <u>thâdthaa</u>

37. <u>kàchəə</u> or <u>sàd</u> for measuring rice, woven

38. <u>kàbuŋ</u> or <u>lûug sàd</u>

39. lever pestle, for pounding

40. lever-pestle mortar of wood, buried in the ground

41. tail of lever

42. pestle for pounding

43. pestle for <u>sɔ́ɔm</u>

44. hand mortar, of wood

45. big hammer-shaped pestle, for hand mortar

46. pestle for hand mortar

47. rice mill, woven

48. winnowing basket woven of bamboo bark with wooden crosspiece, for winnowing rice

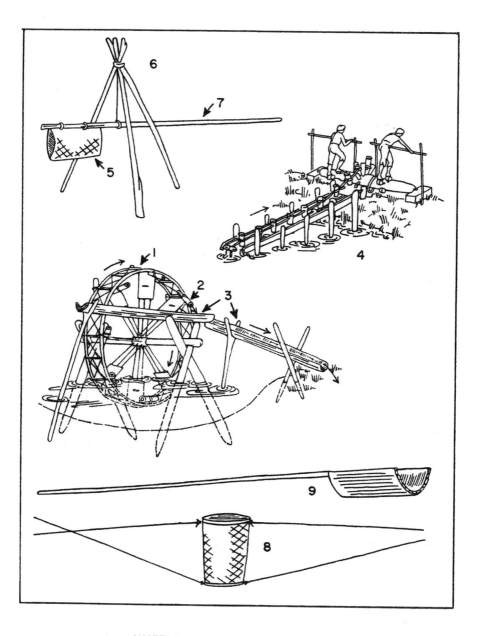

WATER WHEELS AND WATER SCOOPS

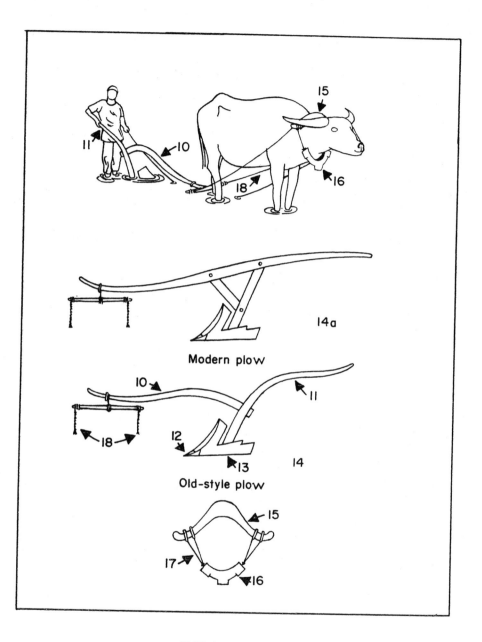

14a

Modern plow

Old-style plow

PLOWS AND YOKES

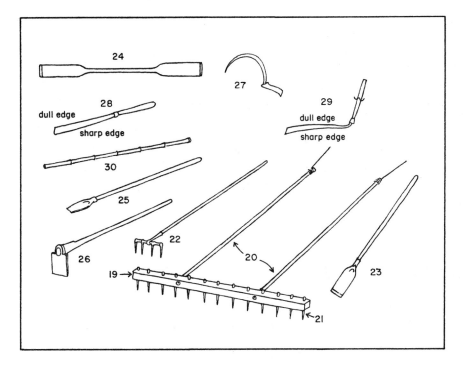

SMALLER FARM IMPLEMENTS

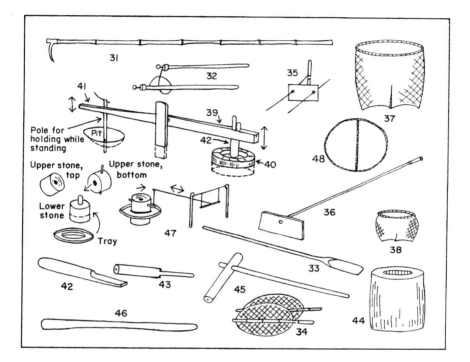

Labels within the figure:

31

32

35

41

Pole for holding while standing

Pit

39

42

40

37

48

Upper stone, top   Upper stone, bottom

Lower stone

Tray

47

36

38

42

43

45

33

44

46

34

THRESHING, POUNDING, MILLING, WINNOWING,

AND MEASURING IMPLEMENTS

Footnotes to The Life of the Farmer

1. Tylor, Edward B., Primitive Culture (London, John Murray, 1871). A.R.

2. The people of Nakhon Ratchasima and the northeast call a spade còɔb, and call a hoe còg. A.R.

3. See Old Textbook of Rice Planting (National Library, 1924) and "Days Forbidden for Ploughing" in Royal Ceremonies of the Twelve Months, in the section on the first plowing. A.R.

4. See Textbook of Farming According to Ancient Methods (Bangkok, Canthánáphlin Printing Press, 1930) by Dr. Chěɲ Cajtroɲ. A.R.

5. See "Kinds of Rice" in Manners and Customs, Part 3. A.R.

6. See the section on plows in the chapter on "Farming" in History of the Ministry of Agriculture. A.R.

7. Through the kindness of Phrájaa Wínîd Wánandɔɔn (Too Koomêed).

8. See "Banners" in Encyclopaedia of Religion and Ethics, Vol. 2, p. 348. A.R.

9. See "Concerning Singing Games" by PhráɁ Phínîd Wannákaan (Sěɛɲ Sǎalítun) in Manners and Customs, Part 25. A.R.

10. The answer is rice: it is cooked in earthenware pots, or can be cooked in bamboo tubes, or for certain kinds of sweetmeats is put through an elaborate series of processes involving three cookings.

POPULAR BUDDHISM IN THAILAND

Table of Contents

POPULAR BUDDHISM IN THAILAND

The Wat

To gain any true insight into the culture and character of the Thai of Thailand, it is necessary to learn something of their religion. Here I mean the religion, not of the educated or of scholars, but of the people in general; for religion is the mainspring of behavior as manifested by the people. The national religion of Thailand is Buddhism of the Southern School, technically known as Hinayanism. It is the religion, as generally professed, of Ceylon and the nations on the mainland of Southeast Asia (with the exception of Vietnam, which adheres to Buddhism of the Northern School or Mahayanism, as professed by China and Japan). Buddhism in essence is a religion of ethics and philosophy rather than a religion in the strict sense of the word. In Buddhism "man is as he has made himself; man will be as he makes himself"; the individual has to strive by himself to be pure of heart and deed for his own salvation without the intervention of God or any other divine being. This is the gist of Buddhism. But the Buddhism of the people, as a result of almost inseparable accretions through long popular practice, is otherwise.

In Thailand, as in the other Buddhist nations of Southeast Asia, the countryside is dotted with Buddhist temples and monasteries popularly called wat (wád) in Thai. The wat is divided into two sections: the first comprises the temple with its chapel, called bood in Thai, where the monks assemble for their religious duties, together with the wíhăan (vihāra in Sanskrit) where Buddha images are housed; the second consists of the monastery building where the monks live. This is the usual arrangement of the wat in its bare outline. Most wats also include a number of stupas or pagodas of various sizes, called phrăʔ ceedii in Thai. They are roughly pyramidal in form, tapering to a plain or decorated tip and supported by a round or square base; bigger ones may rise from a terrace added for circumambulatory purposes. Originally a phrăʔ ceedii was a tumulus containing relics of the Buddha, but the smaller ones in many instances have been built to contain the cremated bones of some deceased persons. It is the Buddhist Thai custom that a corpse be cremated and the incinerated bones and ashes deposited in a phrăʔ ceedii or elsewhere within the precinct of the wat. This is equivalent to the Christian custom of burial beneath a cross in consecrated earth.

In every wat there is also an open hall called a săalaa where the congregation meets to hear sermons or to make merit, as occasion demands. The săalaa may be utilized as a rest house for wayfarers; or, in a bigger wat, it may be used as a place of religious instruction. In such a case it is called in Thai a săalaa kaan pàrian or the hall of learning. A wat also contains a bell tower and sometimes a drum tower as well. If there is no tower for the purpose, the drum is hung somewhere in the monastery. The bell or drum is used to summon the monks or the congregation to their religious devotions, or to assemble them for other purposes. Some of the bigger wats have a library to house the Tripitaka or Buddhist scriptures. Occasionally the library building is built in the middle of a pond to prevent insects, especially white ants, from getting access to the library.

As to the monastery where the monks live, it is divided into groups of houses, if the monastery is a bigger one. In each group there is usually an open hall surrounded on all four sides by the monks' cells, each separated by narrow open spaces. This hall is used as the dining place by the monks occupying the cells around it, as the recitation hall where monks chant their evening devotions, and sometimes also as a schoolroom where a monk-preceptor teaches boys of the monastery a rudimentary knowledge of reading and writing. A monks' kitchen is attached to each group of cells. For the purpose of saying something about Thai life in connection with the wat, I am going into great detail in describing a typical wat, though certain features are omitted in the larger wats, especially those in Bangkok.

Wherever there is a village of reasonable size, there is always at least one wat. The village folk regard the building of a wat as their first duty, unless one exists already. The act of building a wat is regarded as highly meritorious and as a praiseworthy sacrifice of time, labor, and wealth; so it was if we go back to the old days, when communal activities and the attractions of life were centered in the wat. Religious and social gatherings as well as most artistic and educational activities were to be found nowhere except in the precincts of the wat. The Thai rite de passage of life from birth to death has been inseparable from the wat. It was the desire of every Thai, from the king down to the common people, according to his means to build a wat, either individually or cooperatively, in order to gain the great merit accruing from such an undertaking and to gain the approval of his compatriots. A wat is also sometimes built to commemorate some great achievement or success in life. A victorious general on his return from a war must, if possible, build a wat to commemorate his achievement and no doubt also to atone for having deprived a number of human beings of life, which is deemed a great sin in Buddhism. One may wonder why there are a number of wats left in ruins -- why, instead of repairing them, people have continued to build new wats. Before King Vajiravudh's time, every king had built a number of wats. King Vajiravudh himself did not build a royal wat, giving as his reason that there were already a more than sufficient number and that making repairs to certain old deserted wats that were in ruins would surely bring as great religious merit as the building of a new one. But the popular belief persisted that merit for the repair of a wat would accrue to the original owner, so that the only way to gain merit for oneself was to build a new wat of one's own. Although the selfishness of this reasoning might seem all but to preclude the repairing of wats, there have been many cases where an old site has been restored and renamed as a new wat. Today there is seldom a newly built wat in Bangkok (with the exception of Wat Sri Maha Dhat near the Bangkok Aerodome which was built nearly two decades ago) but in the provinces the building of a new wat by an individual, or by a group in cooperation, is controlled and sanctioned by a faculty from the Buddhist Council of Elders.

A person desirous of making merit on behalf of deceased relatives may assign some of his immovable property to a wat. Such property may be a piece of land, a rice field or an orchard garden, or a piece of vacant land with or without buildings. In the old days such assigned lands were worked by a class of people called "wat slaves" under the supervision of a wat supervisor who ministered to the wants of the monks. Wat slaves, or in other words pagoda slaves, were household slaves or prisoners of war whose owner, as an act of merit, had transferred them to the wat as a religious offering. The status of wat slaves was in no way different from that of household slaves, but perhaps they fared better in some cases than the latter in their manner of living, for they were treated tolerantly and not as outcasts. The institution of wat slaves was based on traditional custom; and though slavery was abolished by King Chulalongkorn nearly a century ago, the institution survived implicitly by the consent of the people in certain parts of the country. It came to an end automatically in 1932 with the commencement of the present regime.

When a wat has been built and consecrated, monks from another wat or perhaps several wats are invited to take up their abode in it as a nucleus for the new wat. The monk who is going to be the abbot of the wat is usually selected by the villagers but in some cases will be sent by the church. The abbot-designate is usually a monk with at least ten years' standing in the monkhood who has thus earned the right to be called "thera" or elder. He is a man of learning in religious matters and if possible a man of sanctity with a knowledge of traditional lore such as is needed in a typical small community. A monk who has some knowledge of the healing art, or exorcizing and incantations, is always in demand by the villagers. Here I speak of the situation in the past, though it still exists in the present in some outlying localities. In certain instances when a monk who is desired by the villagers as the abbot of their wat is not able to place himself permanently in such a position, he may be asked to grace the wat for at least a few days as the first abbot of the wat and as a good omen for its prosperity. The coming of the abbot-designate is fixed beforehand on a certain auspicious day and at a time calculated according to the knowledge of astrology, which is to the present day a determining factor in many decisions. There may be a procession and other signs of rejoicing at the approach and arrival of the abbot-designate.

In his old age the village elder may become a monk and later be made the abbot of the village wat. In common language, particularly in central Thailand, an old monk is called as a sign of respect lǔaŋ puu, lǔaŋ taa, or lǔaŋ phɔ̂ɔ, meaning respectively, "great (paternal) grandfather, " "great (maternal) grandfather, " and "great father. " Other monks who are unlikely to attain such a status are addressed as lǔaŋ luŋ, lǔaŋ ʔaa, lǔaŋ náa, or lǔaŋ phîi, that is, "great uncle" or "great elder brother. " (In Thai an uncle is luŋ if he is an elder brother of the father or mother; a younger brother of the father is called ʔaa, and a younger brother of the mother is called náa). The custom of addressing monks with such words as an expression of relationship and intimacy points to a time in the old days when the monks in the village were no strangers but kinsmen.

It may be said that traditionally a male Thai whose parents are Bud-dhists ought if possible, on reaching a full twenty years of age, to become a monk for a while. Many of the monks have in their younger days been mon-astery boys learning elementary reading and writing at the monastery or wat, and some of them have been novices observing the rudimentary rules of the order. This gives them some experience of the religious life, thus smoothing the way to becoming a monk in later years. It is a popular belief that by be-coming either a novice or a monk one gains great merit and so also the per-son or persons who sponsor the undertaking. A childless person desiring re-ligious merit will sometimes sponsor someone, not his own kith and kin, as a candidate for ordination. He will sometimes even go so far as to relieve the man of his financial debts; or, in the old days, if the candidate was a slave, the sponsor might redeem him from the state of slavery, as otherwise he could not be ordained. For a person to become a monk he must be free from both pecuniary debt and other obligations. For instance, a government official is traditionally a king's man and must receive the royal sanction be-fore he can be ordained. Also a candidate must be a normal and healthy per-son free from leprosy.

A son who becomes a novice or a monk is in popular belief a mysterious agent for helping save his parents from hell when they die. A novice will be able to help his mother from such an unhappy state in the next life, and a monk will do so for his father. Thus parents are desirous of having at least one of their sons become a novice, or better still a monk. If possible, the son-candidate ought to be an unmarried man; if he has been married, all the merit thus gained will go to the wife instead of to the parents, and more-over his thoughts are likely to be more on his young wife than on religion. With rare exceptions, the Order of the Church will not allow a married candi-date to be ordained without the implicit consent of the wife. If it is desired to gain religious merit for a person when he dies, his son or, if he was child-less, anyone else, may on the day of the cremation become a novice, if he is a boy, or a monk, if he is a man. By so doing he expresses his gratitude to the deceased, and shows that he holds his memory sacred. Such an act is deemed highly meritorious to the deceased person, even if it is done only for one day. When King Chulalongkorn died, a certain high official became a monk expressly as an act of devotion and gratitude to his late majesty, thus transferring to his king all the reward of good deeds or merit accruing to him. Similarly, when King Vajiravudh died, one high official became a monk in sacred memory of his majesty: this person is still in the monkhood (1957).

A man who has not passed through the monkhood is regarded as a "raw" or "immature" man. The people will have an unfavorable opinion of him as an uneducated and imperfect man who is not "a son of the Tathagata, " that is to say, a monk. It will be difficult for him to find a wife, for decent folk will look at him askance wondering whether he is a proper and suitable man to be a husband or a son-in-law. Here I speak of the good old days but the custom lingers to the present time, especially among the country folk. A man who has passed through the monkhood and again become a layman is called dìd, an abbreviated form of the Pali word familiar in Anglo-Indian as pandit, which means a scholar or a wise man. The word dìd has now in certain instances degenerated in meaning, to imply that there is something in the man of a clumsy person who is a tyro in the ways of worldly life. An ex-monk who has graduated from some school of Buddhist religious instruction is called máhǎa, which means "great" in Pali. The word may be used as an honorary prefix to his name, but sometimes a man may be annoyed or object implicitly to being addressed by such a prefix, for no other reason than that he will not seem up-to-date in the eyes of his modern-minded compatriots.

All I am discussing here pertains to a time in premodern days, when the culture-pattern of the people, especially in central Thailand, was more or less identical. It is still the culture-pattern of the personality of the Thai, despite the fact that there are some radical changes in behavior and thinking among present-day people, mostly in modern towns or cities through contact with modern civilization. In the old days when schooling was practically limited to the wat, it was no wonder that the people were desirous of having their male relatives become at least temporary novices or monks. When a man becomes old he sometimes as a devotional act becomes a monk for life, or if for various reasons he is not able to do so, he will frequently on Buddhist holy days repair to the wat and observe certain religious precepts and hear sermons. Many retired officials in Bangkok still observe such a practice. In the next section I will speak of life in a wat.

The Ordination

The ordination of monks can be performed by a council of Buddhist elders at any time. But in practice there is a certain time of the year when ordinations usually take place: this is in the month before Buddhist Lent during which the monks make a religious retreat lasting throughout the three rainy months from the full moon of the eighth lunar month to the full moon of the eleventh lunar month (roughly from August to October).

A young man who has reached the full age of twenty years or more can become a monk. If he desires to do so either on his own initiative or, usually, through that of his parents, the first step is to prepare a salver containing one or more wax tapers, incense sticks, and fresh flowers, which he carries to his senior relatives or to his superiors, to pay formal respect and inform them of his intention of becoming a monk. He hands the salver of offerings with both hands to the appropriate person, who ceremonially receives and places it in front of him. The young man, assuming a demeanor of worship, prostrates himself thrice before this person, first placing his palms together and then bending his head until his forehead touches the floor between his hands now outspread palms down on the floor. Then sitting on his heels with hands raised and placed palm to palm, he solemnly addresses the person in formal language thus: "May any act or acts of mine, whether of thought or word or deed, which have trespassed against you, be kindly forgiven as an act of cancellation." The person thus addressed, while his right hand touches the salver, will say a few words congratulating the young man on the occasion of his entering the monkhood followed by a short exhortation and blessing. The young man then makes another triple prostration to the person and takes leave bringing back with him the salver, which may be similarly offered to other appropriate persons.

Now if the young man has a fiancée, he ought to inform her too of his intention of entering the monkhood. His fiancée will, as a matter of fact, make no objection, knowing very well that it is a tradition for a good young man to enter the monkhood before he marries. Of course, the girl will show mild surprise when hearing the first news and there may be some questions and answers between the two. For instance, the girl will ask how long he will stay in the monkhood. Why should she ask such a question, since she knows full well that the normal period a man spends in the monkhood is not more than three months, during the lent term only? But who knows for certain that the man will be in the monkhood for such a brief period? There have been instances when a young man, in the course of his novitiate, has become attracted and inspired by the noble teaching of the Dharma or Law of Buddha, and continued to stay on after the prescribed time. In such a case a decent girl is in a difficult position. She, by custom, cannot marry anyone else for fear of public opinion, and no other young man dares to marry her when it is known among the villagers that she is the betrothed of such and such a monk. Such has been the custom of the people but it is now weakening. Sometimes if the young man has remained a monk for a longer period of years with no decision that he will again become a layman, he will in conformity with custom and in justice to his betrothed inform her that probably he will continue to lead the life of a monk for how long he cannot say, and express a wish that she marry someone else if she wishes. Thus the girl is relieved of her moral obligation, and becomes free to marry anyone, for she is a "chaste woman" in the eyes of the villagers. In rare cases if the girl is determined she will reply to her man, the monk, thus: "If you do not intend to leave the monkhood then I will wait and marry no one at all."

There is a well-known folktale prevalent in central Thailand of a certain powerful giant who was killed by Phraʔ Raam (or Rama, the famous god-hero of the Indian epic, Ramayana) with his magic arrow made from a sedge stem. The giant died lying flat on his back and became a huge mountain with a sedge arrow still sticking in his breast. This mountain is said to be at Lopburi, a town some 154 kilometers to the north of Bangkok. In the course of time the sedge arrow, which pierced deep into the heart of the giant, will little by little withdraw from the wound, and in a thousand years it will loosen and fall out; then the giant will come to life again and devour all the people. Phraʔ Raam, therefore, created a magic cock which he stationed at a place near the stone giant. If the sedge arrow becomes loosened the cock will give a crow as a signal. On hearing such a sound, Hanuman, the monkey king and an ally of Phraʔ Raam, will proceed through the air to the stone giant; and with a mallet he will strike at the sedge arrow until it penetrates to its former place. It is believed that if a quantity of vinegar is poured on the wound of the stone giant, the sedge arrow will by its effect be withdrawn from the wound and the giant will revive from his death and devour people.

Now this giant has a daughter, who up to now has lived in a mountain cave a few miles north of Lopburi town. She is the betrothed of Phraʔ Sĭi Ann (Sri Arya Mettraya in Sanskrit), the embryo Buddha (Bodhisatva in Sanskrit), who will attain Buddhahood in succession to the present Buddha whose Dharma or Law will come to an end after the lapse of five thousand years after his death. Half of this number is now begun in either 1956 or 1957 A.D. as computed by the Buddhists in Thailand or in other countries. His betrothed, the giant's daughter, is still waiting for him, and she comes day by day weaving a piece of cloth made of the filaments of lotus stalks. She intends to present this piece of cloth as a robe to him when he becomes the Buddha. Such a story may inspire a betrothed girl to take it as an example of being faithful to the end to her lover who is still in the monkhood. The story bears traces of Mahayana Tantric Buddhism, and has also a resemblance to an episode in the Raamákian, the Thai version of Indian epic, Ramayana which contains no such story. However we will leave the study of this tale to the folklorist.

In village life where each man is a law unto himself, every man carries a weapon for self-defense if he goes beyond the village. A young man on his rounds to pay his respects to someone in connection with his expected ordination as a monk will go accompanied by defensive weapons as a safeguard. Why does he have to do so? If an enemy of his knows that he will become a monk, there will be no way for that enemy to square up the feud or avenge an injury, as is his right. The yellow robe of the monk will act in most cases as a protection, for no one will dare to injure a monk with his yellow robe, a symbol of sanctity. The last and only chance for an enemy to take revenge is the little time left before the young man becomes a monk. Hence the carrying of weapons, and traveling in company, are necessities for the young man. In some cases and localities when the young man goes round on such an occasion, a gong is beaten at intervals along the way. This is to inform the villagers that the young man is going to become a monk. A person on hearing such a sound and seeing the young man pass by, will raise his hand in a worshiping attitude as an expression of rejoicing and approval. This is the pattern of custom in general among religion-minded persons. When one is informed that a friend or any other person is doing some meritorious act, or one sees a procession in connection with the making of merit go by, one raises the hands automatically in such a worshiping attitude to express one's approval. One usage among the folk when doing a meritorious act, or when one has achieved such an act is to announce it by beating a gong and by word of mouth. This was the way of making a public announcement in the old days. It is called in Thai idiom tii khɔ̌ɔŋ rɔ́ɔŋ pàw or "to strike a bell and proclaim in loud voice." If you ask someone for a share or a subscription for any meritorious project you say bɔ̀ɔg bun which literally means "inform (to make) merit."

On the eve of ordination, there is a great stir in the house of the sponsor. Neighbors will bring presents either in money or things to the sponsor "to help in making merit" as we say in Thai. Some of them will give a hand in cooking or doing other things as may be required. The stir continues throughout the night, and there is fun and flirtation among the young people while they are working. Here in Bangkok when one is invited to any social function such as a wedding ceremony or a funeral ceremony we sometimes say paj chûaj ŋaan; this means literally "to go (and) help a function" which reflects the old spirit of the people in which there has been always cooperation and a helping hand in such social functions among neighbors whose social status is more or less on the same scale.

Now we have to speak of the young man who is going to receive ordination as a monk. For a month or two, and sometimes three months, the young man, if he can, will reside as a layman in the monastery training himself in matters relating to the ordination of a monk. He learns how to make responses in Pali to questions which will be put to him also in Pali by the officiating elders, to worship in the prescribed way, and to commit to memory certain Pali verses in the devotional service. On the eve of the day of ordination in a village, or on the actual day in Bangkok, the young man has his head, eyebrows, and moustache shaved and is dressed in white, a symbol of purity. His attire will consist of a lower garment gathered in pleats in front like that of a Thai female dancer and a robe similar to that of a monk.

On the afternoon before the day of ordination the candidate makes a progression in procession through the neighboring villages. The candidate walks with someone holding an umbrella over him; a wealthy one may ride a pony or an elephant. The procession moves from one village to another. Passing the open fields and villages on a hot afternoon, sometimes the procession has to stop for a rest under a shady tree where the fun and amusement of the folk continues; the procession starts again in progression when the sun has passed its highest point after two o'clock in the afternoon. The procession returns home sometime after dusk, when there is an entertainment with food and drink. After that there is a ceremony of tham khwăn which means strengthening or confirmation of the khwăn.

Khwăn is a Thai word identical in sound and meaning with the Chinese word for "soul." Owing to the adoption of a Pali word for "soul" in Thai, the word khwăn has lost its original meaning. Its present-day meaning is vague and denotes something definite but invisible in a man. It gives health, prosperity, and happiness when it resides in him, but if, on the contrary, its fickle nature causes it to leave the man and fly away, then if it does not come back in time, that man will die. Khwăn is translated in English as "vital spirit." At every formal turning point in a man's life and on other appropriate occasions, the ceremony of tham khwăn is performed. As for the ceremony in connection with ordination it is called tham khwăn nâag. The word nâag is nāga in Sanskrit and Pali, a generic name for a class of mythological snakes. A candidate for monkhood is called nâag. Why should he be called by such a name? A folk story supplies the explanation that during the Lord Buddha's time, a certain nāga or mythological snake, by its magical power turned itself into a man and became by ordination a monk. One day the nāga monk during a deep sleep turned back into a nāga and was seen by brother monks. The matter was reported to the Lord Buddha, and the nāga monk had to relinquish his monkhood, for no kind of creature except a human being may be ordained as a monk. The nāga asked a favor of the Lord Buddha that his name as a nāga might be given as a namesake to a candidate for monkhood in memory of the fact that it was once a monk. The Buddha consented, and so the word nāga is given as a name to all candidates for the monkhood. The above story bears a trace of a snake cult in far-off days. To come back to the word khwăn, in the Thai language khwăn is a word that enters into not a few Thai idioms which reflect how the building of words and expressions was done in the old days. To describe the ceremony of tham khwăn further here is to interrupt the thread of the story; for treatment of the khwăn requires a monograph of its own.

The time for ordination may be any time of the day by arrangement with the wat. Usually when the ordination takes place in the morning, there is a morning feast for the monks beforehand, which means some time after eight o'clock in the morning. If the ordination takes place in the afternoon, there is a forenoon feast, the last meal that monks may partake of on that day. A feast for monks may be presented by an individual or by a body of people when there is more than one candidate. I speak here of life in a village, while in Bangkok such a presentation of food to monks on the occasion is sometimes omitted.

The candidate proceeds from the house to the wat in procession. He is usually dressed, whether in a village or in Bangkok, as a conventional celestial being with a white conical hat studded with tinsel, a brocade lower garment, and a long thin embroidered robe worn over a shirt or singlet (a university gown of Chulalongkorn University is one of this kind). He may walk, ride on a pony, or sit in a palanquin or in a car, and he has to hold a wax taper, an incense stick, and a flower (usually a lotus) between his palms in an attitude of worship. He is shaded by a kind of umbrella with a long handle. Included in the procession are the eight requisites of a monk: an alms bowl; the customary lower garment, a mantle, and a shoulder scarf all dyed yellow; a girdle, a razor, a needle, and a water strainer. There are also robes and other things appropriate for presentation to the monk who will be the future spiritual teacher of the candidate and to other elders in the council who participate in the rite. We will leave out the details of such a procession, which of course includes music and other entertainment. In some cases, as in Bangkok, the candidate and his party proceed to the wat in the ordinary way without the attraction of a procession.

On reaching the wat, the procession enters the precinct of the bōod, or the wat chapel, and makes a circumambulation thrice round the chapel in a clockwise direction. The candidate, who has already dismounted before entering the precincts of the bōod, walks directly to one of the boundary stones in front of the bōod where he makes an obeisance to it and says a formula in Pali. He rises after paying respect to the boundary stone and walks into the bōod. But before doing so, he sometimes stands by the portico of the bōod and throws handfuls of cash to the crowd below as alms.

Why does the candidate worship a boundary stone? In one of the two sects of official Buddhism in Thailand such an act is deemed unnecessary. Perhaps the worship of the boundary stone of the bōod is a survival of animistic belief that at the boundary stone either of a city or some sacred places, there is a guardian spirit which requires a propitiation before any important undertaking. Beyond the boundary stones of a bōod one steps actually on sacred ground. Here everybody who wears shoes takes them off and places them somewhere. In old days the people wore no real shoes. They went barefoot or in slippers, and if one wore anything on his feet he had to take off his footwear when entering a house. There was a water jar or water container at the foot of the stairway at every house. A person washed his feet at the water jar before entering a house, where the floor was kept clean. Instead of sitting on a chair, which was not a necessity, he sat in a squatting position right on the floor or on a mat, or in later times on a carpet. The typical Thai house is raised on piles, unlike the western-style house, with a ground floor which in the old days was actually on the ground; hence the necessity in the West for evolving a chair. Accustomed to the traditional way of life, a Thai, even if he wears western-style dress, will in most cases take his shoes off before entering a sitting room, because although he may sit on a chair he feels he may bring mud and dirt into the room on his shoes. With the introduction of chairs in the European style, there is of course no necessity to take shoes off when entering a house, except for those who do not ride in a car who might bring in mud from the muddy roads. Now in a bŏod, which is a consecrated place, if there are no chairs provided and one squats on the floor, if he does not take off the shoes, apart from soiling his own wearing apparel, he may be the agent of soiling other peoples' apparel. One will also notice when entering a bŏod or other places where a religious ceremony takes place, that there is usually a raised platform expressly provided for the monks. Sometimes this platform is raised relatively higher, while chairs are provided below for the laity, for monks must not be allowed to take a lower position than a man.

When entering the ordination room in the bŏod the candidate or nâag is led by the hand by his parents or his sponsor and followed by a number of his relatives and others who desire the merit which will accrue from their participation. Everyone walks in line, touching or holding lightly a piece of string made of unspun cotton yarn which is attached to the candidate. The string acts, so to speak, as a conductor of merit, so that all the participants may have an equal share. One will notice also that the persons who lead the candidate by the hand are usually the parents of the young man. The one who carries a monk's alms bowl on his shoulder by a sling and holds a monk's conventional long-handled fan made of palm leaf is the father, and the one who carries the yellow robe is the mother. The rest of the monk's requisites and presents for monks are carried by other persons.

Once they are inside the ordination hall, after all the articles mentioned have been put in their proper places in front and every one has sat down, the candidate lights a wax taper in adoration of the Lord Buddha, whose sacred image rests on a high dais in front of him. Below the image sits an assemblage of elders. The candidate fixes the lighted taper at the place provided and performs the usual act of worship. The fixing of a lighted taper is popularly deemed a prognostication of the candidate's monkhood. If he fixes the taper in an upright position he will be in the monkhood serving the religion a long time; if there is an inclination of the taper, he will not be very long in the monkhood; relatively the more inclined the taper from its upright position the shorter will be the time in the monkhood.

The yellow robe, a set of three pieces, is handed to the candidate, whose head by now is shaved. His gown was removed before he entered the ordination hall, as he advanced toward the assembly. He sits on his heels before the assembly with the robe in his hands in the respectful position, that is holding it with both hands. He then asks the assembly in a loud voice in Pali words for his ordination as a novice. When consent is given, he goes out to robe himself. Here someone with experience will help him robe. He comes back to make his vows and accept from an older monk who performs the ceremony the ten Buddhist commandments for a novice. He is now a Buddhist novice. Next he asks the assembly if he may join the brotherhood. He presents the alms bowl to the president of the assembly, who hangs it on his shoulder by a sling. Someone may have secretly put amulets and talismans in the alms bowl as there is a popular belief that such articles will obtain an increase of miraculous power. The novice is now directed to a place at a short distance from the assembly where two elder monks will ask in Pali the prescribed questions concerning his status as a free and healthy human being. He will reply in Pali with yes or no. It is hard for a man to understand the questions in a language he does not know. The only thing he can do is to repeat the yes's and no's in the order of the series of questions which he has committed to memory. Sometimes in his apprehension he may reverse his yes or no: for instance, when asked whether he is a human being, he says no, and whether he suffers from leprosy he says yes. Then the formula has to be repeated. The questioners go back to give a report to the assembly while the candidate stands waiting. Then a pronouncement is made and the assembly ordains him with formal words and manners as a member of brotherhood. He now becomes a full monk. The actual time of his ordination as a monk is noted, as there may be a number of monks ordained; monks must go by seniority of ordination in their religious functions rather than by seniority in age. In old days when there were no timepieces, the noting of time was by the sun where a shadow of man was measured by the man himself in so many footspans. There is a superstition that when the assembly makes the actual pronouncement of ordination no pregnant woman may be present. Unless she leaves before the pronouncement is made, she will have to suffer a hard labor. Presentation of articles to the elders by the new monk begins and he in turn receives articles from friends and relatives who have been invited to the ceremony.

Life of a Monk

The young man has now become a monk and a changed man as far as his manner is concerned. He is meek and mild in strict observance of the exacting rules of the Buddhist brotherhood. A lay person who is very humble or shy in manner is compared in the Thai idiomatic expression to a newly ordained monk. A monk after ordination may reside in the wat where he has received his ordination, or he may select the wat of his choice as his residence. Usually he resides in his village wat for obvious reasons; for he has to rely on the support of his own people for his subsistence during the term of his monkhood of three rainy months, and at the same time serve as a means for his folk to "make merit." The old folk, especially the women, are always glad and happy to "make merit" through the newly ordained monk who is their own kinsman. Usually the wat where the young monk resides has an abbot or a monk who is an elder relative of his; so much the better. He will not feel a stranger in his new way of life. In fact the young man may have been a novice or a "monastery boy" during his boyhood days, in which case he is no stranger at all and will not feel lonely in his new mode of life.

During the first few days after his ordination, the new monk is busy adapting himself to his new life and receiving visitors who come to present him with the articles necessary for monks. These are the individuals who have been unable to attend the ceremony on the day of the young man's ordination. Perhaps his fiancée will pay her visit too. Customarily there is a celebration of rejoicing by the parents of the new monk at his old home. In such a case the new monk will, of course, have to be present and receive the customary alms from the people. A monk usually goes out for his morning alms; for it is his duty to do so. Such an act by a monk is called in Thai prood sad, which means literally "to show mercy toward creatures." It is through monks that there is an opportunity for a "creature" to make merit, for the monk in such an instance acts indirectly as a priest ministering a merit to the donor of alms. It is thus logically the donor of food to the monks who has to express thanks to the receiver, that is the monk, instead of the monk having to express thanks to the donor of food.

Now we come to the daily life of a monk. Every morning at dawn, about four o'clock, a bell in the bell tower of the wat is sounded at intervals. This is to arouse monks from their sleep and also to awake villagers to prepare food for the monks on their morning visit for alms. The main food of the Thai is rice, and it requires boiling for at least half an hour before it can be taken as food. No rice left over from the last meal is suitable to present to monks as an act of merit. The young monk after rising out of bed robes himself in the customary way. Within a wat compound monks will robe themselves with their right shoulder bare, but with both shoulders covered when they leave the wat. The young monk will recite such appropriate portions of the Buddhist scriptures as he at that time has been able to commit to memory. This is how a monk learns by heart gradually a fair portion of the sacred text, by practicing every morning. Such a recitation as chanted by a chapter of monks in ritual and ceremony is not prayer in a strict sense of the word. Logically there is no prayer in Buddhism, but in popular practice, there is, of course, a prayer to the Lord Buddha or to unseen beings. The young monk, after a short recitation of the text, goes out on his morning round of alms gathering. In the village, monks of the same wat go for alms in single file with the abbot at the head and the most recently ordained monk at the end of the line. In Bangkok or in large towns such a practice is now inconvenient,

because of traffic; therefore each monk goes by himself, although when receiving alms monks line up in queue. If a monk, owing to sickness or other
adverse circumstances, is unable to go out for his usual morning alms, he is
allowed by custom to send his "monastery boy" to represent him.

During the act of putting food into the monks' alms bowls, a person
who is wearing slippers or other footwear that leave the heels uncovered must
take them off as a sign of respect. A monk may not "show mercy toward a
creature" who by an impudent manner pays no respect to the religion. After
putting food into the alms bowl, the donor will raise his hands in worship. By
etiquette no one must stand with his head above that of a monk. One ought
to bend one's head low or stoop down a little as a sign of respect before a
monk, just as one might show a respectful attitude by bowing before a superior.
This practice is observed also toward a superior or an elder layman. If such
a person is sitting on a chair, one ought to stoop a little as a sign of respect
while going near or passing by. If the person is squatting on the floor, one
has either to crawl or sit down. To speak to a person squatting on the floor
while one is himself in a standing position above that person is a sign of dis-
respect, for one must not overshadow a person's head. The average Thai
deems his head a tabooed part belonging to his personality. His fortune or
prosperity will be weakened if perchance anything undesirable touches his
head, and he deems it a grave insult if anyone dare to do so without his permission.

After presenting alms to a monk, the donor will perform a libation by
pouring water from a basin or other utensil with a continuous running down of
water without interruption into a clean place. This is a ritual act of allowing
one's merit to accrue not only to one's own deceased relatives but generously
to all other sentient beings as well.

Here we have to say something of the "monastery boy." In Thai he is
called lûug sìd, which means a pupil or a disciple. But actually a lûug sìd
or a "monastery boy" is a boy who serves a monk by doing his chores. In return the boy receives religious instruction and knowledge of reading and
writing. In premodern days there were no schools in the modern sense. It
was only at the wat that teaching was carried on by some of the monks voluntarily during their spare time as requested by the abbot. The knowledge of
reading and writing thus gained by a monastery boy was relatively rudimentary or higher in level according to the monk-teacher's knowledge. Parents
desiring their boy to know something of religion, reading, and writing sent
him to a certain monk in a wat to be trained. If the monk who would be a
guardian of the boy was the parents' elder relative or an acquaintance, so
much the better. The boy might be a young child some eight or nine years
of age, or already a grown-up boy. If the boy was a young child the monk-
guardian would look after him as a father looks upon his son. Thus an old
monk was called by the boy lǔaŋ phɔɔ or lǔaŋ puu, that is, great father or

great grandfather. In some cases the monk-guardian was himself the actual grandfather of the boy. People at present call an old highly respectable monk lǔaŋ phɔ̂ɔ or great father as an honorific prefix to the monk's name. The boy stayed either in the wat with his great father, or he might return home every evening if his home was near by. The boy, if he was not too young, would serve the monk with whom he stayed after his school hours by arranging the monk's food, clearing the plates, sweeping and cleaning the monk's quarters, and so on. The boy might be ordained as a novice if his parents desired. The life of the boy in the wat was interrupted every now and then during the year. His parents might require him to do some light work as a helping hand in getting their livelihood, which, in central Thailand, was by rice growing; and this required more help at certain stages of its growth.

Monks of the Hinayana or Southern School of Buddhism can take their daily meals only in forenoon. There are two meals a day, one in the morning and the other, the last meal, at eleven o'clock in the morning; and he has to finish this last meal before the sun has passed the meridian. Before the introduction of the mechanical clock the time was measured by the sun's shadow. A drum hung in the wat is sounded at eleven o'clock in the forenoon for the monks to partake of their final meal of the day. It is the duty of monastery boys to arrange the place and to present food in the customary way to monks. Monks usually take their meal in groups in a particular dining hall. There are rules and manners for the partaking of food by monks as laid down in the Buddhist Code of Discipline, which we need not go into. The monastery boys take their food after the monks and then clear the place. What about an evening meal for the monastery boys? They eat the food that is left after their last meal if there has been any; or after a few days of getting accustomed to the life in the wat they do not take any evening meal. As for a young boy, if his home is near, he will go back home to take his evening meal and return later to the wat.

The newly ordained monk, after partaking of his forenoon meal, will proceed to the abbot's quarters to receive instructions and training in religious matters. It will take him many afternoons or sometimes a month or two to finish the course of instruction and training for newly ordained monks. He is to learn by heart certain formulas and texts in Pali as required of monks. This is relatively easy for a literate monk, for he can learn by heart from a book, but not so with an illiterate monk. In the old days most of the monks, not only of the village folk but also of the people in towns, were illiterate. In such a case the monk had to learn the text and formulas by heart orally either from the abbot or from his deputy.

As to a monk who has been in the monkhood for a number of years, or in the Pali idiom for a number of "vassa" or rains, he has time at his own disposal for he no longer attends instructions from the abbot. He may take an afternoon nap to compensate for his early rising. In a village wat all is comparatively silent in the afternoon. A layman will hardly pay a visit to any monk unnecessarily in the first hours of afternoon, for he is aware that probably the monk is taking his siesta. In Thailand there is a certain set of common words in the vocabulary as used in connection with monks. For instance, to sleep for monks is not nɔɔn, the ordinary term in the language, but cam wád; to partake of food is not kin but chǎn; to take a bath is not ʔàab náam but sɔ̌ŋ náam. A monk, if he does not have his afternoon nap, may choose to pursue his own studies or go out on certain personal business or follow a special course of study elsewhere not available in his wat.

If he is a teacher to the monastery boys, the first thing he does, after partaking of the forenoon meal, is to turn the dining hall into a schoolroom. The boys will sit around the monk-teacher with their wooden slates and pencils. Both articles in the old days were home-made. The slate was made of soft wood cut to a required length and width and blackened on one side with soot. The pencil was made from a certain kind of hard subsoil clay. The boys squatted on the floor in a sideways sitting position with legs bent backward and soles upturned. One will often see people sitting on a carpet or a mat in this position, for it is deemed graceful or good-mannered to do so. No one will dare to sit cross-legged in a sacred place or before a superior where there are no chairs provided. To sit cross-legged is done only among intimates or by a person assuming an air of superiority. A Thai woman will seldom sit cross-legged, or sit with legs wide apart, for it is deemed indecorous for a woman to do so. The only conventional way of sitting for a woman on the floor is to sit sideways as mentioned. A person unaccustomed to such a conventional sitting position will not be able to continue long in it; indeed one has to change from one side to the other every now and then to relieve the discomfort.

Learning to read and write by the boys in the wat is in outline like this. A tray containing a wax candle, an incense stick, a bunch of flowers, and a handful of jâa phrɛ̂ɛg (Bermuda or dub grass) is offered by the boy with both hands to the monk who is going to be his teacher. The boy makes an obeisance by thrice prostrating himself before an image of Buddha and then to the monk, his intended teacher. This is the customary way of offering oneself as a pupil or as a protégé. The monk accepts the tray and places the articles in it on an altar or shelf before the Buddha image. The boy is now a pupil of the monk. The ceremony of offering oneself as a pupil either to a monk or to a layman is always done on Thursday, which in Thai is called wan khruu or "teacher day." The teacher in this instance is the Hindu divine tutor of the gods, whose name, Brihasapati, is honored in Thai as both the name for Thursday and the name for the planet Jupiter.

The ceremony itself is called wâaj khruu or the ceremony of paying respect to a teacher. It is traditionally carried on by schools and colleges right up to modern times. The ceremony takes place on a Thursday after the opening of the first term of the year. The flowers used by a pupil, as prevalent in central Thailand, are flowers from a shrub of the "Ixora" family and "Solanum" family. The former bears flowers in florets, which, when not yet in bloom, resemble needles. It is called dɔ̀ɔg khěm in Thai or "needle flower." The latter, called dɔ̀ɔg mákhy̆a or mákhy̆a flower, bears purplish white flowers in clusters. Its edible fruit contains numerous seeds. A person invoking a blessing on a pupil cites these two kinds of flowers figuratively thus: "May your intellect be as sharp as the needle flower, and may it develop and grow profusely like seeds of mákhy̆a flower and the dub grass, and (in addition) salty like salt." "To be salty" is an idiomatic expression for cleverness.

A boy student, if he is a beginner, will begin by memorizing the first series of the letters of the Thai alphabet which his monk-teacher writes for him on his slate. He will learn them by rote, repeating them in a loud voice, and also trace each letter with a small piece of wood as his first act of learning to write. A test of his learning will be made by the monk-teacher later in the day. The monk-teacher will test his boy pupil by erasing certain letters in the series, or by rewriting new ones by shifting their places. The boy will write the right letter in its place or read the letters in their jumbled positions. This goes on from day to day until the boy has a command of all subsequent series of the alphabet both by reading and writing. He now learns to read and write in syllables and words, as laid down in the Thai system. Such a process will take him some time, the period varying according to his intelligence and effort. When he has mastered all these he can now read and write fairly well.

But the average "monastery boy," if he comes from a village, does not stay long in the wat. He has to go back home every now and then to help his parents in their livelihood and finally leave the wat before he has completed his learning. How much he has learned is, therefore, dependent on the individual. Here we speak of the learning to read and write of the average people as conditioned by time and social surroundings.

The school hour of the wat in the first part of afternoon will take only half an hour or so by the monk-teacher if there are only a few students under his charge, which is usually the case. The monk-teacher leaves the rest of the time to the boys themselves. The boys will read aloud what has been given to them as lessons, while the monk-teacher retires to his cell for an afternoon nap or does other things. Here it must not be taken for granted that the boys will always adhere to their studies for the time prescribed by the teacher. At first they will read aloud the lessons, but will stop reading them if they think their teacher is by that time sound asleep. After a few minutes silence to assure them that their teacher is not awake, they will play pranks and get into mischief as monastery boys will always do if left to themselves. "As mischievous as a monastery boy" is a saying in Thai.

The monk-teacher wakes up from his siesta about three o'clock. He
tests the boys as to how much of their lessons each one has committed to
memory. There may be, of course, some whippings for lazy boys. After
this the monk will take his afternoon bath, usually about four o'clock. Monks
who have nothing to do in the afternoon will sweep the ground of the wat or
give a helping hand in any work as required by the wat.

During Buddhist Lent the number of monks in a wat will be more than
usual; for most of the young men ordained as monks stay in the monkhood for
a period of three months during the rainy season only. Some of them for
various reasons will stay longer, or for life, which is a matter for the individual concerned. A monk may further his studies by becoming a preacher, a
doctor, an astrologer, an artist, an artisan, or so on. In the old days such
callings for certain monks in a village wat were a necessity. The average
villagers, unlike the monks, had no time for such studies because most of
their time was occupied in the arduous work of rice growing. Monks with
ample time at their disposal would take some course of study as a hobby or a
vocation. A monk with such knowledge, especially a doctor or an astrologer
or one well versed in magic, was in demand by the people. The specialized
service was given free by the monk, and in return the villagers would present
to him an offering of all the necessary things befitting a monk's use. Where
would a monk acquire such knowledge? Usually in some of the wats there
were monks who specialized in such knowledge. If a monk required some
knowledge, say of astrology, and there was not a monk-astrologer in the wat
where he was staying, he would retire to another wat where there was such a
monk-astrologer. He would present an offering to the monk-astrologer of
tapers, incense stick, and flowers, in the same manner as a boy student to
his monk-teacher, and ask for initiation as a pupil. The monk then would
attend the study at his monk-teacher's residence regularly every afternoon.
He might have a layman for his tutor if he could not find a suitable monk-
teacher. There was no teacher-fee in the modern sense. The teaching was
given free to accepted students. When a monk-student had completed his
course of learning he might become an astrologer himself and give his services
free to the people of his village. Every year at a certain period of time and
always on Thursday he held a wâaj khruu or "worshiping of the teacher."
Those who had received help from him would come to the annual wâaj khruu
commemoration to pay respect and present him with necessary things. Such
a practice has been observed traditionally up to the present day. A doctor of
the old school, whether he is a monk or a layman, will give his professional
aid free of charge, save small expenses as incurred. He will tacitly collect
his full professional fee from his clients on the day of wâaj khruu. Such a
practice survives, though weakening, to the present day.

An abbot of the village wat, if he is a man of age, full of lore and
wisdom, is a highly respected person in the village. He is called lǔaŋ phɔ̂ɔ

or "great father" by the villagers. His counsel is eagerly sought in case of difficulties and differences. The villagers seek his advice and decision even in a serious case rather than refer the case, if they can, to the official authority for decision. A decision by the authority or the legal court will take days, and also a certain amount of money has to be paid out in fees and other expenses. But not so with the venerable abbot, their spiritual father. The abbot in his spare time will make a round of afternoon visits to the villagers, giving advice or distributing his home-made medicine or other things as needed.

Some monks, after having been a number of years in the monkhood, leave the brotherhood to lead a layman's life. Whatever knowledge a monk has gained during his monkhood will be turned into useful occupation. If, for instance, he has learned something of a certain craft, he will turn to it as a profession if the village he resides in is a big one where there is a demand for such craft. If he is a successful and recognized artisan or artist, there will be one or two young men apprenticed to him. A young man in apprenticeship, if he comes from another village, will stay with the master-artist, with free board and lodging, as one of the members of the family. He learns his art and trade while at the same time serving his master in all domestic matters. If he has attained sufficient skill in his art, the master-artist will put him to some easy and odd jobs ordered by someone. Any fee received will be apportioned to the young pupil as his share. After staying for some time as an apprentice and intimate of the family, he may marry a daughter of his master or one of the master's female relatives. He now becomes one of the members of the family. After he has finished his apprenticeship, he may carry on his professional calling independently but live in a combined house and workshop of his own in the vicinity. Seldom will a young artist, whether he marries into the family of his master or not, live and follow his profession far from the master's house or in another village unless he is a recognized skilled artist. No one will hire him for a job, for most jobs come usually through his master. As time passed there would arise in that vicinity a village of artists most of whose inhabitants have a connection somehow or other by blood or marriage with the master artist. Such a village usually bears traces of the name of the inhabitants' profession -- for instance, as in names of districts in Bangkok, Bâan Môo or the Potter's Village, Bâan Lòo or the Image Caster Village. The latter still exists as a place where the casting of bronze Buddha images is carried on as a profession by many families in the district.

The Sacred Recitation

Among the Buddhist Thai, important events in a person's life (birth, coming of age, birthdays, marriage, death) as well as all feasts, festivals, or other special occasions (New Year's Day, the erection of a new house or building) are marked by a tham bun or "merit working" ceremony. A tham bun in the usual form consists simply of the presentation of food to the monks on their morning round of visits for alms, but in an extended form the tham bun will consist of inviting monks to one's house or to some particular place to recite certain texts from the Buddhist scriptures. An extended tham bun will ordinarily consist of a recitation in the afternoon followed by a feast for the invited monks the next morning. Nowadays, especially in Bangkok or other urban areas, such a ceremony is often shortened to one day, the sacred recitation being given in the morning, followed immediately by a feast for the monks. In addition, the recitation itself will be shortened to half an hour instead of the hour or so customary in former days. This abbreviation of the ceremony has been made necessary by the changed conditions of economic life among urban populations where free time is not always at one's disposal. But to devout people in a rural district, the shorter recitation is regarded as less spiritually satisfying. In rural areas where there is more time, the people want to hear more of the sacred recitation in order to gain more merit, for the recitation represents something mystically inspired. Of course there was no mysticism originally in Buddhism. The recitation itself, if one knows either Pali or a translation of the texts recited, is a selection of certain incidents in the life of the Lord Buddha containing words of wisdom appropriate to the occasion. To hear a recitation by monks as mentioned one has to sit in a solemn and respectful manner with one's hands raised in a worshiping attitude.

In all religious ceremonies in connection with auspicious occasions, a certain kind of mystically consecrated cord made of unspun threads is essential. This cord is bound thrice in a clockwise direction round the pedestal of the image of Buddha on the altar. The image of the Buddha is usually placed facing east or north. The cord is then passed out of the house through a window or other opening from the place where the ceremony is going to take place. It encircles the perimeter of the house also in a clockwise direction and returns to the altar where it is bound thrice in the same manner to an alms bowl and other vessels filled with water which are placed nearby. The remainder of the cord is rolled into a ball and placed on a tray near the altar.

The chapter of monks invited to the ceremony must number more than four, so as to form a monks' quorum. Although four is a quorum at a monks' council, the number is exclusively used for the recitation of certain formulas in connection with funeral or memorial ceremonies and therefore it is tacitly accepted that it should never be used for an auspicious one. The monks sit in a row according to seniority in age and rank in the brotherhood. A special place has been prepared for them, arranged so that their right shoulders face the altar where a Buddha image is installed. When the time for the recitation arrives the host or the honored person in the congregation will light the candles and incense sticks placed before the flower-decked altar and perform a triple prostration before the image of the Buddha. Whoever is acting as master of ceremonies on the occasion will pronounce in Pali a formula denoting an act of faith in "the Three Gems," i.e., the Buddha, the Law, and the Brother-hood of Monks. The head monk who sits first in the row will hold a monk's conventional fan (an adaptation of the ancient palm-leaf type) before his face and pronounce thrice in Pali the three "refuge" formulas of the Buddha, i.e., "I take refuge in the Buddha, I take refuge in his Law, and I take refuge in his Brotherhood of Monks." The congregation repeats these word by word. The head monk then pronounces in Pali the code of five precepts of the Bud-dhist religion beginning with the first one: "I undertake to abstain from kill-ing, I undertake to abstain from stealing, I undertake to abstain from com-mitting adultery, I undertake to abstain from lying, I undertake to abstain from alcoholic drinking." The congregation will repeat the formula word by word as a declaration of intention to observe this fivefold commandment. Such a ritual is necessary as a preliminary to any Buddhist ceremony. The head monk then removes his fan and places it nearby. Next the master of ceremonies must make a formal request, also in Pali, to the monks' council for a recitation of the sacred texts for the welfare of the congregation, in-tended to disperse ills and calamities. Thereupon the head monk will take the roll of sacred cord placed in a tray, unroll it a little and hold it in his hand, then pass the remaining ball to the next monk, who does likewise and again passes it over. Now the monks begin to recite the ceremony of the rec-itation of sacred texts. Before we go on with the ceremony, there are some things to be described incidentally in order to have a better understanding of the subject.

One may ask the meaning of the sacred cord tied in the elaborate man-ner described above. The popular belief is that the sacred cord acts in a mystical way like an electric wire, carrying the sacred words as recited by the monks at one and the same time to every place and corner where the sa-cred cord reaches. It is a realistic and a practical device, for at one stroke everything within the orbit of the sacred cord is consecrated and receives the mystic words of the sacred texts which give it a protection and blessing. Even the water in the monk's alms bowl and other vessels, or other ceremo-nial paraphernalia that are used in some cases becomes hallowed and fit for lustration. The binding of the sacred cord to the pedestal of the image of the Buddha is evidently to render the mystic influence of the Lord Buddha as real-istic as one can imagine. It gives a psychological feeling of satisfaction to a devout person similar to what a Christian feels for his cross.

The sacred thread made of unspun threads is a traditional one. In the
old days most of the Thai households in rural districts wove their own clothing.
Unspun threads or yarns were to be found in every home; when a cord or a
long string was required, and nothing else of this kind that was suitable could
be found, it was logical to utilize the unspun threads. A single thread was
too thin and easily snapped; hence either three or its square nine, the mystic
number derived from "the Three Gems" or Buddhist Trinity, are made into
one strand with ritualistic elaborations of process due to later development.
Unspun threads thus made into a single strand might be used also for various
purposes other than religious ceremonies but, with the introduction of better
things, are seldom seen nowadays. The sacred cord is commonly called săaj
sĭn; the last word is from the Pali word sĩncana which means "to sprinkle."
No doubt it has something to do with the water in the alms bowls and other
vessels which turn into consecrated water after the ritual recitation and which
is sprinkled on the congregation and also used for lustration. The Cambodians
call this sacred cord a "boundary line," which points to the fact that it is
used as a mystic protection for everything within the radius of the sacred cord.

The ceremony of the recitation of sacred texts originated in Ceylon
and was undoubtedly brought to this country in the latter part of the thirteenth
century during the time of Ram Kamhaeng the Great of the Sukhothai Dynasty
when the Thai had adopted the Ceylonese sect of Hinayana or the Southern
School of Buddhism. The Thai, like all peoples of primitive times, were
animists. They probably adopted Mahayana or the Northern School of Buddhism before they came to Thailand; this was more or less true of the ruling
classes as in the Thai kingdom of Nan Chao in southern China. When they
came to Thailand they adopted Hinayana Buddhism, no doubt from the Mon
of Dvaravadi, and later mixed this with Mahayana Buddhism as imported
from the Srivijaya Empire in the middle of the tenth century through the con-
quest of a king of that empire. To add more to the melting pot of religion,
Hinduism was apparently also an element in the beliefs of the Thai, especially the ruling class, through the influence of the Cambodians, at certain
periods of history. In looking therefore at the Buddhism of the Thai on its
ritualistic and popular side one must bear in mind the above facts. To ana-
lyze the component parts which came to be integrated as a whole into Thai
Buddhism requires laborious work and an unprejudiced mind.

The conventional monk's fan which forms a part of a monk's equipment
in religious ceremonies is peculiar, as far as is known, to Thailand and Cam-
bodia. The fans used by the Ceylonese and Burmese monks are natural ones
made of the big rounded leaves of the toddy palm. They are utilized as
monks' sunshades only. In Thai Buddhism the monk's fan is made also of a
toddy palm leaf but is artificially shaped in an ovate form with a long handle
made of wood with a pointed tip. This is used by an ordinary monk. Another
kind of monk's fan is made wholly of silk, wool, or brocade and is either

embroidered with artistic figures or letters or is plain. The long handle is made either of wood tipped at both ends with ivory, or made wholly of ivory. No precious metals such as silver or gold can be used for monks, as by the rules of discipline he cannot touch them, though gold and silver are sometimes tolerated in a veiled form, for instance, as part of the brocade. One sometimes sees such fans with beautiful artistic designs worthy of a work of art. Monk's fans presented by the king to a prelate or to a monk with official status are different from the unofficial ones. Fans of this group have various shapes or forms, colors, and decorations as befit the rank of the monks. One may be able to recognize, provided one has some knowledge, a monk's rank in the hierarchy if he carries his fan with him. Such a fan is used exclusively in a royal ceremony when the king or his deputy is present. A Buddhist prelate wears no uniform to distinguish him from other monks. Hence the difficulty in recognizing a monk's hierarchical rank unless one knows him personally. Perhaps a king in the old days instituted such a gradation of monk's fans and these have become a tradition. Later, in King Vajiravudh's reign, a special kind of monk's fan bearing a royal cipher with many grades was instituted and presented by the King to monks as a royal personal favor. In short, these fans, both the official and the royal cipher ones, are used on occasions in the same manner as one wears a uniform with decorations and medals. Perhaps as an extension of the above practices, people have also made fans of their own to present to monks on occasions of making merit, replacing gradually the primitive fans made of palm leaves, which are now seldom seen. A monk with many unofficial fans in his possession may use any one of them on suitable occasions.

A monk's fan may be used on five special occasions only: when he pronounces the three "refuge" formulas and the five precepts; when a recitation begins; when he expresses formal thanks; when a monk is in the act of drawing to himself a robe laid on a coffin during a religious service; and when a quartet of monks chant certain sacred formulas before and during cremation. The drawing to himself of a robe laid on a coffin is called pamsukula in Pali which literally means a "dust heap." In ancient days monks collected discarded robes and rags from dust heaps and washed, dyed, and used them as robes. This act of the monks has developed into what is described above. Why a monk's fan may be used only on such five occasions, or when, where, and why it originated is for me impossible to say.

The stories and substance of the recitations that are ceremonially chanted by monks are too long to be included here, even in their shortened form. We will therefore omit them and continue with the ceremony.

After the monks have continued with their recitation for some quarter of an hour, the head monk will light a wax taper attached to the rim of the alms bowl. After a while, when the recitation reaches a certain point appropriate for the occasion, he takes the lighted taper in his hand and begins to drop molten wax from the taper here and there into the water in the alms bowl. When the recitation reaches a certain text the head monk dips a lighted taper into the water, stirring it for a while; and the recitation continues on until the end. The sacred thread is re-rolled into a ball and replaced in the tray. The ceremony then comes to an end. The monks sit for a while drinking tea or chatting with members of the congregation and then take leave.

An enquiry into the ritual dipping of a lighted taper into the water in the alms bowl in the northern and northeastern areas of the country elicits an identical ceremony but one that sometimes varies in certain details. In northern Thailand three tapers are used for dipping. This is the same number of candles as is used by a Roman Catholic priest in consecrating water for baptism. No doubt the dipping of a lighted taper into the water is a ritual act to purify the water for sacred purposes. In the Roman Catholic ritual such consecrated water has a little mixture of saliva (see W. J. Wilkins, Paganism in the Papal Church, pp. 93-94). It finds a parallel also among the Thai but in an indirect form. In certain cases a monk famed for his mystical power is asked to blow out from his mouth consecrated water or medicinal solution in a spray on a person who is sick or possessed by a malignant phǐi or evil spirit.

The next morning the same group of monks who gave the recitation on the previous afternoon arrive at the appointed time, either in the earlier part of the morning or at a time a little before 11 A. M. to partake of the food provided by the owner of the house. If the appointed time is the earlier one, the monks have to bring their own alms bowls too. This is a necessity for monks. If they partake of their earlier meal at the house, there will be no food for them when they return to the wat to take their final meal of the day. The alms bowls they bring with them will therefore be handed over to the people to present food for their final meal after returning to their wat.

Before partaking of their feast, the monks will recite a eulogy describing the Buddha's Eight Victories over certain heretical beings, as found in the episodes of the traditional story of the life of the Buddha. This may be compared to saying grace before a meal. A special tray filled with various foods in small quantities is placed in a formal way on a white cloth before the image of the Buddha at the altar. After placing the tray, the person will kneel with hands upraised in a worshiping attitude before the image of Buddha and pronounce thrice the usual Buddhist opening formula invoking the name of the Buddha, and then recite a certain word in Pali presenting the food to the Buddha. After the presentation the monks may begin their feast.

By Buddhist rules a monk cannot handle food or other gifts unless they are presented or offered by someone. The presentation is done by approaching him in a respectful manner. The food or other gifts are held with both hands, or a small thing may be held with one's right hand only but with the left hand raised a little. The gift is raised and then lowered directly into the monk's hand. If the presenter is a woman, the thing presented to a monk cannot be put directly into the monk's hand in this way, but is to be placed on a piece of cloth laid before the monk where he can take it after it has been offered. It is sinful for a monk in his celibate life to touch the body of a woman whether willingly or unwillingly. The practice extends also to other creatures of female kind.

During the meal, music is played if any is available. In strict discipline a monk cannot enjoy music, which is an enemy to celibate life. In popular practice music is permissible if played during a feast. The people want their monks to enjoy the feast, and they are delighted if monks take more food as it is offered. The more food taken by monks the more merit it is believed will accrue to a person who offers it to them. On the other hand, by discipline a monk must not take more food than is necessary for the sustenance of life. Music plays a subsidiary part in Thai ritualistic Buddhism. It is played to mark stages in the ceremony. There is music in the ceremony when the monks arrive, when a preaching or a recitation comes to an end, when the monks depart, and so on. There is a particular tune appropriate to the occasion, and a person familiar with the tune will know when he hears it what stage in the ceremony has now begun.

Among the people in central Thailand a person serving monks at their feast or taking part as master of ceremonies usually wears a piece of cloth on his left shoulder with both ends hanging down across the torso in something like a loop or a sash, or better in the manner of a Scot wearing his tartan. A cloth, called phâa khǎawmáa or "khǎawmáa cloth," worn in this way is a symbol of respect before a superior or sacred thing. The phâa khǎawmáa is a piece of fabric woven in a distinctive checkered pattern of different stripes and colors which may be utilized in many ways. In a hot country, the unsophisticated wear shirts only when they work in the field, to protect themselves from the intolerably hot sun. On other occasions they usually leave the upper part of the body bare if they can. The only piece of cloth they have with them is the phâa khǎawmáa which they put to various uses. It is used as a shawl, a turban, a sash, a bathing cloth, a bag, a binding or for such other practical uses as one can devise. The people take their bath in the open, therefore a bathroom is not a necessity. But a phâa khǎawmáa is necessary. Accustomed to such a behavior pattern a Thai, and not only the villager, wears a phâa khǎawmáa when taking a bath even in a bathroom. Only the sophisticated ones take a bath in the western style. The women wear their sarong-like lower garment when bathing. In his traditional way of life, a person usually has a phâa khǎawmáa hanging on his left shoulder; if the air is hot he may wet his phâa khǎawmáa to relieve the heat. A dandy will drape his costly phâa khǎawmáa across his shoulders in a showy and careless manner. Hence when he comes before a superior or a sacred thing, or into a wat, he will take his phâa khǎawmáa off or wrap it around the upper part of his body as already mentioned. As to a woman, she wears a piece of cloth wrapped around her breast and another piece of cloth used as a shoulder shawl. She will take off her shawl and arrange it in the same manner as a phâa khăawmáa when entering a wat or meeting the monks.

When a householder is feasting monks, he does not forget the house spirit or tutelary guardian of the house, whose shrine is a miniature house perched on a single pillar found at most Thai houses. The spirit also receives a share of the feast, but he takes his portion after the monks. He is only a lay spirit whose status is below that of a monk; similarly the monk does not partake of the feast until after a special meal has been offered to the image of the Buddha. The tradition is obviously a popular animistic survival from primitive days.

The monks after partaking of the feast will return to the seats where the recitation took place on the previous afternoon. They will then recite a formula of gratitude and blessing to the donor of the feast. During this recitation the donor will pour water from a vessel in the same manner as already described as a libation to departed relatives and to other creatures and beings as well. Libation as defined in the dictionary is a pouring of a liquid, usually wine, in honor of some deity. It develops into the drinking of wine in honor of some person or, as we say, drinking a health to such and such person. In Hinduism after a feast is given to a body of Brahmans, a pouring of water called tarpana is performed to transmit to departed souls the merit gained through feasting Brahmans. Evidently the feasting of monks and the pouring of water for the benefit of departed persons, the tarpana of the Hindus, and the drinking of wine in honor of some person developed from the same primitive source as the libation in honor of some gods as performed by the ancient Greeks.

After a recitation of thanks and blessing by the monks, the ceremony comes to an end. Certain articles befitting a monk's use are now presented. If there is a present of money to monks on the occasion, the money is given in his name to a reliable monastery boy or to any other person acting as an agent or a banker for the monk or monks. A slip of paper written in a formal wording informs the monk that a certain sum of money is made over to such and such agent of the monk. If he wishes to acquire certain articles as befit a monk's use, he may call on that person who will buy them for him. In theory a monk cannot touch money.

Before the monks depart to their wat the head monk will bless the congregation by sprinkling consecrated water from the alms bowl. He sometimes sprinkles sand along the boundary of the house also as a protection against the unseen evils that may lurk in the vicinity. The traditional instrument for sprinkling consecrated water is a bunch of lalang grass, which is used as a thatch grass of the villagers, or a bunch of májom branches (star gooseberry). There is some reason for the use of these two things, though a superstitious one. The former has to do with a story of popular Hinduism. A semidivine being, half-man, half-bird, named Garuda stole the water of immortality from the gods, and a few drops of this elixir fell on lalang grass, hence its sacredness. The latter, the star gooseberry, bears the name in Thai májom, the last syllable being identical in sound to jom in Thai or yama in Sanskrit and Pali, the King of Death of whom evil spirits are in fear. The sprinkler made of májom branches is tantamount to Yama's rod with which he chastises evil spirits.

Buddhist Feasts and Festivals

Feasts and festivals observed by the Thai Buddhists are mainly religious and are related to the changing seasons. Here we have to say something of the Thai traditional calendar, for most of the feasts and festivals are based on it.

The Thai traditional calendar, like all the calendars of this part of Southeast Asia, is a lunar one, consisting of twelve moons or lunar months of twenty-nine days and thirty days alternately. The former are called odd-number months, the latter even-number months. There is an intercalated month between the eighth and ninth months every third year. The Thai name their lunar months in numerical order; the first month begins at nearly the same time as December, except in northern Thailand where the first month answers nearly to October, two months earlier than in other parts of the country. Evidently this first month, as its name shows, marked the first Thai New Year's Day in former times. The old Thai word for their first month of the year was ciaŋ or ceŋ month, a word no different from the name of the Chinese first month. Nevertheless the Thai traditional New Year's Day is now otherwise.

A month, called dyan in Thai, which means "moon," is divided into two parts, the waxing moon from the first to the fifteenth or full moon of the month, and the waning moon beginning with the sixteenth which, however, is counted as the first of the waning moon; the waning moon ends on the fourteenth or the fifteenth according to whether the month is an odd or an even one. Hence there are two numerical series of days in a month. The days, like the months, have their odd and even numbers also. No marriage ceremony is performed in an odd-number month, with the exception of the extra month added in an intercalary year. This month is the beginning of the Buddhist lenten season when no marriage ceremony is traditionally performed. No cremation takes place on an even-number day of the waxing moon or on an odd-number day of the waning moon, for its first day is regarded as the sixteenth day of the month considered as a whole, and sixteen is an even number. Everything in number that pertains to a marriage ceremony is in pairs, and everything that pertains to a cremation is in odd numbers. Logically a marriage ceremony requires a pair of man and woman to consummate the ritual, and a cremation is confined to a dead man alone. Any odd or even number of either month or day is viewed superstitiously and with apprehension with the notion that "like produces like." A marriage ceremony performed in an odd-number month will result in one of the wedded couple not surviving long in married life. So also the cremation performed on an even day to a superstitious mind requires another living man to follow the dead one to complete such a number. The superstition is now weakening in urban areas, especially in Bangkok perhaps because of the reckoning of days and months by the solar system.

The Thai New Year's Day traditionally takes place on the first day of the waning moon of the fifth month, roughly in the latter part of March. Nothing in the nature of feasts or festivals is observed, except the usual presentation of food to monks on their morning round for alms. Until a decade or so ago there was an official ceremony called "the cutting of the year" with a ritual driving away from the city evil of spirits lurking behind from the old year. Evidently the ceremony was introduced from Buddhist Ceylon with indigenous animistic beliefs added. However, the New Year was actually celebrated with feasts and holidays from the thirteenth to fifteenth of April, the so-called Sŏŋkraan, better-known as the Water Throwing Festival, of which we will speak later. In 1888 King Chulalongkorn instituted a calendar on a solar basis beginning on the first of April. The first of April became an official New Year's Day but the popular one was the Sŏŋkraan Day. The months of the newly instituted solar year are named from the twelve zodiacal signs with a suffix of aakhom for a thirty-one-day month and aajon for a thirty-day month. February, with twenty-eight or twenty-nine days, has aaphan as a suffix peculiar to its name. In 1951 the official New Year's Day was changed from the first of April to January 1 and this remains in force to this day. The celebration of this official New Year's Day is like that of Sŏŋkraan. In fact it is a replica of the latter, but the people at large still observe the Sŏŋkraan celebration.

Now we will begin a description of the seasonal feasts and festivals beginning with Sŏŋkraan. As this festival has been described and analyzed by me in detail elsewhere (see my story of Sŏŋkraan in Thai Culture Series No. 6 and The Journal of the Siam Society, Vol. XLII, part 1, July 1954) we will give it only in its bare outline. Sŏŋkraan is a Thai word derived from Sankrānta, of Sanskrit origin, which means the entry of the sun into the sign of Aries, the Ram. It begins on the thirteenth of April and ends either on the fifteenth or the sixteenth in accordance with the actual time when the sun enters the Aries. It is therefore a fixable feast on a solar basis. In fact, Sŏŋkraan is the celebration of the vernal equinox. Though Thailand has no spring season, the month when the Sŏŋkraan occurred coincided splendidly with an opportune time of the year, when the mass of people of Thailand are unoccupied with their agricultural work.

Early in the morning of the first day of Sŏŋkraan, the thirteenth of April, the people in their new clothes repair to the wat of their village to offer food to monks. A long bench, either temporary or permanent, is erected in the compound of the wat where monks' alms bowls stand in a row on either side of the bench. There is a special alms bowl bigger than the rest placed at the head of the row. This is meant as the alms bowl peculiar to the Buddha. Into the alms bowls, first into the so-called Buddha's alms bowl and then into the others, the gathering crowd in pious mood queues up to put boiled rice, and into the covers of the alms bowls lying upturned other food, fruits, and sweetmeats. Paradoxically there is more food than a monk can take in a day even though a monk by discipline cannot take food offered to him if any is left after his last day's meal. Economically it is really a waste, but it was not so in the old days when food, especially rice and fish, were in abundance and money to a people with simple needs was not a necessity. The people attached the highest value to their religion; and this is the only way for them to express their faith.

In the afternoon and on the next days there is a ceremonial bathing of the Buddha image and also of the abbot of the wat, followed by the well-known "water throwing festival" which in the old days was considered a magic means to cause abundance of water or rain but which has degenerated into a form of amusement pure and simple. On this day and also on the succeeding days there is a ceremonial bathing of elder relatives and respected persons carried out by the younger generation. A memorial service to the departed ones and the releasing of live fish and birds are also performed as deeds of merit. During the three days of Sŏŋkraan young people of both sexes amuse themselves by throwing water at one or another, playing games, dancing, singing, or other such pastimes as they can devise.

The month of April is the hottest month in Thailand, and about the middle of May comes the beginning of the southwest monsoon rain when the people are busying themselves with their ploughing. There are no feasts and festivals this time of the year until the Buddhist Lent begins in mid-July. The only exception is Visakha (Wísǎakhǎa) Day, the anniversary of the Birth, Enlightenment, and the final entering into Nirvana (death) of the Buddha, which coincides with the full moon in the sixth month (May). The observance in commemoration of this great triple event in the life of the Buddha is mainly among the monks, but the people also participate. In rural areas the commemoration is observed for three days, commencing on the fourteenth of the waxing moon, and ending on the first of the waning moon (or the sixteenth of the month). On the first day there is an evening recitation of the sacred texts at the wat followed by sermons on the life of the Buddha. At dark the ceremony comes to an end for the first day. Next morning, that is, on the day of the full moon, there is an offering of food to the monks. There is also a circumambulation round the chapel three times in a clockwise direction with lighted tapers. In some places such a circumambulation is performed on the previous day also. Sermons as a continuation from the previous day are preached from morning until evening and further continued to the third and last day.

In Bangkok Visakha (Wísǎakhǎa) Day is a one-day observance in the evening of the full moon. There is a circumambulation, after which there are sermons preached by monks in succession and continuing throughout the whole night. In some of the bigger wats there are huge crowds of people circumambulating the chapel. In the Royal Chapel of the Emerald Buddha the king and queen, followed by the royal family and officials, honor the Buddha by thrice circumambulating the sacred building with lighted tapers in the evening. Hung around the royal chapel are decorated candles and lights with which the royal family and officials honor the Buddha on this important occasion. These candles and lights are mostly decorated with fresh flowers in many beautiful designs. In some wats there may be exhibits along the corridor of the chapel of altars decorated with rare and beautiful pieces of brass or porcelain ware.

After Visakha (Wísǎakhǎa) Day there may be a ceremony of presenting milled rice and other unprepared food to the monks. It is called the ceremony of "placing milled rice in alms bowls." Actually it is usually done in the afternoon. Milled rice and unprepared food contributed by the people are placed in a common heap, then divided proportionately among monks in the wat. Each monk receives his share, which is carried to each particular kitchen of the monks by the monastery boys or other persons. Such a ceremony shows forethought on the part of the villagers. They are too busy with their ploughing and their planting of rice, which is a race against the time of the coming rain. Most of the villagers go out to the fields very early in the morning, before dawn if the fields are some distance from home. In many cases the whole family leaves the house together, carrying with them their young children if there is no one left to look after them. To leave one's house unoccupied does not mean that a thief or thieves will steal something in it as there are of course no valuable things worth stealing. What about the monks in the wat? They will have an insufficient amount of food for their daily needs in their morning round for alms. Few people will be in the village to present them with food. The milled rice and unprepared food presented in this ceremony therefore will keep them supplied with their daily wants for the time being until the time of Buddhist Lent when there are more people making merit.

The ceremony of placing milled rice in alms bowls is shifted in time in urban areas to the period during the three months of the Buddhist Lent, when there are unusually more monks in the wats because newly ordained monks swell the number. These monks, owing to their increase in number during the lenten season, will sometimes have insufficient food in their morning alms if they have to depend on the usual number of donors of food. The ceremony further develops into a means for raising funds indirectly for the wats at any time of the year. The milled rice presented by some wealthy persons will be in big bags, and these are sold to bidders. The money realized from the sale will go into a fund to be used as needed by the wat. People will part willingly with anything if it is done in the name of religion.

There is another Buddhist ceremony called "food tickets" in which food belonging to a group of monks in a wat is distributed to the monks by tickets. This is done at any time when occasion arises. In Thailand it is usually performed by the people when any kind of fruit is in season. A group of families each contributes food to a monk with such seasonal fruits forming the predominant part of the offering. The food with sweetmeats and the fruits are placed in a tray or trays which are again placed in two baskets suspended from the two ends of a shoulder-carry (the Thai never carry things on their heads). In rural districts the carrying pole made of bamboo with beautiful curved ends is a thing treasured by a village girl. On festive occasions, such as this instance, the carrying of food to the wat is done by a girl in her best dress. Each girl in the file proceeding to the wat will vie with the others in carrying her pole on the shoulder. If the pole is gracefully curved, giving a beautiful rhythmic movement, it is greatly admired. At the wat the food is distributed to the monks by ticket. The ceremony in this instance is to provide monks with special fruits of the season, which monks seldom have from their usual morning alms.

On the first day of the waning moon of the eighth lunar month (roughly in July) comes the beginning of Buddhist Lent when monks make their retreat for the three rainy months. It ends on the full moon of the eleventh month (roughly October). During this period of time the ploughing and planting of rice have begun. The farmers have comparatively little to do but to wait until the rice ripens, in December or January at the latest. Before the lenten days begin the people cast a big candle of molten beeswax. The ceremony may take place at a village or, as is usually the case at the present time, in the compound of a wat. This candle, called the lenten candle, is lighted and kept burning continuously throughout the three months of the lenten period. If the lenten candle is cast in the village, it is borne in a decorated cart or other conveyance with a procession to a wat, where there is a celebration. People also present articles to the monks as befits the occasion. These things are decorated with artificial flowers and leaves of varied colors and designs. There are more persons than usual presenting food to monks on their morning alms. Devout and elder people go to the wat every day to hear sermons. A Buddhist sermon preached by a monk always begins with the triple "refuge" of the religion, i.e., the Buddha, the Law, and the Brotherhood, followed by the five precepts for ordinary days or the ten precepts for the Buddhist holy days for observance by the layman. In the old days all theatrical or other amusements were voluntarily suspended during the lenten period; even a habitual drinker of spiritous liquors will sacrifice his delight and turn into a sober man, at least during the three months, as an offering to religion.

During the interval there is an autumnal feast called Sàat in Thai which occurs on the last day of the tenth lunar month (early October). Sàat is a Thai form of the Sanskrit word śārada, which means "autumn." In central Thailand there is a certain kind of special sweetmeat made of pounded-flat glutinous rice, groundnuts, teelseeds, popped rice, and green peas mixed with molasses and formed into a sticky mass of brownish color. This is presented to monks with a certain kind of ripe bananas to neutralize the great sweetness of the sweetmeats. There are variations in the details of the Sàat feast and dates of performance in other areas of the country -- in fact, the feast is called by various names and in some places no such sweetmeat is known. But the feasts, though different, betray themselves as an autumnal feast in connection with the "first fruits" as an oblation to departed ancestors. The Sàat feast forms a subject of its own on which I have written elsewhere.

The full moon of the eleventh month, usually in the latter part of October, marks the last day of the three months of Buddhist Lent. On this day the people make special merit by offering food to monks and listening to special sermons preached by the monks at the wat. The next and succeeding days until the full moon of the twelfth month (November) make up the well known Kàthin or the period of presentation of robes to monks, which subject was treated at some length in my article, "The End of Buddhist Lent" (The Journal of the Siam Society, Vol. XLII, part 2, January 1955). On the last day of Buddhist Lent there is the ceremony of Lɔɔj Kràthoŋ or the floating of lights in leaf cups which has nothing to do directly with Buddhist festivals. After this date there is a lull in feasts and festivals. The people, especially the farmers, are busy harvesting their rice. On the full moon of the third and fourth month (February and March) there is the festival of pilgrimage to Phràʔ Bàad or the footprint of the Buddha. During these times the people have in most cases finished harvesting rice, and there is the usual ceremony of recitations of Buddhist texts and a morning feast for the monks. The people have a time of comparative leisure to make the pilgrimage to the famous footprint and enjoy their vacation, though it is of a semireligious nature. There are pilgrimages to other sacred shrines, which are to be found in many parts of the country, and fairs and amusements for the people to make their vacation enjoyable. Some shrines in urban areas such as the Golden Mount in Bangkok and the big pagoda of Phràʔ Pàthŏm have their festivals during the full moon of the twelfth month (December) when the rains come to an end.

On the full moon of the third month (February) comes the Buddhist Maakhá Buuchaa or Buddhist Saints' Day. It was on this same day during Buddha's time that 1,250 arahantas or Buddhist saints met coincidentally at Veluvan Monastery in Rajagriha, then capital of the Magadhan Empire in

India. Because the 1,250 arahantas assembled at the place, and all of them had been ordained as monks by the Buddha himself, and they had come by themselves without any previous notice, and it was the full-moon night when the moon entered the sign of the Maakhá asterism, it is commemorated as one of the Buddhist festivals. The observance of the Maakhá Buuchaa is a one-night festival, and the performance is done in the same spirit and manner as the Wísáakháa Buuchaa, the anniversary of Buddha's birth, enlightenment, and entering the final Nirvana, save that the sermons preached in the chapel have as their subject the Buddhist Code of Discipline for monks. It was on this day that this Code of Discipline or the Vinaya was promulgated or preached by the Lord. No decorated candles and lights are hung on this occasion as is done during the Wísáakháa Day.

To complete the cycle of feasts and festivals of the Thai people it is necessary to include the "Festival of Thêet Máhãa Chãad" which means the festival of a recitative sermon of the Great Birth in connection with the Buddha's last but one life on earth in his transmigrations of births before he perfected himself and became the Enlightened Buddha. The festival is usually performed during the Sàat or mid-year autumnal feast in October, or on any special occasions such as the raising of funds for the wat. The recitation is done in the preaching hall within the precincts of a wat. The recitations begin early in the morning and continue sometimes to late midnight. It is a traditional belief of the people that whoever hears this recitation of the "Great Life" in its complete story will gain great merit. The recitation is in Pali verses, and a free translation in the form of a Thai prose poem forms the best literary work in the Thai literature. The story of this Great Birth is a very well-known one in Thailand and influences immensely the life of the mass of the people. The story serves as an inspiration to Thai poets and artists, for the story contains noble sentiments, humor, pathos, and beautiful descriptive scenes which give play to their power of imagination and artistic expression. The story is very popular not only in central Thailand, but also and not less in the northern and northeastern areas of the country. There are many versions of the story both in the standard Thai language and in other Thai dialects. The oldest version, dating back some four hundred years, is used as a subject of literary study in Chulalongkorn University. I have written a detailed descriptive story of this festival as a separate subject.

I now have described the customs of the Thai people in connection with their religion and traditional way of life. As one will see, the wat or monastery played a significant role in shaping the life of the Thai. In former days, and to a large extent in the present, the wat was and has been the place of education in arts and crafts and for the social gatherings of the people. One will wonder why there are so many feasts and festivals in the year. The answer is not difficult to discover if we imagine ourselves back in the old days among the unsophisticated folk who formed the great mass of the population.

Unlike their brothers in the cities, they had few attractions other than in the wat. The wat provided, and still provides in the villages, everything for them in what we call arts, literature, morality, and philosophy. Theatrical performances, music, fireworks, and exhibits of artistic works are to be seen frequently at the wat during certain festivals and ceremonies. Poets, artists, and craftsmen generally originate from the wat. If one wishes to witness a fashion show, if I am permitted to use the word, it may be found in a social gathering at the wat during festive occasions. We have a saying in Thai that "such and such a girl may go to the wat" meaning that she is an attractive girl. The wat is also a sanctuary for animals both wild and tame. People will never dare to shoot birds or to fish in the compound of the wat. Even fish in a river in front of a wat find a sanctuary there. If any person disobeys this traditional custom he, if caught red-handed, will receive his punishment by being beaten by the monks in the wat. An arbitrary punishment given to a person is called idiomatically in Thai "to punish in a wat manner." A fowl, if the owner deems it to be unlucky, is not killed but released in the compound of the wat. Such a fowl is shorn of its tail before release in order that people may recognize it as a fowl belonging to a wat. A delinquent son expelled from home is said metaphorically "to be shorn of his tail and released in the wat." If all the highly valued things are to be found in the wat, so also there are things to the contrary. Everything has a reverse side. Animals found in the wat, especially pigs and dogs, are parasites of their kind, and to say that a man is a "wat dog" is an insult to the person in Thai idiomatic expression. To say a man's knowledge of reading and writing is of the wat's kind is to mean that the knowledge is only elementary. It reflects, therefore, the fact that the teaching of such knowledge in the wat was carried in former days no further than the elementary stage, unless one stayed longer in the wat and learned Pali. But such literary language in a village was incompatible with their way of life. Leaving this minor drawback out one is justified in saying that the wat was a great civilizing influence in the past in rural districts, and it is still a living force which, as a Thai, one cannot ignore without harming one's own foundation of culture, unless one builds a new one on that of the old.

A VILLAGE WEDDING: INFORMAL MERRYMAKING ON THE SIDE

A wedding in Bang Chan, as anywhere, is an occasion for good fellow-ship. The bride and groom receive the blessings of their elders and make merit through their first joint offering to the monks. Family and friends celebrate the event with festive hilarity.

MERIT-MAKING: NEVER TOO YOUNG

Children learn ritual merit-making from a very early age. Here a
child places his merit offering onto an alms receptacle. In the pulpit
a monk recites a sermon from a palm-leaf manuscript while the adult
audience listens reverently.

MERIT-MAKING: NEVER TOO OLD

As a person enters middle age his or her thoughts will turn more and more to earning merit for the next life and lives. The merit-maker places a little rice in each of the alms bowls, one for each monk in the temple plus one for the Lord Buddha.

PROCESSION TO THE ORDINATION

Above we see candidates for the monkhood parading from home to the Bang Chan temple. Ornate umbrellas, a regal symbol, shade the candidates and the ceremonial receptacles containing the orange robes that the candidates will soon be wearing.

ORDINATION: SUPREME MOMENT

The elderly bishop in the center of the picture receives the new monk
into the order of the Sangha. The newcomer is resplendent in his
bright orange robes with alms bowl suspended from his right shoulder.

PILGRIMAGE: MEMORABLE PERIOD IN THE ANNUAL CYCLE

After the holy season, during the coolest months of the year, many monks leave the temple, in small groups or alone, on pilgrimages to holy places. A monk is sometimes gone for weeks and may travel a distance of hundreds of miles, much of it on foot. The monk in the picture, equipped for his pilgrimage, carries an alms bowl over his left shoulder, a portable tent and an all-purpose travel bag over his right shoulder, and, in his left hand, a teapot.

Topknot Cutting

The raising of a child's topknot is a Brahmanical tradition now on the wane in Bang Chan. When the boy or girl is seven, nine, eleven, or thirteen years of age—odd numbers are considered auspicious—the topknot is ritually cut.

CUSTOMS CONNECTED WITH BIRTH
AND THE REARING OF CHILDREN

Publisher's Preface

Colonel Lǔaŋ Te·châsě·na·, in preparing to conduct the funeral of
Mme. Te·chá·sě·na· (Can Te·châsě·n), his wife, at Wat Mǎkǔd
Kàsàdtr'ja·ra·m on 8 December 1949 requested permission of the Fine Arts
Department to publish the book <u>Customs Connected with Birth and the Rearing
of Children</u>, by Phya Anuman Rajadhon, for distribution at the ceremony.
The Fine Arts Department feels this to be appropriate, because the deceased
was a close relative of the writer of this book, and so has granted permission
to publish as desired.

[Two paragraphs concerning publication omitted.]

Fine Arts Department
24 November 1949

[Three-page dedication by publisher omitted.]

Author's Preface

Customs are always undergoing changes, because they are easy to imitate; when people like others' customs, they adopt them. Old local customs
gradually disappear, and new customs move in to take their place; or the old
customs are retained but altered to fit new living conditions. Customs therefore consist of complicated and overlapping layers. It is difficult to trace the
reasons for practicing them, or why they are performed in one way or another,
and to what nationality or what locality they belong, and when they originated. When one asks people about customs, he usually does not get detailed
information. People who are old enough to have witnessed old customs, when
asked, are unable to give very much information, because they did not observe and remember; they are able only to tell about things they have seen.
Persons who can give complete information are therefore very few. It is necessary to ask a great many people, learning a little from one person and a
little from that one, and noting down and putting together whatever one gets.
This procedure enables one to get better information, but it takes a long time;
if one is not interested he cannot do it, for one receives no reward except
knowledge and personal satisfaction.

Originally I never thought of collecting old customs, because I had no
interest in learning about them. Later when I had read books on customs
written by foreigners, I came to see from those books that customs are an

important feature of a society; they are like a mirror reflecting the life and minds of the majority of the people of the nation, showing the stages of progress they have passed through, and this information helps us not a little to understand our conditions of life at present and in the future. If we regard old customs with a generous spirit, we know that customs originate for a reason or because of necessities relating to surrounding conditions or the spirit of the times. When they are performed continuously over a long period, the reasons and necessities for some customs disappear; some are given up but some remain. They follow the general rule that if the people still regard them as good, they still observe them and do not give them up; if they regard them as bad, and acquire others in their place which they regard as better, then the old customs must be abandoned. But do not forget that the people who make up a nation are complicated, forming classes having thoughts, knowledge, and mentalities not all of the same level. It is possible to make them uniform only in larger matters; smaller matters that are characteristic of particular localities and agree with surrounding conditions always exist. It is impossible to force all of these things into a uniform mold. One need look only at the Thai people. The majority have Thai facial features, manners, and speech, but if one looks at the minor characteristics he sees that no two Thai are exactly alike in facial features, manners, and speech; at best, they are merely similar. If my wife were exactly like me in every way, cast in the same mold, then she could certainly not live with me.

I feel regretful that when I became interested in learning about old customs of the Thai, not so very long ago, and thought of asking this person or that, in some cases it was already too late, because many of those who had known about these old customs were already dead. Some customs must be investigated in localities where they are understood to be still extant, but I had no opportunity to go there because I was busy with my work. I have therefore been able to investigate only as much as I had opportunity for, and have arranged the results according to categories, like the old things in a museum. Doing only this much is still better than doing nothing at all, because if there is further delay it will perhaps be impossible to obtain anything, since customs will have vanished.

I have divided my books on Old Customs of the Thai into five parts, namely:

1. Customs Connected with Birth, the Rearing of Children, and Education.
2. Customs Connected with Marriage.
3. Customs Connected with House-Building.
4. Customs Connected with the Life of the Thai, such as Merit-Making, Amusements, and Occupations.
5. Customs Connected with Death.

Of these books on customs, I have already published Part 3, "Customs Connected with House-Building," and Part 5, "Customs Connected with Death." The books have not been published in numerical order, because I work on them according to whim; when I am satisfied with any part I publish it as opportunity affords. Part 4, "Customs Connected with the Life of the Thai," has had various sections published separately, because it is a big subject. Parts already published are "Life of Monastery-Dwellers," which at that time I called "I Shall Take Holy Orders," and "Life of the Farmer." Besides these there are certain short sections which have been published in the Journal of the Fine Arts Department as opportunity afforded. "Customs Connected with Birth," that is to say Part 1, is here published for the first time, but it is not here printed in full, because it still lacks the last part concerning education, which I am not yet ready to publish. "Customs Connected with Marriage," that is to say Part 2, has not been published because I am not yet satisfied with certain details, for these are customs which differ in almost every locality and every case, depending upon individual models or individual textbooks; besides there is always a mixture of the old and the new, as well as influence of Chinese, Vietnamese, and western customs.

To speak in particular of the customs connected with birth described in this volume, I am fortunate in having acquired most of my information from my own wife. According to western custom, when anyone has compiled something and has acquired information from any book or has received help from any person, he states this and renders thanks in his book; even if it is his own wife that has helped, he thanks her. I approve of this custom, and so will follow it here, and take the opportunity to thank my wife for giving me information of many kinds on the subject of birth, I thank her even though I know that I can thank her without having to announce it to other people in print; the western custom is like this, and I approve of it and so follow it, feeling that it does no harm. I must also render thanks with the deepest respect to my elders who have been kind to me, and there are also many others who have given me help on this subject whom I am unable to remember and note down, having obtained a little from this person and a little from that person. I have also obtained information from a great many books, and so I render thanks here collectively. . . .

Sàthĭan Ko·sè·d
[Pen name of Phya Anuman]
22 February 1949

Table of Contents

CUSTOMS CONNECTED WITH BIRTH AND THE REARING OF CHILDREN

Preliminary Matters

Birth and death are things that go together. Birth is the beginning and death is the end of the life of every person. Birth and death are therefore closely connected. Humans regard both these events as important, because they are the beginning and the end of life; they must be attended by traditional ceremonies for the purpose of seeking happiness in this world and the next world. To speak only of birth, even though there are fewer required traditional customs than at death, there are many small matters which today are regarded less seriously than formerly and so are gradually disappearing. People are changing over to modern opinions and beliefs in accordance with medical knowledge and progress.

Beliefs of people of former times which have been handed down traditionally, if considered from the point of view of modern opinions, may perhaps be regarded as foolish and unreasonable. This is because we are using the new as a yardstick to measure the old, or using our own measuring basket to measure other people's rice. How can they be the same? Beliefs of people of any given age or any given locality are always suited to the life and needs of that period or that locality, for customs which arise must always have a reason, so that they are regarded as beneficial or useful to the majority according to the opinions and beliefs of people of that period or that locality. When later on the opinions of the people in the group undergo changes according to the progress of the times, any custom which is appropriate to one age but perhaps is not appropriate to later ages declines and disappears, or is altered to make it appropriate. Gradual alterations and additions occur cumulatively and steadily through many generations, until national customs arise. Every nation thus has its own independent set of customs.

As a rule if anything is handed down traditionally as a custom, it survives for a long time. If there is no forcing circumstance, people dare not change; even though the usefulness or necessity is gone, people still believe in it stubbornly, for if they change from what they have been familiar with, they usually have a vacant and uncomfortable feeling. It is as if after one has eaten his meal he is accustomed to eating dessert; if he has none he feels strangely unsatisfied. Customs which have been handed down and still survive to the present are usually of the sort which have successfully passed the test of collective opinion of the group. Nations which have advanced therefore preserve their original customs; even though they no longer serve a useful purpose, they are stubbornly observed, for customs are national symbols, causing members of the nation to feel that they belong to one and the same nation and have for long generations. There is an exception only in the case of customs that are harmful or that obstruct or delay progress, being no longer appropriate to the times. These must be dropped or cast aside, or else changed and improved to render them more convenient. In such cases they are not maintained stupidly; people do not cling stubbornly to one way without change or alteration; nor, if they are not stubborn, do they cast aside everything old because they regard it as out of date, and seize upon new things which are not suited to the mentality or lives of all the people of the nation as a whole. Both of these methods result in damage.

Customs are an important branch of knowledge, because they give evidence regarding the life and opinions of people in former times which cannot be obtained from any other source. When we study history or any other subject whatsoever, we desire to learn about its development and expansion in order to know how to apply this information to the work of adapting new things appropriately and smoothly to our conditions and mentality. The same principle applies to the study of customs.

Books that deal with our customs connected with birth are hard to find, because these are regarded as matters that everyone knows and has seen. We therefore do not have old manuals on this subject like the Gṛhyasūtra and the Yajurveda of India, which contain much material concerning birth. We have only the textbook called Pàthŏmcindaa, which says that Phráʔ Máhǎathěen Tamjee was the author. Whether Phráʔ Máhǎathěen Tamjee was an Indian or of some other nationality, what he has written in this book is in accordance with the beliefs of those times. His intentions toward his fellow human beings were good, and he should receive some credit, but his name is instead an object of scorn, because it happens to coincide in sound with the name of a kind of plant which has an irritating poison all around the edges of the leaves. [1] Moreover, we call the person who delivers babies a tamjɛɛ doctor; but nowadays it is necessary to change this, because tamjɛɛ is regarded as an impolite word, and midwives[2] are regarded as skilled in magic spells and enchantments, which are ancient knowledge now out of date. Indeed for the most part this is true, and it is the misfortune of Máhǎathěen Tamjee that his name ought to be an object of praise but instead has become a low name which no one likes to pronounce.

If one were to classify beliefs and ceremonies connected with birth, he might classify them according to the reasons that give rise to them, which may be grouped under three headings:

(1) For prevention of dangers which might befall a pregnant woman, because formerly it was believed that a period when one is liable to danger is the period when one is about to be a mother.

(2) For facilitating delivery and preventing dangers resulting in death; the period of giving birth to a baby was regarded as so important that pregnancy was compared to a woman going forth into battle or, as they say, like setting out in a little boat to cross the sea, one foot in the water and the other on the gunwale of the boat.

(3) For protection and care of the newborn child, at a time when its body is frail and weak and it may easily die, in order that it may survive to grow up later.

All three of these reasons were originally for the most part matters connected with protection from and driving away evil spirits which, it was believed, would come to molest and harm the child and mother. This was the belief of people in former times, when it was thought that anything not known and understood was to be assigned to the effects of spirits and gods as the agents which caused them. Later when there had been some advancement, even though the belief in spirits as cause faded out, the fear remained, because this belief lies deep in the bones. It is hard to eradicate; it varies only to a degree according to the time and locality. If anyone stubbornly refuses to follow the customs in which others believe, he offends the spirits and traditions to the point that he may cause suffering to the majority or to members of the group. It is therefore necessary to act alike in order not to go against tradition.

The customs connected with birth which I am about to describe have been compiled from old stories insofar as I have been able to seek them out. There are some that are still observed in certain localities, and some that have been given up. Even in the same locality there are practices and beliefs which are not uniform; there are certain omissions, additions, or alterations, depending upon the ability, beliefs, nationality, class, and knowledge of the people. I will not, however, speak of things which I regard as modern methods, which have nothing to do with research into old things, the purpose of this series of books.

Conception

It appears that formerly there was a belief that at the time of conception, the pregnant woman usually had a strange dream which was a token to inform her in advance whether the child in her womb would be a boy or a girl, whether it had good or bad characteristics, and what sort of person it would be in future when it grew up, as in the story of Khŭn Cháaŋ Khŭn Phɛ̆ɛn, at the birth of Khŭn Cháaŋ, where it says:

> Lady Thêebphathɔɔŋ lay asleep. She rolled and tossed, spoke in her sleep, and dreamed that a male elephant died and rolled down a steep bank; it bloated up and its head rotted and sent forth a foul odor.

> There was a bald-headed pelican that came flying aimlessly from the great forest. It took the elephant in its beak and laid it down, entering the central house where she slept.

In the dream she called the bird, "Come here, you old bald-headed fellow." She took hold of the bald-headed creature and lay embracing the bird and the elephant happily.

When she awoke she straightway awakened her husband. She vomited and trembled, unable to restrain herself. The foul odor of the elephant and the bird clung to her. She retched and cried, "O husband, I beg you, thump on my neck."

Khun Sĭi Wĭchaj was much alarmed. He started up, his eyes bulging, and stroked and massaged her neck with his hand till she recovered from her nausea, and then she told her dream.

Khun Sĭi Wĭchaj interpreted the dream: "You will be with child; nothing is wrong. Our child will be a boy, according to the prediction, like the big pelican that came carrying an elephant in its beak.

"He will be wealthy and prosperous, my love, but this child of ours will disgrace us. Bald-headed from birth, he will be rich, possessing more than five cartloads of money."

When one has dreamed of anything, he must relate the dream to someone who knows how to interpret it. Interpreting dreams is a good thing, because if the dreamer has a dream that seems bad to him, it causes him worry and uneasiness; one who relates his dream and has it interpreted feels relieved. This applies only to people who still believe that dreams are signs of good or evil; if one does not believe in them that is the end of the matter.

As a rule persons who conceive are not at first aware that they have conceived, and it is a waste of time to speak of dreams. They occur often only in stage plays; when a woman has conceived she has a dream, and then someone interprets the dream. This appears to be a convention of literary composition, not a convention of ordinary people. If one writes a book, when someone conceives she must dream that she eats something inedible. Perhaps the woman who conceives has heard many stories of this sort; she happens to dream about it and so it comes to be regarded as a convention that when one has dreamed she must tell the dream and have the dream interpreted. However, this is a question of individuals, not a convention that is held everywhere.

The period from conception to delivery is regarded as a time when there are dangers all around one. The pregnant woman must risk various dangers until the period is passed, and this makes her uneasy and unhappy. It is therefore necessary to find methods of protecting and defending her by various devices, for example:

They find a phĭidsàmǒon talisman to tie on the wrist or hang diagonally over the shoulder for protection. A phĭidsàmǒon is a sheet of palm leaf on which a magic formula is written, called loŋ khun phráʔ. Then it is folded into a small square, and is usually strung on a cord or cotton thread. It is

tied or hung around the neck for a long time, many months. As time passes
perspiration turns it black, for it is a cord that is worn constantly until the
child is born and the mother leaves the fire; then she takes it off and keeps
it in a jar containing turmeric and delivery articles. It is odd that this
phǐdsàmɔ̌ɔn talisman is similar in name and characteristics to the talismans
for tying around the neck to ward off dangers used by people who hold the
Moslem religion, which have magic formulas praising Allah and are called
Bismallaha. The phǐdsàmɔ̌ɔn [Siamese] talisman is tied on to ward off evil
spirits which might cause harm to the pregnant woman. In the times when
beliefs of this sort were general, anything harmful that might occur was as-
cribed to spirits, and especially in the case of a pregnant woman, because
both mother and child might die if careful precautions were not taken. No
doubt people had heard of such cases. As regards the death of a mother and
child at this period, if they die before delivery, they are said to die thǎŋ
klom. The word klom is said to be Cambodian, meaning "completely,"
that is to say, both mother and child die. If they die after delivery they are
said to die phraaj, and usually become fierce phraaj spirits waiting and watching to harm pregnant women because of a feeling of disappointment and envy.
This causes people to be all the more fearful and uneasy, and so they use
whatever devices they have as protection.

    Also, pregnant women are usually inclined to feel very thoughtful;
they like to think of various things, and usually think more of unpleasant
things than of pleasant ones. If they have magic objects that they firmly believe can be used for protection, their fear is somewhat relieved. It is not
only we who have these notions; other nationalities have them as well. For
example according to Indian belief, spirits like to molest and harm children
and women because they are weak, whereas spirits do not dare molest men
with strong hearts, just as dogs like to bite children and women. At the time
of pregnancy and the time of delivery there are likewise many methods of protection against spirits that might come to do harm. I will relate these here
in order.

    Pregnant women may not go to a cremation, and may not go to visit
persons seriously ill. This is probably protection against thinking too much,
which might cause fear and loss of confidence. They are also forbidden to go
and see other women give birth, because it will make delivery impossible,
the children in the womb being embarrassed by one another and so refusing to
be born. If one were to guess at the reason for this prohibition, it is probably
that the person who goes might lose confidence when she sees the intense pain
of delivery, and so she might be made uneasy. When monks conduct the
sǎŋkhǎkam ceremony and chant the jádtĭ , it is forbidden for pregnant wom-
en to enter the precincts of the ceremony; it is believed that they will have
a hard time giving birth. Probably they regard the sound of the word jádtĭ
as similar to the sound of the word jád [meaning "to stuff in, cram in"] and

so they forbid it. Actually it may also be a question of the ceremony, in which purity is desired, for according to Indian custom when a ceremony is held, I understand that they forbid pregnant women and strangers to enter, regarding this as a defilement of the ceremony. Besides these things, it is also forbidden to fish, to kill animals, to tell lies, to drive nails or tacks, or to sew up the end of a pillow or mattress which has been stuffed with kapok but is not yet sewn up, for this will have an effect upon delivery, causing accidental closing of the passage in the same way. It is forbidden to sit, lie down, or stand in a doorway. When ascending or descending stairs, one must ascend or descend at once; it is forbidden to stop midway on the stairs. The reason for these prohibitions is easy to understand, and they are very widely observed. When sleeping, one must lie on the side; it is forbidden to lie on the back because it is believed that the child will bulge out and cause the belly to break open. I have asked women who have been pregnant and they say that if they sleep on their backs they feel uncomfortable.

When there is a solar or lunar eclipse, they are to fasten a sewing needle in the waistband of the lower garment, believing that this prevents the unborn child from having squinting eyes or a deformed body or facial features, such as a misshapen mouth resembling the eclipsed sun or moon. This belief is similar to a belief of Indians who hold the Moslem religion; they believe that a lunar eclipse is caused by evil spirits which eat the moon. They forbid pregnant women and their relatives from eating anything at this time; neither may they smoke cigarettes, for it is a time when spirits have come out and are roaming about. Moreover, if one chews betel at that time, the child to be born will have folded ears like betel leaf. (When Indians chew betel leaf they fold it rather than pleat it as we do.) It is also forbidden to twist or cut anything, for this will cause the child to be born with deformed fingers or swollen lips.[3] I do not understand why they fasten a needle in the waistband, believing that this will prevent squinting eyes. Perhaps it is a protection against spirits, which the Indians believe to be roaming about at that time. There is nothing that spirits fear so much as a sharp piece of iron; this is a belief held by many nationalities, as I have related elsewhere.[4] Concerning prevention of deformities in the child to be born, we also forbid deformed or ugly people from walking behind a pregnant woman, fearing that the child in the womb will be affected in the same way.

It is forbidden for pregnant women to "rub themselves" at night, because it is believed that at the time of delivery they will be pained by excessive liquid or will give birth to "water twins." If it is necessary to bathe, they should disrobe completely to bathe and then there is no danger. Women formerly did not bathe often; at best they "rubbed themselves" instead. "Rubbing oneself" here does not mean actually rubbing oneself; it is a method of bathing by pouring water on the upper part of the body without wetting the lower part of the body, which is covered by the lower garment. When they are going to "rub themselves," they must tuck up the lower garment as high as possible, bend over low, and then pour water from the vessel onto the middle of the back. If they do not bend over low, or if they do not pour the water exactly in the middle of the back, the water may run down and wet the lower garment. "Rubbing oneself" instead of bathing all over is not much seen now; this is different from former times, when it was still popular. The custom arose from not wishing to change the lower garment frequently, or from not having a lower garment to change to. The original source may have been shortage of water; it was necessary to economize on water because there were not enough vessels such as jars and jugs. If one were to bathe, it was necessary to go down to the landing in the dark when it was impossible to see and one might fall or be harmed by wild animals, and so bathing at night was forbidden. This is a supposition based on conditions of life in the country where things were formerly like this.

The prohibition on pregnant women bathing or "rubbing themselves" at night is not a belief confined to us. Other nationalities, so far as I have ascertained, also forbid it. For example, according to Vietnamese belief it is forbidden to bathe at night, because it is thought that it will cause a chill to the body of the pregnant woman, and at the time of delivery she will not give birth easily. According to Indian belief, besides forbidding bathing, they also forbid combing out the hair. When asleep it is forbidden to place the head on a high pillow, and it is also forbidden to sleep with the head low. On this subject of forbidding bathing, I have been told that the peasants in some localities in Thailand -- I am sorry that I cannot remember what localities -- believe that on the last day of the month pregnant women should seek an opportunity to take off all their clothing and bathe at night, but they must take care to allow no one to see them; what will happen if they are seen, my informant did not say, but he said that if they can do this they will be able to give birth easily. This belief concerning nakedness is strange. It is believed that spirits are very much afraid of it; no doubt these are spirits with culture! For example, if one is going out to collect herbs to treat illness, he must go naked, and must not allow his shadow to touch the medicinal plant. If there is a spirit in a tree acting as if it were going to haunt one, one must take off his clothes and tie the garments and some illuk grass to the tree, holding one's breath while tying them. After these things are tied, the spirit will not be able to come down from the tree and haunt one again.

Pregnant women must find work in order to exercise, such as carrying water or pounding rice, which are normal duties and tasks of women in the country. This is in order to keep the womb loose, and to prevent the child in the womb from becoming so fat and big that delivery will be difficult. This agrees with the belief of the Vietnamese, who likewise recommend heavy work.

Besides this they forbid reaching the arms out to full length, believing that the child in the womb will have trouble sucking the umbilical cord, because the cord of the afterbirth will contract and rise up high. They also forbid driving nails just as we do, but their prohibition is broader; even other people in the same house are forbidden, because it will cause the child in the womb to have a deformed body.

Concerning our prohibition against pregnant women fishing, killing animals, and telling lies, probably it is desired that they should be pure in heart. This is similar to the Indian custom of having one speak only auspicious words and perform sacrificial rites. This is all good; they say that it causes pregnant women to have beautiful clear complexions and happy dispositions. As it says in one place in the story of Khŭn Cháaŋ Khŭn Phĕɛn:

> I will tell of Thɔɔŋ Pràsĭi, who was heavy with child. She was
> truly lovely, her hair becoming to her face. Her complexion was
> as if burnished with gold, and her face like the orb of the moon on
> the night when it is full.

> Her two cheeks were like golden fruits, and her two breasts were
> full and firm. Her skin was soft and beautiful to see, and her
> countenance radiant and fair.

> She observed the precepts and said her prayers regularly, humbling
> her heart and raising her folded hands above her head. She made
> religious offerings with lotus blossoms, and had no fear of danger.

The quotation that I have cited here shows the beliefs of people in former times as to how pregnant women should behave. Besides this, the lotus blossoms which they had offered were boiled and eaten in the advanced stages of pregnancy, because they were regarded as a medicine beneficial to the fetus, making the child strong in body, and preventing the mother from vomiting with morning sickness. Sometimes they took the lotus blossoms and had monks say magic spells over them; this is still believed and practiced today. It is associated with strong belief in the efficacy of the Buddha, fostering religious faith and cheerfulness. This is also very helpful. If one desires really good results, she should wrap the stamens of giant lotus blossoms with black candle seed (Abroma augusta sterculiaceae) in a cloth as a massaging pack, boiling it in the milk of a young coconut. This is a specific medicine for the fetus. Coconut milk has certain properties which help the fetus. People in former times used it and saw the benefits, and so they handed it down as a prescribed treatment. People of this day and age may not agree, but their disagreement is not the result of chemical analysis of the constituents of coconut milk to see what elements it contains. So long as they have not really tested it scientifically, they cannot pronounce any definite opinion. Recently I read in an Occidental newspaper that coconut milk contains certain substances which are good for unborn children.

There is another belief connected with pregnancy. If she would like to rear her child easily, a pregnant woman must seek an opportunity to walk under the belly of an elephant, but it is necessary to choose an elephant with a kind disposition. If she has passed under the belly of an elephant, the child that is born will be easy to rear. The reason for this is not clear, but it is strange that many nationalities have beliefs similar to this. For example, Arabs and Iranians believe that if a pregnant woman has passed under the belly of a camel she will give birth easily. Peasants in Sweden, if they desire to give birth easily, must pass through a tunnel formed by shrubs and trees; sometimes they pass through a tunnel beneath stones, or pass through an iron barrel hoop. It is even believed that if children who are ill pass under an animals's belly or through a tunnel three times, they will recover.

Besides the miscellaneous beliefs already described, there is another matter that must be taken care of. One must entrust one's unborn child to a midwife, paying an amount of money as a sort of deposit, customarily one-half tamlyŋ or one tamlyŋ, that is two bàad (tical) or four bàad, or it may be more or less than this according to cases, depending upon the status of the patient and the locality. After this agreement is made, if anything occurs in connection with the pregnancy, one can summon the midwife to help, no matter what the time. Usually it is a matter of raising the womb, by lifting the womb with the hand, in order not to allow the fetus to drop down low, for this will make it difficult for the pregnant woman to walk because the fetus has fallen low.

Pregnant women usually have a desire to eat strange things. Usually these are things which human beings do not normally eat. This condition is called phɛ́ɛ thɔ́ɔŋ, and is the result of changes in the nervous system. It is a matter of psychology, causing a temporary desire to eat very sour things, very salty things, or strange and unusual things. There is also nausea and frequent vomiting. This is the opinion of modern doctors; you can make your own inquiries. This condition sometimes causes one to feel almost gluttonously hungry; I do not know whether this is because the woman deliberately says that she is hungry or because she is really hungry, for it is very difficult to judge the hearts of women. I will quote an instance of this pregnancy sickness from the story of Khǔn Cháaŋ Khǔn Phɛ̌en, as follows:

I will tell of Lady Thêebphá̂thɔɔn. Her belly was huge and protuberant. She rose and sat with difficulty, and so she shuffled about, and trembled with hunger for liquor and meat.

Her saliva drooled like that of kàsy̌y spirit, and she wept and moaned, imploring her husband. It was as if she were possessed by a ghost. The more one gave her to eat, the more she craved.

Eels, chickens, frogs, turtles, lizards, caterpillars, bullfrogs, all were insufficient to her guts. She snatched up huge bites and gobbled them down. In a moment the liquor jug was empty; it was impossible to buy it fast enough.

Strange things that pregnant women like to eat include pitch from torches, hard chalk, diatomaceous earth, uncooked white rice, and burnt earth (mud baked in sheets in the sun and then burnt). Formerly one saw hard chalk stacked up for sale in shops (I have seen it at the Big Swing; more recently I have seen it for sale at Sàphaan Hăn). At present one does not notice it; probably the fashion for eating it has gone out. This hard chalk is not in long thin sticks like the pencils which school children use for writing on slates; it is a kind of diatomaceous earth of a soft yellow color and friable, for use in writing on blackboards and black paper books like chalk. The good variety is called "widow chalk" because it writes easily and need not be touched up with saliva frequently to make it soft and possible to write with. Some women when they are pregnant feel nauseated and feel that their own husbands are malodorous. The husband cannot come near, but must sleep in a different place, or sleep at a distance from her; if he comes near and she smells him, she feels nauseated. This is very strange.

In the textbook Phromcindaa the symptoms of pregnancy sickness are described as follows:

If the mother desires to eat meat and fish and raw things, they say that a creature of hell has come to be born.

If she desires to eat honey, cane sugar, and palm sugar, they say someone has come down from heaven to be born.

If she desires to eat fruit, they say an animal has come to be born.

If she desires to eat earth, they say that Brahma has come down to be born (because Brahma came down to eat delicious earth).

If she desires to eat hot, spicy things, they say that a human being has come down to be born.

It is probably because of the belief that they like to eat earth because Brahma has come down to be born, that women formerly liked to eat hard chalk and burnt earth, so that Brahma would come down to be born as their child. Also, during pregnancy it is necessary to be careful for the child in the womb. Even if the woman desires to eat hot, spicy food, which is something she likes, she must refrain from eating it. When she sits or lies down or moves about she must be careful of her body, not to fall down or jar herself too much. This is to prevent the child in the womb from being hurt or damaged in any way.

When pregnancy approaches the seventh and eighth months, the flesh of the belly around the navel stretches and protrudes, closing the navel. If it protrudes above (the navel), the navel is said to be supine; if it protrudes below (the navel), the navel is said to be prone. If any woman's navel turns up, they say that the child in her womb will be a boy. If the navel turns down, they say it will be a girl. This prediction is probably based upon the characteristics of being turned down or turned up. At this time when pregnancy is far advanced, the belly is very large and protuberant. The skin of the abdomen is very taut, making it necessary to have medicine to smear on the belly to prevent cracking. They say this is because the child in the womb has grown very large, stretching the skin of the abdomen to the point of cracking. For this medicine they use the rind of the bael fruit dried in the sun and ground up with clear lime-water in an earthenware potlid. Some women have white streaks on the belly; this is said to be the result of the belly cracking at childbirth. Besides applying medicine, they also tread on the front of the legs, saying that this relaxes the tendons in the groin and facilitates delivery. It is also necessary to take medicine to nurture the fetus as already related.

When pregnancy is far advanced, the man who is the husband must go and cut firewood in advance, for the wife to lie near the fire after the birth of the child. It is forbidden for other people to cut it for her. He is to select the wood of Combretum quadrangulare or tamarind wood, and the pieces must be large. The reason for selecting these two kinds of wood is that in some localities they grow in open woods and are easy to find, and it is said that when these two kinds of wood burn to charcoal they leave only a little ashes, not causing much annoyance or inconvenience. If it is another locality which does not have these two sorts of wood, they may use other woods, depending upon their traditional practice. When they have cut the wood and brought it in, they cut it up in sections. Then they must stack it up vertically in a suitable place. In some localities they have a belief that the cutting of the firewood for lying near the fire should be done very near the time of delivery, that is, in about the eighth month after conception. Also, in the matter of the kinds of firewood, besides Combretum quadrangulare and tamarind, there should also be wood of Erythrina lithosperma. But the wood of Erythrina lithosperma is said to give off a great deal of smoke; probably they put only enough into the fire to observe the custom. The use of Erythrina lithosperma wood when lying near the fire is said to prevent pains in the womb and to cure bad blood. But if it is a first child, they are to use wood of the "five species," [5] because this is supposed to accustom the woman to lying near the fire made from woods of various kinds when she has her later children. There are omens observed in cutting firewood. If the firewood is cut in long pieces, the child to be born will be a boy. If it is cut in small pieces, the child will be a girl. This is a matter of predicting from the characteristics of shortness or longness, similar to the question of the turned-up navel or turned-down navel. Similarly when the firewood is assembled in a stack: if the stack of firewood is observed to be high in the center, the child will be a boy. If the center is not high, but flat and normal, the child will be a girl. This is a matter of omens of the same sort.

According to the beliefs of the Mons (as recorded by R. Halliday in The Talaings, Government Press, Rangoon, 1917, p. 55), the firewood for

lying near the fire must be cut in the seventh or eighth month. Halliday goes
on to say:

> If, however, one stick is cut in the seventh month the rule is
> considered to have been observed and the remainder may be cut at
> any time. It is usually green wood, smoke evidently being desirable
> as well as heat. [But the Thais use slightly moist wood, not too
> fresh and not too dry, because it is desired that the wood not burn
> quickly and that it form coals; it is not desired that it produce much
> smoke. Phya Anuman Rajadhon.] In cutting the wood (young sap-
> lings) the first tree must fall clear to the ground. Should it fall and
> lie against another tree it is rejected. [Because it is stuck halfway,
> this will affect the delivery of the child. Phya Anuman Rajadhon.]

The belief restricting the cutting of the firewood to the husband is probably handed down from olden times when there was yet no hiring for wages
and no purchasing. Also, it is a small matter not requiring the calling in of
neighbors to help. Thus every family must do its own work and depend upon
itself. Later on, even if it were convenient to hire someone to go and cut or
purchase the firewood, there were those who believed firmly in the original
custom and still observed it. This is to be regarded as a good thing; it is an
act that shows the feelings of man and wife toward one another; no doubt
the pregnant wife is made happy. But in localities where firewood is hard to
find, or in times of progress and advancement, there are probably few people
who still stubbornly observe this custom, because its usefulness and necessity
are gone and it is out of date. Persistent observance of it causes hardship,
and it is not progressive or appropriate to the times.

On the stack of firewood that is piled up vertically they must lay Indian
jujube thorns (the Mon use bamboo thorns), believing that they ward off spirits.
At the time of cutting these, they are to speak the following formula: namo
buddhatassa.[6] When they reach the syllable hat they are to cut[7] at once
with a knife. (This formula makes use of syllables of similar sound, that is,
námoo = năam, thorn, and phúd [tàd] sáฺ = phúdsaa, Indian jujube.) In any
case, the spreading of thorns on the pile of firewood is a good thing. Besides
warding off spirits, it also keeps away animals and naughty children who
would get up and walk on the stack of firewood and knock it down. Why is it
necessary to use Indian jujube thorns? Cannot other kinds of thorns be used?
The answer is that they probably can, but Indian jujube thorns are easy to
find, since they grow in forests and deserted places, and so it is stated flatly
that the name is auspicious as explained above.

The central meaning of the spreading of thorns is protection against
spirits. If these are kràsῠy spirits, they fear thorns more than spirits of other
kinds, for kràsῠy spirits are said to be people like ourselves. Usually they
are old women. At night in the dark of the moon when it is very late and
everyone is asleep, the woman who is a kràsῠy spirit goes out in search of

food, taking along only her head and entrails from her body. Wherever she goes she can be seen as a flickering greenish light forming a big orb. The things that a kràsy̆y spirit likes to eat are raw meat and excrement. She is especially fond of women who have just given birth and have tiny pink babies. She usually seeks an opportunity to enter the belly of the woman and devour the delicious entrails of the woman and baby with enjoyment. For this reason persons who are thin and dry with only skin covering their bones, and fruits such as small flat bananas without much flesh, are called "people sucked by a kràsy̆y" or "bananas sucked by a kràsy̆y." In the matter of spreading thorns to ward them off, it is necessary to spread them also under the house where there are cracks and holes, because wherever a kràsy̆y spirit goes she drags her entrails along with her. If she tries to pass through the thorns, her entrails catch on the thorns. She is therefore very much afraid of thorns. When a kràsy̆y spirit has finished eating the thing she normally likes, namely excrement, her mouth is smeared. If she sees anyone's clothing hung out at night outside the house, she will usually wipe her mouth with it. If in the morning one sees clothing that has been hung out faintly marked with round brown spots, one knows that a kràsy̆y spirit has wiped her mouth with it. If one wishes to know who the kràsy̆y spirit is, one is to boil the soiled cloth. The woman who is a kràsy̆y spirit will be unbearably hot at the mouth and will have to come and ask to buy the cloth. Clothing that is soiled in spots because a kràsy̆y spirit has wiped her mouth with it is usually seen in the rainy season. The cause is that the clothing is moist and gets no sun and so becomes mouldy; if it is hung in the sun for a long time the spots disappear of themselves. The saying that kràsy̆y wipe their mouths with it is a good thing; people take care not to leave their clothing out in the dew till it becomes mouldy and is damaged.

Persons who are kràsy̆y spirits are said to die very hard. When they are to die they must suffer very much. Thus they do not die easily, until some child or grandchild[8] accepts the heritage of being a kràsy̆y spirit by receiving the saliva of the kràsy̆y spirit, who spits it out on her. Then the kràsy̆y spirit can die. This matter of saliva is strange. It is usually regarded as something peculiarly magic or the like. In the Northeast it is believed that if a person who is a pɔ̀ɔb spirit spits on anyone, that person must be a pɔ̀ɔb spirit, [which is a spirit of the] same category as kràsy̆y spirits in that area. When I was a child I lived in a locality where kràsy̆y spirits abounded. It was an area where there were many people of Mon and Tavoy descent. I have often heard stories of kràsy̆y spirits. Next to my home there was an old lady who lay ill for a long time. The neighbors said that she was a kràsy̆y spirit and died hard because she had no children or grandchildren to receive her saliva and carry on as a kràsy̆y spirit. I was so frightened that I did not dare trespass into her yard to play. Later she died; I don't know whether it was because someone consented to be her heir or not, but I remember the story well and so have related it here. By coincidence recently an old lady who had lived at my home ever since girlhood came to visit me, and so I took the opportunity to ask her about this story. She said that the old kràsy̆y spirit had no children or grandchildren to accept the heritage of being a kràsy̆y spirit, and so she had to have a cat accept it instead; that is, she smeared her saliva on the cat, and so she could die. This is very amusing.

An elderly person once spoke to me about kràsy̆y spirits as follows: "This name kràsy̆y is peculiar. The world regards only bright lights as kràsy̆y, for example kràsy̆y worms[9] and kràsy̆y lamps.[10] But because it is known that there are only female kràsy̆y, a male was invented and called kàhăaŋ, but what they speak of is a mere concoction, said to be made with flat baskets for wings and a rice-pounding pestle for a tail. The thing as described would seem to be half man and half bird, but when one draws a picture which is half man and half bird, it is rather called ʔarăhăn.[11] This name is strange. Why they should take the name of an enlightened person with divine wisdom and apply it to a filthy figure like that, I don't know."

In the north they do not trust mere spreading of thorns. They also make a fence around the area under the house directly beneath the delivery room, and then put thorns all around the fence. Around the delivery room upstairs they make a circle with a magic cord, hang up cloths on which magic figures are drawn in all directions, and then stretch a net across the ceiling with a peak in the center. These strong defenses they say are to ward off phooŋ spirits (probably from phlooŋ, that is, they have a shining [phlooŋ] light like kràsy̆y spirits). They usually make holes in the floor (probably floors made of flattened bamboo strips) and come up to suck the blood of the mother where she lies. They like to drink the blood at the tip of the heart of the mother and child who are lying near the fire, and they are capable of transforming themselves into cats, pigs, birds, or whatever they please. It is therefore necessary to take strict precautions.

Labor Pains

When the time of labor pains arrives and the child is to be born, the people in the house must hurry to knock down the firewood that has been piled up, and then pull out two or three sticks of it, and go and light a fire to boil water in preparation for the time of delivery. They use a piece of wood from this fire to start the fire that the mother will lie near later.

They must open the doors and windows and unlock all bolts and locks of cupboards, drawers, and anything else that is locked up. Also pieces of wood and other things that are fastened or stuck under the beams or roof must be removed. In the northeast amulets which are "closing-the-portal" charms must be taken away elsewhere; only after the birth can they be brought back and put away in their original places.

It is forbidden to sit or stand in a door or midway on the stairs, or to speak the words "stuck," "fastened," "hung up," "stuck midway," "difficult delivery," or other words of similar meaning; none of these can be spoken, because it is believed that they might come true.

It is forbidden for pregnant women to come in and visit, because the children in the womb will be embarrassed and refuse to be born.

These prohibitions are superstitions to prevent obstruction and facilitate delivery. They are ideas remaining from olden times and are common to all nations. Among the Arunta in the middle of the continent of Australia, the husband must take off all personal ornaments; whatever he has in bags or pouches must all be poured out; anything tied up in a coil or knot must be undone. The matter of opening doors and windows, unlocking cupboards and drawers, and untying knots and coils at the time of labor pains before delivery, are beliefs held by many nationalities, both Occidental and Moslem. It is even believed that corks in bottles and spigots must be taken out. Domestic animals in pens, coops, or sheds -- such as horses, oxen, ducks, and chickens -- or those that are chained up -- such as dogs -- must be set free temporarily. Hair that is coiled up must be unfastened and let down. Jackknives that are closed must be opened. In sum, no matter what it is, if it is fastened, or stuck, or closed, or tied, or locked up, it must be released, freed, or undone.

At the time of delivery the direction must be selected. Usually it is good if the face can be turned toward the east, or the head may be pointed toward the north; the child will be able to move down easily.[12] In some cases they have a master of magic select the direction for them. Some select the direction according to a hen which is laying an egg; in whatever direction the chicken turns its head, the face should be turned in that direction in order that the mother may bear the child as easily as the hen lays its egg. In some cases they have the woman in labor turn her head toward a door, which is a "way out."

When the labor pains become frequent, they are to light candles and incense sticks and worship the spirit of the plot of land as an act of begging forgiveness and in order to inform him, for they have taken the liberty of coming and giving birth on his land. Probably they regard giving birth to a child as a blemish. This is a belief held by many nationalities. They do not say outright that it is a blemish, but one can tell from various prohibitions of theirs that they so regard it. I will save these and relate them in the section discussing reasons for lying near the fire. Besides this, if one wishes to make vows to any other spirits or gods, it is up to one's beliefs. In the book, Khŭn Cháaŋ Khŭn Phĕɛn, in the section, "Birth of Khŭn Cháaŋ," it is said:

> Some spoke charms and sprinkled white rice, their lips mumbling incoherently.

In another place, in the section, "Birth of Naaŋ Phim," it is said:

Some took cowries and stuck them on the wall, making vows and mumbling incoherently.

Speaking charms and sprinkling white rice are still popular with some people, because this period is one of emergency, and whatever knowledge or beliefs one has, he puts them into action. The Palaung, who are a hill people living in the north of Burma, sprinkle sacred water all around the room to ward off spirits; this is the same sort of thing as our sprinkling of white rice. In the north of Thailand they make holy water and float the unripe pods of Acacia concinna in it; then they tie leaves of the camphor plant, which spirits fear, in bunches, dip them in the holy water, and sprinkle it all over the delivery room, as well as in every corner and cranny of the house in case a spirit is hiding somewhere; when touched by the holy water the spirit cannot endure it, but must flee away. But the custom of sticking a great many cowries in the roof or fastening cowries on the wall and making vows, as in the story of Khŭn Chǎaŋ Khŭn Phɛ́ɛn, is a belief which at present no one seems to observe or to have seen. And why was it necessary to use cowries? I have found evidence that rural people in some areas, at the time of labor pains before delivery of a child, take fýan or salŷn coins and fasten them with beeswax to a cotton thread, and then hang them up at the head of the woman in labor. Or they may hang them up at the spirit shelf in the house. When they hang them up there are also betel and areca, flowers, incense sticks, and candles as offerings. When the incense sticks and candles have been lighted they are taken down and set upright below. This is a way of making a vow and asking for an easy delivery. After the child is born, they take the money and buy things to put in a monk's begging bowl or offer to a monk. If one considers this he will see that the cowries are simply money offerings, because in former times cowries were used as small money. Even at present, sàtaaŋ coins or banknotes may also be used instead. In those days if one wished to insert a silver bàad coin in the wall or roof to make a vow, he could do so, but this was a very large amount, and if it disappeared the owner might be ruined, for a silver tical in those days was not a small sum, even to royalty. For example, it is known that His Majesty the Second King of the Third Reign received from the king only ten catties of silver per year, or eight hundred bàad. This was regarded as a fabulously great amount, sufficient to maintain the honor of the palace of the Second King. His Majesty King Chulalongkorn once told a story that country girls said to their mothers as they paddled their boat past the King's palace, "No doubt the King has a whole catty of silver, and eats glutinous rice with coconut cream every day." Little did they realize the accuracy of their remarks. When the King ascended the throne he had one catty, or eighty bàad, of personal money left.

There is an important requirement connected with the time when the delivery is about to take place; they must go after the midwife to whom the womb was entrusted. When the midwife has come, they are to arrange a bowl filled with an appropriate amount of white rice, with three areca nuts (some people say five nuts or seven nuts, or in some cases slices; this is indefinite), three bunches of betel leaves (some people say five or seven betel leaves), one bunch of bananas, three incense sticks, and three candles. There is silver fastened to the candles according to custom; this may be one tamlyŋ, two tamlyŋ, or three tamlyŋ (four bàad, eight bàad, twelve bàad, depending upon the fee in the locality. There may be other things added to the bowl; this is not restricted. All of this is called "setting up the rice bowl"; that is they take the bowl filled with rice, money, and various things mentioned above, and set it up in a suitable place as an offering to show their gratitude to the midwife for coming to assist in the delivery. When the mid-wife has performed the delivery and has for three full days come to help make other arrangements in connection with the delivery, the duties of the midwife are finished. Then they turn the rice bowl over to her; this is called "presenting the rice bowl." In some cases they present the rice bowl when the mother has left the fire; some people leave it set up for a longer time than this, for what reason I do not know. The rice bowl of the Mon has no rice; it has only areca, betel, and silver, with a cotton thread for tying the navel of the child when the umbilical cord is cut. The midwife takes a chew of areca and betel and then sets the bowl down in its original place. I do not know what sort of bowl they call it, but they undoubtedly do not call it a rice bowl for there is no rice in it. In the south, according to notes kind-ly furnished me by a friend, they call it the rice bowl only in the case of physicians who treat diseases. If it is a rice bowl for a midwife they call it râad. They prepare a skein of raw cotton thread, one unit of beeswax, one mountain-shaped pile of areca and betel, one unit of white rice, and one unit of cowries or silver coins. These things may vary in amount, depending upon how they are arranged on the stand or in the bowl to look nice. The amount of silver may be six sàlyŋ (one and a half bàad), one-half tamlyŋ (two bàad), one tamlyŋ (four bàad), or at the most one and a half tamlyŋ (six bàad). The money demanded is usually more than for children born later. The mountain-shaped pile of areca is made by smearing lime on betel leaves and forming them into a conical pile like an inverted funnel in the center of the bowl or stand. There is no prescribed number of leaves. The areca nuts are placed inside the funnel, while the other articles are arranged on the stand, except the raw cotton, which they tie around the mountain-shaped pile of betel. This râad bowl is laid at the head of the bed. When the mother leaves the fire, the midwife comes and dismantles the râad bowl and takes the things away. Normally the thread and wax are offered to monks to make candles for worshipping Buddha images.

The things in the rice bowl are all things that can normally be eaten or used, but why do they chiefly use the number three? If one tries to ex-plain this along the lines of a religious catechism, as people are accustomed to do categorically in matters having to do with funerals, one will say that three is the number of the Buddhist Trinity. But why do they not use three bunches of bananas? Probably it is because it is too much to put into the bowl. If one were to use only three bananas it would be too little and make a very poor showing, and so it is preferable to use a whole bunch. Bananas seem to be a usual article of food, because they are grown easily and occur at every house; therefore they use bananas along with the white rice and the areca and betel, which are articles used for food and for chewing every day. As for the bowl, it is used as a vessel for washing the face. Incense sticks and candles are included as articles of worship, but the inclusion of silver seems to be something that arose at a later stage when it was necessary to use silver, but it was nevertheless an amount which, if compared proportionally with the present day, is only a little. No doubt it was sufficient for purchasing needs in those days, which were a period of exchanging labor, and not yet a period when everyone had to do his own hiring.

At the time of labor pains, when the child is almost to be born, there must be someone to support the back; that is, a person is used like a chair back for the woman in labor to lean against. In some cases the person supporting the back sits in turn upon a water jar; this is probably to make it easier for the woman to lean back. Besides this, the person supporting the back also has the duty of being assistant to the midwife. If the midwife says to push, she must press both sides of the belly of the mother with her two hands; this is said to prevent the child in the womb from squirming away in this or that direction. If the midwife says to press down, she presses the upper part of the belly of the mother with her hands in order to cause the child to move downward. If the woman in labor faints, she must pound up lemon grass for her to use as an aromatic medicine. If they have other aromatic medicines they need not use lemon grass.

If trouble arises in the delivery and the child is slow to be born, they must use various devices. One that is much used is exorcising water sprinkled and rubbed on the body of the woman in labor, and also given to her to drink. This exorcising water is made in many ways, for example, by soaking a charmed amulet in water and using this water as exorcising water, or by pouring water over the great toe of the husband and then catching it and using it as exorcising water, or by throwing water up on the roof and then catching it until they have done this three times, and then enchanting the water that is caught the last time with a Buddhist formula pronounced backwards, and using this as exorcising water. Sometimes the exorcising water is enchanted with a spell that is humorous and obscene; it is the sort that I cannot cite as an example here. This spell must be pronounced loudly so that the woman in labor will hear it; this probably gives her some comfort and no doubt makes her laugh at the words of the spell, and so the exorcising water is effective, the woman in labor being relieved of her pain and strengthened in her efforts to expel the child. In the north they use magic formulas, covering the head of the pregnant woman with the hands and pronouncing the spell; this is called "pressing down." Another method is to enchant water and sprinkle the head of the mother with it or have her drink it. This is nothing else but exorcising water, but I don't know whether they have spells for their exorcising water that have obscene wording like our spells or not. According to Indian custom, if the delivery is difficult they likewise drink exorcising water; they write cabalistic figures, soak them in water, and have the mother drink it, or else have them drink water in which the feet of the husband, or the husband's mother, or a virgin girl, have been washed.

Some nationalities have strange methods of facilitating delivery, for example the Arunta on the continent of Australia, as has been described. They take the cloth with which the husband binds his head and wrap it around the upper abdomen of the wife, in order to keep the infant in the womb from moving upward. This is the same sort of thing as our method of pressing downward on the abdomen. If they see that the child still can't be delivered, the husband must remove his clothing and walk past his wife, at a distance, assuming mannerisms and posturing as if to invite the child to come out and follow him. (No doubt this is because the child in the womb will regard a naked person as similar to itself, and so will come out and follow him.) Among the people of some of the islands in the Philippines, when the wife is in labor and about to give birth, her husband must remove his clothing and stand boldly in the doorway of the house, or go up and exhibit himself upon the roof, one hand brandishing a sword back and forth continually; this is to threaten the evil spirits and prevent them from coming and interfering with the delivery. The Ching-paw or Kachin people, who are mountain dwellers living in the north of Burma, when a woman is in labor, must worship and make vows to the spirit of the places; this is the same sort of thing as with us. Then they perform a rite of expelling forest spirits and ghosts of women who have died in labor. If they would perform the rite in the very best way, they must have young men assume obscene postures in front of the woman in labor; when the spirits see this they will be embarrassed and flee. (No doubt these are female spirits and shy.) The Maltese use a flower of the kind called in English "rose of Jericho." It is kept in water in the room. Whenever the flower blooms, this is a signal that the child is about to be born.

As regards devices to facilitate delivery, every nationality whether occidental or eastern or any nationality whatsoever that has people of the peasant class has various methods. Many examples can be found in western books on the subject of birth customs, and so it is not necessary to cite them here. The sum and substance of the matter is that at the time when knowledge had not yet achieved its present level of progress, human beings of every nation have regarded childbirth as an important event. It is a matter of life and death for a woman. When there is difficulty and the child is not delivered with normal ease, she is liable to die easily, and so people view childbirth with great apprehension, and various methods must be devised in accordance with the people's beliefs to prevent danger to the woman who is to give birth. Even at the present time, when people know that childbirth is a natural event not different from the reproduction of animals, there is still feeling about it, and people still hold to the traditional beliefs that any interference with the birth of the child is due to the work of spirits. People who are rural farmers are still frightened about it, and so they seek ways to assist matters by preventing evil spirits from coming and causing trouble. Although such beliefs as these are gradually disappearing as knowledge advances, it will probably be a long time before they disappear altogether.

When the child is almost to be born, that is, the head of the child has passed the portal bones but still remains in the vagina, they are to take fairly large lumps of salt, choosing those with sharp edges, and scratch the "stitches" till they part. [13] At the same time they are to press downward on the abdomen in order to cause the child to slip out. In some cases they use the fingernails to cut the "stitches," but this is probably not so good as salt because the latter is salty and may have fewer disease germs on it than unclean fingernails. This is spoken from the point of view of modern feelings; in former days they had no such feelings because they knew nothing of germs. If anything happened which was due to disease germs, they simply blamed it on spirits. At the present time it is not necessary for the "stitches" of the woman giving birth to be damaged to the point of severance, because maternity doctors have ways of assisting. They wash their hands clean so that there are no disease germs and then gently assist the head of the child to emerge. They have knowledge which they regard as superior, and so they do not consent to call themselves midwives. In the north midwives are called mɛ̂ɛ hâb. [14] Probably they regard her function as that of "receiving" the child as it emerges. The wounds arising from delivery are to be washed with liquor, and then they pound Zingiber casumunar with salt and apply it; it is necessary to endure the smarting caused by this until the flesh feels no pain. Wealthy city people generally apply processed opium, because it is not necessary to endure as much smarting as with Zingiber casumunar and salt. If the wounds occurring as a result of delivery are long because the child that is born is large in size, no matter how much Zingiber casumunar and salt are applied, even though they heal, they do not close as before. When one walks or does heavy work, this causes the womb to move downward into the vagina. This is called dàag ʔɔ̀ɔg [15] (different from the dàag ʔɔ̀ɔg in the rectum). [16] This ailment was formerly very common, because they did not know how to make stitches like modern doctors. In the old times they regarded wombs as of two kinds, namely, lotus-leaf wombs and stone wombs. Women with the former kind of womb were not usually liable to prolapsis uteri. If they had the latter kind of womb they were usually liable to this, because it is round and not flattened like the former kind, and so can slip down easily. Some peasants believe that prolapsis uteri is a dropping of the diaphragm. Diaphragm here is the "pelvic diaphragm," not the diaphragm which is in the center of the body. Also, during the first three days after delivery the mother usually does not urinate. They say that this is because she is shy and so does not urinate. Actually she probably wants to urinate, but no doubt she is afraid of smarting and so she restrains herself as long as possible. In such cases they put warm water in a basin and have her soak herself in order that the flesh, which is to say the nerves, will become adjusted. Then she can urinate into the basin and there is little pain. But in the real old days they probably did not do this; they probably left the matter to take care of itself, but no one was dissuaded from giving birth to children. In these times if there is reluctance to urinate they insert a tube to cause the urine to come out.

Birth

When the child is born and slips out onto the floor they call it "falling to the bamboo floor." Originally the child really fell onto the bamboo floor. An old midwife has told me that at this time of birth it is necessary to spread a cloth to receive the child. When the child slips out, they must first cover it with the "tail" of the lower garment of the mother to keep it from the wind. I think that this is correct, because if a newborn child is touched by the outside air before it has time to adjust it may have convulsions. This old midwife has another special practice of her own which she boasted much of and asked me to put down just as she described it; I ask that it be regarded simply as an old belief. She said that when the child slips out, if it is seen to be a girl, one must first grasp the "golden turtle";[17] if a boy, one must first take hold of "that thing";[18] then one lets go. She said that if one does this, when the child grows up it will have no deformities, but will have very beautiful characteristics, because it was "adjusted" from the very first.

They usually take note of this time of "falling to the bamboo floor" and remember it. If they can read and write they note down the time, day, month, and year in order to have an astrologer make note of the planets' positions and write out the horoscope. If they cannot write they may ask a monk to write it for them. I have seen horoscopes in the north; they were written on palm leaves and then rolled up round and put away. If they have no clock to note the time of birth, they estimate it from the shadows of the sun in daytime and from the cock's crow during the night.

When the child has been born, the person supporting the mother's back must press the abdomen of the woman in labor firmly, in order to prevent the afterbirth from "flying up," that is to say, they fear that the afterbirth will not emerge. They are usually very much afraid in this matter of the afterbirth "flying," because there have been many cases of harm caused by failure of the afterbirth to come out. Nowadays if it does not come out it can be pulled out.

At the same time, the midwife holds the child in her arms, face down, and then puts her finger into the mouth of the child in order to extract mucus or blood in the mouth. If this mucus is not removed at once the child will have trouble breathing; this is called "choking on filthy water." The "filthy water" is the mucus on which the child was nurtured in the womb and which spurts out at the time of delivery. It is like lubricating oil to facilitate birth of the child. If at the time of birth it is observed that there is little of this mucus for lubrication, they put in coconut oil to help. Nowadays they probably use vaseline, or I do not know what oil. When the mucus has been removed from the child's mouth, if the child does not cry they must beat its bottom hard enough to make it cry. If it still does not cry, they must wait for the afterbirth to emerge, and then put a spade or any piece of iron in the fire and heat it red hot, and press it against the afterbirth. The heat will pass along the umbilical cord to the body of the child. When the child feels hot it will cry. If even after doing this the child does not cry, this shows that it will not survive. They say that failure to cry may be caused by a lump of blood stuck in the throat which they failed to notice and remove.

When the child has cried out, they wrap it in a cloth and leave it for the time being. If they do not hurry to wrap it in a cloth, the child may have convulsions and turn blue in the face and die, because the air is too cold. In some cases at this point they take honey and gold leaf which they have prepared in advance and swab the base of the child's tongue. They say that this is a way of preventing pharyngitis. This procedure of swabbing with honey and gold leaf is found only among certain peasants who know it; they generally use honey of the fifth lunar month, which is regarded as good honey. In the north they believe that if they do not remove all the blood from the mouth and do not swab with honey and gold, the child may have pharyngitis which will develop into asthma. According to Indian custom the midwife must clean out the child's nostrils (probably by sucking and then spitting), in order to open the passages and facilitate breathing, and she must clean out the anus in order to get rid of obstructions that may remain there. If the newborn child is a boy they perform a ceremony called játakarma and give the child honey and clarified butter to eat.

When the child has been put aside, they must see to getting the afterbirth out, because this stage is a matter of life and death to the mother, more important than the child. If the afterbirth does not emerge within a proper interval after the birth of the child, that is within about five minutes, they have the mother rise to a squatting position and have someone pound her back with a pillow. Sometimes they lower a rolled-up betel leaf or some other article down the throat or nostrils in order to cause squirming or coughing and sneezing, so that the afterbirth will come out. (In India, if the afterbirth has not come out then everyone present must be perfectly silent; if not, the afterbirth will flee upward.) When the afterbirth has come out, they have the mother take medicine at once. This medicine is a dish of moist tamarind fruit and salt put together (this is nothing more nor less than a purgative). They believe that this washes and cleanses the blood which remains. Later she takes medicine "to prevent action of the blood"; they explain that if the blood rises and floods the heart it will cause a feeling of oppression and difficulty in breathing. It is necessary to take medicine to drive out the bad blood. (In southern India they likewise take moist tamarind fruit.) When she has taken the water of moist tamarind fruit, the mother must lie still for a time, until they have arranged the fireplace for her to lie near the fire. At this point the midwife returns to take care of the matter of cutting the child's umbilical cord.

Duties Relating to the Newborn Child

Cutting the Umbilical Cord. The people take cord or raw cotton thread (sometimes also dyeing it with indigo), and tie two knots in the umbilical cord, drawing them tight, leaving an interval between them at the part which is to be cut. Sometimes they break the thread and tie three rabbit-neck knots[19] and pronounce Buddhist incantations over all three knots. The reason for tying the knots tight is to stop the flow of blood and air. The child will feel numb, and they believe that when the umbilical cord is cut the child will feel little pain. They leave a part of the umbilical cord attached to the child's navel reaching down to the child's knees. They use the outer bark of Thrysostachys siamensis[20] to cut. It is forbidden to cut with an iron blade. (Almost all nationalities in the Indochinese peninsula, so far as I have read in books, use the outer bark of bamboo to cut the umbilical cord.) The reason for leaving a long section of umbilical cord attached to the child's navel is that if they leave too short a length, much blood will flow when the cord has been cut. If this happens they must make haste to untie the cord or thread which has been tied, and retie it closer, tightly enough to stop the flow of blood. Otherwise if the flow of blood does not stop the child will be in danger. They must grind or pound fresh turmeric and apply it. If after applying this the flow of blood does not stop, there is no hope of saving it; the child must certainly die.

The method of cutting is to use a lump of dirt placed under the umbilical cord in place of a cutting board; some people use a ginger tuber instead of a lump of dirt. Then they cut it with the outer bark of Thrysostachys siamensis, sawing the umbilical cord at a point between the places that have been tied until it parts. According to northeastern custom they tie the umbilical cord with black cotton thread, lay it on a lump of charcoal, and cut it with a sharp mollusk shell. These methods of cutting the umbilical cord may be regarded as bits of antiquarian information. An elder has kindly informed me that in the case of a prince or princess who is of the rank of phrâʔ ʔoŋ câaw,²¹ they use a golden wedge as the cutting board. This is no doubt a custom which arose later when people had become wealthy.

Also, the umbilical cord has black lines inside it, called "charcoal lines." If the charcoal lines are close together, they believe that the mother who bore this child will later have children in close succession. If the charcoal lines are far apart, she will have children at long intervals.

Bathing the Child. When the umbilical cord of the child has been cut, they bathe the child in warm water. If there is much grease or mucus sticking to the body of the child, they must first rub the child's body with coconut oil and then rub the grease off with a cloth. They then bathe it clean in water. To bathe it, the bather sits with both legs stretched out straight in front and lays the child down in the hollow between the shins, with its head toward the feet, in order to wash the head and face of the child easily. The bathing is not a mere matter of cleansing. There must also be flexing of the child's arms and legs in order to make the child's arms flexible and its legs straight. If they would "adjust" other parts to make them beautiful as the old midwife did at the time of birth, it can be done. They proceed in this way every time they bathe the child. This method of bathing upon the shins is perhaps a traditional survival from ancient times when there were still no vessels such as basins for laying a child down to bathe it. This is likewise a bit of antiquarian information that has survived.

Bathing a child upon the shins is called "bathing," and bathing a child in a basin is called "soaking." If they are wealthy people, they arrange silver and gold valuables such as rings and necklaces in the basin, if they use "soaking," in order to cause the child when it grows up to be a person of wealth and property. This is a custom which arose after there were silver and gold. According to northeastern custom, when the child has been bathed, a relative takes the child together with its cushion up in the arms and goes down from the house to the ground, to a distance from the house stairs of about two meters or more. Then the person carrying the child bends down low and touches the right foot of the child to the earth three times. They say that they perform this rite in order not to have the child tread incorrectly on the earth, and to make the child as steadfast as the earth. (This is similar to the children's rite of treading the earth in the south and the royal ceremony of touching the earth, which will be described later in the section dealing with rearing children.) When the rite of treading the earth is finished and they have reascended to the house, elderly relatives such as the grandparents tie auspicious white cotton threads around the neck and wrist of child and mother. Then they let the child lie in a flat basket, with a net covering the basket. Sometimes the mother also goes to lie inside the net. They regard the net as an effective protection against evil spirits, because when the spirits see that the net has many eyes they are afraid.

When the bathing is finished, they take a square piece of cloth of adequate size and rip a long hole in the center. Then they slip this over the umbilical cord and lay the cloth around the navel, bringing the umbilical cord up through the hole so that it lies on the cloth. They bend the umbilical cord in a circle on the cloth, and sprinkle turmeric powder mixed with diatomaceous earth on it, or they may apply moist pounded turmeric, in order to dry the umbilical cord so that it will slip loose from the navel quickly. Then they bind the abdomen of the child with cloth, to prevent the curved umbilical cord from moving.

Children Dying at Birth. If after a child is born, none of the methods to make it cry as already described is successful, this shows that the child will not survive. If a child dies at this period, they usually smear the corpse of the child with soot or red lime, on the face or the arm or the buttocks or any part they choose. This is a marker so that when the child reenters the womb and is born again it will be recognized as the same person, for the child that is reborn will have a birthmark on its body at the place where the marker was smeared. If the child born later has a black birthmark, it means that the corpse was marked with soot; if it has a red birthmark, it means that it was marked with red lime. The corpse of the child is to be covered temporarily with a net; this is understood to be a prevention against the dead child's becoming an evil spirit which will do harm to the mother. Then they invite a witchdoctor to come and "do up" the corpse of the child; that is, he places the corpse of the child in a large earthenware pot, makes a cabalistic design at the bottom of the pot, and then covers the mouth of the pot with a square white cloth of adequate size, tying it with a magic cord. Then he sinks the pot in water or buries it, whichever is appropriate.

They are very much afraid of a child that dies at birth, because it may take its mother with it, that is, cause her to die as well. They must therefore protect the mother of the child by tying a magic thread around her wrist; this is a way of summoning her guardian spirit. Soon, when the mother lies near the fire, her breasts will be very taut because there is no child to suck them. The milk must be pressed out into a little bowl and set out at a triple crossroads (see the subject of triple crossroads in my book on death customs) for the spirit of the child to eat. They do this for three to seven days and then tie up Jussiae repens plants in a bundle and beat this against the breasts frequently. They do this for about three days to dry the breasts and reduce the swelling. This is a matter of mingled love and concern and fear.

The matter of covering the corpse of the child with a net is strange.
It is also used in the exact reverse of death. For example, in the Vessantara
Jātaka, when Jāli was born, they used a golden net to receive him, so that
he acquired the name of Jāli, meaning "net." It is said in the book,
Pathamasambodhi, that when the Lord Buddha was born, Indra and Brahma received him in a golden net in order not to hurt his person. Sir James Frazer
says in the book The Golden Bough that nets are characteristically full of
knots, and many nationalities have beliefs that knots are firm and fast and
cannot be untied, so that they are efficacious as protection against spirits or
against harmful magic spells employed by people. For example, in Russia
the peasants in some places have the custom of using a net to cover the bride
at a wedding to protect her from the magic spells of enemies, while the bride-
groom and his assistants have a net tied at the waist. A cord tied in square
knots at intervals is used by Russian peasants as an amulet. According to our
custom, when we tie the guardian spirit or tie the wrists, we tie a square
knot. In the north they must make three or five knots in the cord before tying it on, and when they tie it on they pronounce a magic spell of exorcism.
If these matters are compared with the practice of covering a child's corpse
with a net, as has been described, the meanings are similar; that is, the net
has knots which serve to prevent the spirit of the child from coming out and
doing harm to its mother, or, in the contrary case in matters of birth, a net
is used to cover the child and protect it against spirits that might come in to
do it harm.

Concerning the Afterbirth. When the umbilical cord of the child has been
cut, they are to take the afterbirth and the part of the cut umbilical cord
which is attached to the afterbirth and wash them clean in water. They say
that this prevents skin diseases which might appear later on the body of the
child. Then they take the washed afterbirth and umbilical cord and place
them in any vessel of earthenware which may be procured easily in the locality, such as a sugar pot. Then they cover them with salt to prevent decay.
It is forbidden to throw the afterbirth away. They must bury it, but not until
three days after the birth. I do not know the reason for this. In the textbook,
Pàthŏmcindaa, it says, "Evil spirits will be attracted by the odor and come
to eat. When they have eaten, they will proceed to come after the mother,
causing various dangers." For this reason it is required to bury it. Besides
this there are many other requirements connected with the afterbirth. I will
save these and describe them later. At this time they are to set the pot containing the afterbirth down beside the place of lying near the fire, in order
to cause the umbilical cord of the child to dry rapidly. Also, they must set
the pot containing the umbilical cord up straight; otherwise they believe that
the child will have a crooked mouth.

Bouncing on a Basket. After bathing the child and taking care of the umbilical cord, they carry the child in the arms and put it down upon a flat basket. They use the bottom rather than the top of the basket, because the bottom is convex and resilient, and can be bounced like a spring. They need not fear that the child will roll off, because it is still young and has no stength to squirm about. Nevertheless, sometimes at this point if they have not finished preparing the cushion and diapers (why they do not make them in advance I will explain later), they use other cloths such as blankets to lay the child on temporarily. On the basket in which the child lies, if it is a boy, they are to place a book and pencil; if a girl, they are to place a needle and sewing thread instead; this is in order that when the child grows up it will know how to read and write or know how to do needlework, depending upon whether it is a boy or girl. But this is done among the wealthy and aristocratic people, for these arts are regarded as knowledge befitting the children of aristocrats. The ordinary peasants hardly do these things. Sometimes these things are not done at this point but are done at the time of the rite of placing in the cradle. Besides these, they are to take the outer bark of Thrysostachys siamensis which was used to cut the umbilical cord of the child, and the lump of earth which was used in place of a cutting board for cutting the umbilical cord, and tuck them under the cloth in the basket also.

When this is finished the midwife lifts up the basket and bounces it lightly, enough to serve as a gesture. Then she drops the basket, but lightly also, in order to cause the child to be frightened and cry. They say that they do this in order to accustom the child, so that it will not be startled later on. The midwife does this three times, saying the while, "Three days a spirit child, four days a human child! Whose child is this? Take it!" Some person among those sitting there, one who is a woman who has reared children successfully and is a kind and well-behaved person as well, will answer, "It's my child." The midwife passes the basket and the child to that person. The receiver in this rite is called mêε jôg. [22] She will give money to the midwife, usually in former times an ʔ̀ad, equal to one and one-half sàtaaŋ at present, to serve as a gesture of buying. Then she takes the basket and lays it down in the circle surrounded by a magic thread, near to the child's mother. She must lay the child down gently in order not to frighten it. They usually place the basket on supports resting in water, to prevent ants from coming up and biting the child. In the north they call a midwife "receiving woman",[23] if we compare this with the "lifting mother," the meanings are very close. After this, they take a cloth and form it into a tent covering the basket in place of a mosquito net, in order to prevent much wind from entering which would destroy the warmth and cause convulsions. But these tents are usually made of thick cloth such as blankets, and the space inside is so small and confined that air does not enter easily. This may destroy the strength of the child. Therefore they sometimes use bent rattans to stretch the tent out wide in order to allow a good deal of air for the child to breathe. That part of the subject of bouncing on the basket which relates to the spirit of the purchasing mother involves many matters which must be described and discussed as to reasons, and so I will leave it for the section concerning the purchasing mother.

Children which are newly born are not yet allowed to eat anything. They have them eat only burned cockroach excrement mixed with a little salt and then dissolved in honey in a small cup. They hang a small bit of cloth down in the cup, letting the other end hang over the edge of the cup for the child to suck. They say that this medicine containing cockroach drop-pings is a laxative to expel the child's first faeces. The first faeces are the child's faeces which are in its abdomen when it is born. They are hard and black. It is believed that if they are left and not expelled they will cause the child to be ill. They have the child eat this for three days and then they let it suck its mother's milk. They cannot let the child suck its mother's milk from the beginning, because the mother does not yet have milk which is pure enough to feed the child. Even if she has, they cannot let the child take it until it is sufficiently strong. If they persist in letting it eat, the child may be in danger because its stomach has not yet expanded.

According to Indian custom they have a newborn child eat clarified butter and honey. They likewise use a container similar to a flat basket to hold the child, but they place cowdung, ashes, turmeric, and two or three silver coins in the basket with the child, and they sprinkle holy water on it. If the child is a boy they lay a brass tray there, believing that it drives away spirits. If it is a girl this is not necessary, because the sex of the girl is a protection in itself, and spirits cannot come to bother her.

Lying Near the Fire

I will drop the subject of arrangements for the child temporarily, and return to the subject of the child's mother at the time she lay still after having given birth, when the midwife was busy with the child, as described above. I will speak of the husband and other people; they help one another arrange a fireplace for lying near the fire. It is forbidden to prepare this fireplace in advance. They may only prepare the framework of the fireplace. Similarly they are forbidden to make the cushions and prepare the diapers in advance. If they do not prepare them in advance, when the emergency arrives they will not be able to do it in time. They are therefore allowed to sew the cushions and stuff them with kapok beforehand, but they are forbidden to sew up the mouths of the pillows, as has been described, because they fear that if they sew up the mouths the child will not come out to receive the diapers and pillows which have been prepared. Also, children often die at birth. If they prepare these things in advance and the child dies, the effort is in vain and the diapers and pillows are wasted. In olden times these things were not easily procured.

When they have laid the framework, they cut sections of banana tree trunks, split them in two, and lay them parallel in the frame. They scatter dirt over these and then light the fire. They call this "laying out the fireplace," and if they are superstitious they must seek a good day for it. If they cannot make the fireplace in time, they have the mother who has given birth lie beside an old-fashioned stove at first. (This old-fashioned stove is a portable stove made of baked earth, in shape similar to a horse saddle.) They use three sticks of firewood per day and have her remain for three days. Then they perform the rite of lying near the big fireplace. Banana trees may be used for many purposes and are easy to grow. They grow in every village. Bananas therefore enter into various ceremonies at many points, even though in some ceremonies the necessity for them is no longer present; for example, decorating crematoria with banana tree trunks, or setting up banana trees at the ritual fences in ceremonies such as the preaching of the Vessantara Jātaka. They still survive, however, as customs until the present time. As for the use of banana tree trunks under the fire, it can be seen easily that it is desired that the fire not spread downward to the floor of the house. Nothing can be used so readily as banana tree trunks, because they are more easily procured than other things.

In connection with lying near a fire there are many rites which must be performed. For example, they must perform a ceremony of quenching the poison of the fire, make a circle with a magic cord, and fix cabalistic designs in eight directions around the place for lying near a fire. Sometimes they use as many as ten cabalistic designs; that is, they add the directions up and down as well. For the direction down they place a cabalistic design under the bed. Then they must scatter thorns. Usually these are thorns of Indian jujube, thorns of Manila tamarind, or bamboo thorns, because they are easily found. They scatter these around the pit under the room used for lying near the fire. Wherever there is a crevice or hole in the floor they likewise scatter thorns, to keep off spirits which would come to do harm, especially kràsўy spirits, because the crevices and holes in the floor are generally used for pouring out filthy things onto the ground below; kràsўy spirits will be attracted by the odor of the filth and slip up through the crevices and holes. Sometimes even these precautions are regarded as inadequate, and so they also weave mat-like panels and curl them around to form pipes leading down from the pits and holes in the floor of the house where things are poured out. Besides warding off spirits, probably this prevents domestic animals from coming in and making the place filthy as well. As for upstairs in the house, besides cabalistic designs and the magic thread, they also fasten leaves of the camphor plant at the door to the room. Leaves of the camphor plant have an unpleasant odor; when spirits smell them they are afraid and dare not enter.[24] In some cases they also stretch a net over the place for lying near the fire, to prevent spirits from approaching from above. This protection is like that used by the Thai Lue people.[25]

Planting Magic Pentacles of Bamboo. In the northeast they make magic pentacles of bamboo, equal in size to the lid of a monk's begging bowl. They wind black, red, and white cotton threads around the angles of the pentacle, but alternating the colors, and then tie the pentacle to the end of a piece of bamboo and plant it to the right of the foot of the stairs of the house. They leave it planted there until the mother emerges from the fire, and then they pull it up and throw it away. The purpose of planting the pentacle is to serve as a symbol to tell visitors to be careful of their speech. At the time of lying near the fire it is absolutely forbidden for anyone to speak the words "warm" or "hot," because it is feared that the person lying near the fire will have prickly heat or rashes and blisters, called "fire spots." These bamboo pentacles may also be used in other affairs; they are not limited to lying near the fire. Thus they are planted at the edge of pools, wells, or fishponds to inform everyone that it is forbidden to go down and dip up water or catch fish in that place. In funeral ceremonies in the north they also plant pentacles in the area of the house at the time when they remove the corpse from the house. This is no doubt to prevent the spirit from returning.[26]

According to Vietnamese custom, they scatter thorns of Indian jujube and pineapple leaves outside the room. Inside the room they plug up all cracks and holes with cloth; in the room it is therefore dark and close, for the air cannot pass in and out easily. They must keep the fire in the room burning all the time, both day and night. Then there are cabalistic designs hanging in the four corners of the room. These things which are done are self-explanatory as being protection against spirits. The lying near the fire of the Vietnamese is more violent than the lying near the fire of the Thai, because besides lying beside a charcoal stove, under the bed on which the woman lies there are three more charcoal stoves burning. This is tantamount to broiling, and is the same sort of thing as Yogis practicing austerities and burning their passions to a crisp. As for the Thai method of lying near the fire, at first they kindle a fire to produce only a little heat, enough to boil water for drinking. Later on when the flesh and skin of the person lying near the fire are accustomed, they increase the heat of the fire gradually. Otherwise they say that "fresh boils" and "fire spots" will occur. (These are bumps with pussy heads similar to those of smallpox but smaller in size.) These are poisonous and cause one to feel sore and hot. In lying near the fire there must be someone to keep watch. If the fire is seen to be too strong and is spreading to too much of the fuel, there is a cloth wrapped around the end of a piece of wood and a pot of water kept in readiness to dip the cloth in the water in the pot and extinguish the fire.

When someone is going to lie near the fire, there is first a quenching of
the poison of the fire. They must find a person who knows to come and enchant white rice and salt with a Pali stanza as follows: "Buddho lokanātho
maggallāno aggīsayāyam mama." (What this means is not clear; we know
only that it has to do with fire.) The reference to Maggallāna is probably
due to the story that this chief disciple once went to relieve the creatures in
hell. When he arrived the fires of hell all went out. This spell should be
called "Maggallāna extinguishing the fires of hell." When he has pronounced
this spell, he chews up the white rice and salt and spits it out onto the belly
of the woman lying near the fire three times, onto her back three times, and
into the fireplace three times. Then he sprinkles thɔɔrániisǎan holy water on
the fireplace.[27] They obtain exploded rice, flowers, incense sticks, and
candles, together with a banana-leaf cup of offerings including prawn and
fish salad; these are an offering to the supporting columns of the fireplace
and an act of begging forgiveness of the god of fire. Generally they use four
incense sticks and four candles, setting them up at the four corners of the
stove.

Before the mother lies down upon the fire board, it is necessary first to
perform the "fitting the rafters."[28] This is done by lying on the side and
having the midwife tread on the hips. They believe that this makes the "rafter
bones," which spread apart because of childbirth, reenter their proper position.
Then she can lie down on the fire board. Before lying down she must prostrate herself and implore forgiveness of the fireplace, because it is believed
that the fireplace is a magic thing inhabited by a guardian spirit. (This belief is similar to that of the Chinese in a lord of the stove, that of India in
the grhyāgni fire, and that of the Romans in the penates.) This is to ask for
protection in order to live happily, and she is to think of the goodness of the
god of fire, the god of wind, the earth goddess, and the goddess of water,
asking to regard these gods of the four elements as her refuge. Besides this
the midwife enchants turmeric and red lime and smears these on her belly,
and pounds up Zingiber casumunar with salt and applies it to the wounds in
the vulva to prevent infection and facilitate rapid healing. If they have liquor, they wash the wounds first with liquor. What has been described seems
like a terribly arduous affair. One would think they would never want to
have children again. But they must endure it and act according to the customs of olden times, which are beliefs surviving from the worship of spirits
in ancient times. Such customs as these, when the beliefs of the owners of
the customs have changed, will normally of necessity disappear of themselves,
because they conflict with or hinder progress in living. It is not necessary
to force the people to drop them.

During the time of lying near the fire, neighbors who know of it come
to visit. In visiting they do not come empty-handed. If they have nothing
else, they bring anything that comes to hand and offer it in a friendly spirit,

such as turmeric, diatomaceous earth, [29] dried fish, or bananas, usually the kind of bananas called broken-faceted bananas. These are all things which are used and which can be eaten, not being harmful foods. This custom is now fading out because of the pressure of modern progress. Formerly no matter what sort of affair it was, whether a wedding or a funeral, those who went to assist in the affair always carried something along to help. Nowadays social conditions have undergone a great change, and it is too much to do this always, except in places where social conditions have not changed greatly. When one speaks of the necessity in going to visit of carrying something along, one is reminded of the Indian proverb which says, "Persons who go to attend upon the king, or visit children, or visit pregnant women, or visit teachers, and those who go to worship an idol in a temple -- these visitors should not go empty-handed." Our proverb has it: "When one goes to attend upon the king, when one goes to see a religious preceptor, when one goes to see a judge, when one goes to see a young woman, when one goes to see an old woman who has a daughter that one loves and covets, the ancients forbid going empty-handed." I should like to add another group in order to make it fit present times, but I do not dare add it.

Persons who go to visit a woman lying near the fire are forbidden to speak of heat or cold, of prickly heat or boils, of illness or fever or death or anything of that sort; these subjects are regarded as inauspicious because it is feared that the woman lying near the fire will lose morale, and what is spoken of will come true. (Some people believe that after three days it is not forbidden, observing the rule of three-day and seven-day prohibitions.) In this matter of forbidding people to speak of things which should not be spoken of, peasants are rather strict. In visiting the sick they also have this sort of belief. I have asked many persons who have formerly lain near the fire, and they all answer that what is spoken will come true. Probably it is because they believe it, and are already on the watch for this sort of thing, so that when what is spoken of happens to come true they become excited. Besides this, in lying near the fire it is forbidden to kindle another fire from the fire in the fireplace, or to use this fire to roast meat or fish. Fires that are forbidden in this way are of three kinds, namely a fire for lying near, a fire for cremating corpses, and the fire of incense sticks and candles which are lighted for worship. The reasons for these prohibitions are self-evident.

The person lying near the fire must wear a loincloth, and has turmeric and red lime mixed with liquor into which she constantly dips cotton to close the navel and swab the abdomen and the back. They say that they do this in order to quench the poison of the heat and care for the body. Besides this there is also medicine to sprinkle upon the coals of the fire in order to steam the eyes, to prevent infected or sore eyes. There is also a jar or jug of water placed beside the fireplace. When the fire in the fireplace blazes up excessively or becomes hotter than is desired, they can take a long dipper (or a stick with the end wrapped with cloth, if they have no dipper), and reach out and dip up water in the jar in order to splash it on the fire and put it out; or if it is desired to dip water out into a vessel to boil for drinking, it will be near at hand.

As for food of the person lying near the fire, normally she eats rice with dried fish or rice with salt for many days before she has some curry. They say that eating mild curries causes production of much milk. Besides this, for water they usually drink hot water placed in a coconut shell or a thick dish which can be held without being hot in the hands. For washing and cleaning various impurities they mostly use coconut half-shells, because after use they can be thrown away. In the north they likewise have women lying near the fire eat rice with salt, but they have a special item in that they require that the husband be the person who prepares it for her to eat. For the most part they make rice balls for the women to eat. Rice balls are cooked glutinous rice formed into balls, impaled on a stick, and toasted in the fire; they are eaten with salt. They eat these for ten to fifteen days, before they are allowed to eat rice with salty fish. Persons lying near the fire, besides eating rice with salt, must also take special medicine for the blood. They must take this morning and evening every day until they leave the fire. According to Vietnamese custom, during the first seven days that they lie near the fire they eat rice with salt and pepper. Some say that they eat mild curries also. Later on they eat Vietnamese-style boiled salt pork; this is really salty, with no sweetness in flavor.

Doors and windows, if any, in the room for lying near the fire must always be kept closed, because it is feared that if the wind enters and touches the body of the person lying near the fire she may contract a fever. The susceptibility to fever is said to be due to the fact that the person lying near the fire is still weak. Perhaps they also fear that spirits will slip in through the windows and doors. According to Indian custom they must also close the doors and windows, but they must keep a light burning both night and day because not much light can enter, and they do not lie near the fire; the room is therefore dark and close, and a light must be kept burning. But the excuse they give is that if they keep a light burning spirits will be afraid to enter. This is clever reasoning, because fire and light are enemies to spirits (to say nothing of spirits, thieves also dislike them). They believe that the god of fire stands guard against evil spirits and is the destroyer of evil for the gods, because fire can be used as a cleansing agent. They say that ladies are his attendants, and the menses of women are his person. Probably the meaning of this is that blood is red, which is a symbol of the god of fire and of fire. Various nations therefore regard the color red as powerful, feared by spirits, and auspicious.[30] European peasants, for example those of some parts of England, Germany, and Sweden, keep lamps or candles burning all around the child, believing that this keeps spirits from coming to carry off the child. Our custom of closing doors and windows of the room for lying near the fire to make it dark and close is said to be because of the desire for warmth and the dislike of cool air. They also use hot medicines, believing that if coldness is encountered the womb may swell and be poisoned. I believe that this is a later opinion; originally it was more likely a matter of warding off spirits, for when spirits enter we do not see them, but know that they have entered because a gust of cold air touches the body, and so fever is contracted.

Concerning the making of a circle with a magic thread and the hanging up of cabalistic designs, this is because cabalistic designs are magic objects, having letters of the alphabet and designs drawn in mysterious fashion and containing magic spells; thus they have power to ward off danger or are capable of retaining things which it is not desired to have lost or disappear. The cabalistic design which is popular as a preventative of danger particularly in the matter of lying near the fire is called trinisimhe. [31]

The magic thread which is laid all round the place for lying near the fire is the raw cotton thread used in chanting the paritta stanzas. [32] They wind it around the pot of holy water, and then carry it to the monks who take part in the chanting ceremony, and they hold onto it. Everybody has seen this often; it is not necessary to give a great deal of explanation. This thread is regarded as a magic article, because it leads from the pot of holy water, and so they use it as a protection in auspicious ceremonies. The technical name for it is parittasūtra, that is, the cord of the paritta chants. Siñcana [33] means to sprinkle or scatter with water. If we were to interpret from this translation, we are tempted to understand that originally it was a cord for sprinkling holy water, and so it is believed that the magic thread in a sense contains holy water in itself. When it is used to make a circle around a place, it is as if that place had been sprinkled with holy water, and there is a general prohibition against the husband's trespassing inside the circle formed by the magic thread; they believe that if he has any magic spells they will lose their efficacy. This prohibition is good; why it is good, please judge for yourselves. The magic thread, besides being used to encircle the place, is also used to cut in short lengths to tie around the wrist for protection against danger. Used in this way, it is probably similar to the "protective thread" worn by the Brahmans (rakṣabandhana). It is related in the Viṣṇupurana that when Kṛṣṇa was a child he was tormented by spirits as he slept, and so his father Vāsudeva had to tie a protective thread around the wrists of the boy Kṛṣṇa.

While still in the house of fire, if the weather is cold or it rains they say that the child will have convulsions (that is, it is affected by the weather). It has blue, pale hands and feet, trembles like a young bird, and has a stiff chin; it may die. They have a method of prevention, to wit: they burn the shell of a horseshoe crab or duck and chicken feathers, the shells of sea-crab claws, camphor leaves, onion, garlic, buffalo horn, or leaves of the "rank smell of vultures and crows" plant; what other things there are I do not know. They may select any one or another of these things to burn, depending upon which they can procure. When it is burnt the odor is all-pervading and unbearable, reaching to eight or nine houses. [34] No doubt readers have experienced this odor and know how bad it is; if not, try burning some and you will know. If a child has pharyngitis they likewise burn things for the child to inhale, such as the bones of a black dog, the horns of an albino buffalo, cat hair, and many other things, all of which are things which when burned give off an unbearably bad odor. I do not think these are things which can cure disease. I suspect that the burning of them is connected with the driving out of spirits also, which is a belief surviving from olden times; when the spirits smell the odor they flee. Diseases of children and infants, as will be related in the chapter on the purchasing mother, are said to originate from the action of spirits. I will cite an example given in the invocation of the purchasing mother called sǎaradèed wǐthii jàj:

Hail! O great one, I salute you. I fold my hands in reverence and raise them above my head, and prostrate my body to you. May the pure precepts, and goodness and virtue, in which power inhere, be bestowed upon me. Come and destroy the hosts of evil spirits, the ghostly ambassadors of wickedness who harass the three worlds, who destroy by means of invisible diseases, diseases that are visited upon us, of which the one called cholera is the most prominent. There are both bird-spirits and convulsions. Heat rashes are caused by the demon Rahu. Foreign ailments come in countless numbers, all of them evil spirits, ghosts, giants, powerful in various ways.

Some diseases transform themselves
Into various shapes.
Some have a crow's head and a dog's body.
Some have a giant's head and a horse's body.
Some have a dog's head and elephant's feet.
Some have a deer's head and a crow's body.
Some have an ass's head and a tiger's body.
Some have a stag's head and a lion's body.
Some have a monkey's head and a human body.
They command a powerful army.
Diseases of the forest, of dry land and water,
Diseases in caves and marshes,
Diseases that fly through the air,
Come to the fire,
I will burn you all up with fire.

Phrá Theewaa Phǐnimmíd (Chǎaj Theewaaphǐnimmíd) has kindly noted down the texts for exorcising convulsions and children's diseases for me, and so I print them here, for purposes of research, as follows.

Various Spells. Before reciting any spell, one must first pronounce the following, which is called "Invitation to the Teacher to Enter Me":

Behold the Blessed One! I will raise all ten fingers of my hands in reverence. I invoke the blessing of the Lord Shiva to come to my left shoulder. I invite the Lord Vishnu to come to my right shoulder. I invite the God of the Wind to come and be my breath. I invite the Lord of Serpents to be for me a belt. I invite the Goddess Kali to be my heart. In whatsoever I may do, let no spirits come to interfere or cause annoyance. I invite my revered teacher, who is most exalted, to come from his dwelling. Bestow upon me your blessing. Reverend lord, bring me success. Let my enemies be destroyed.

Spell for Exorcising Convulsions. Prostrate yourself three times, saying: Hail, O Lords of the three worlds! O Sariputta, O Lord Buddha! Let me drive out all kinds of convulsions, the one whose body is a buffalo and whose head is a human head, with evil feet and hands, a bad convulsion; the one whose head is a snake's head, terrifying in form, with the body of a stag; the butterfly convulsion with yellow head, red chin, and flashing eyes, with the head of a lion; the one with an evil mouth and the head of a dog, carrying a stick; and demons and all enemies of every kind. The purchasing mother shows her teeth and makes gestures; she gazes at the roof and cries 'Ah, ah, ' curling up her fingers and toes, and moaning; she hides in the heart. Bring the spirit of this child; bring back the spirit of this child. Bring it back at once, and don't come yourself. The Lord Shiva has sent me to drive out all convulsions. Don't you recognize me? My name is the great king Sĭi Kan. My mother's name is the Earth Goddess. My father's name is the God Kuvera, who is a master of all the hosts of spirits. If you don't go out I will cut off your heads. O Lord Buddha and the Three Gems! I will flog you with rattans. Hail to the Buddha! Hail to the Law! Hail to the Order!

Another Spell.

Hail! Convulsions of the rocks, convulsions of the cliffs, convulsions of cloth, convulsions of the pillow, convulsions of the bed and of the head of the stairs -- all these convulsions I know. I know your birth and your death. Your father was named ฦฦฦ ฦaaj. and he died in the middle of the forest. Your aunt had a ghostly name and she died a violent death; she fell out of a tree and they stabbed her. Your mother was named ฦii phɛɛŋ. You make children cry every day. I will spray magic herbs on you. I will put a heap of iron upon you. Hail!

(To be pronounced while spraying water with the mouth, in the evening or when the child is sick.)

Spell for Exorcising Children's Diseases.

Behold the Blessed One! I will make obeisance to the Sage who planted medicinal herbs all around Mount Sumeru, the stems in the land of demons and the twigs in the land of gods. I have counted nine hundred thousand twigs of medicinal plants. I will exorcise the disease of spots in the tongue and in the eye. I will exorcise the disease of wicked spirits. Let the disease of gourds come out beyond the skies. I will exorcise yellow diseases and fiery diseases, the wicked ones; I will slash you and knock you together. I will spray water to extinguish the poison and effect a cure. Buddha, cure him! Law, cure him! Order, cure him!

(To be pronounced while spraying water with the mouth, in the morning before sunrise.)

The subject matter in the invocation of the purchasing mother as quoted above shows that convulsions originate from the action of spirits, and so it is necessary to burn things which create a foul odor in order to drive away the spirits. But because the burning of things makes the air in the room closer, this affords some help to the child which has been affected by the weather and has convulsions. If it recovers from the illness they assume that the spirits fear the foul odor and flee. The rightness or wrongness of this opinion is up to you to consider, but it is strange that many nationalities agree in having the practice of burning things to create a foul odor in order to drive away spirits. Probably they believe that even humans regard these odors as unbearable, and it is unnecessary to mention that spirits will be similarly repelled. According to Vietnamese custom they burn duck and chicken feathers, ox and buffalo bones and horns, and other things which when burned have a strong unpleasant smell; this is a way of driving out spirits. According to Indian custom, when a child is ill, they burn rice bran, dry chilis, lettuce seeds, salt, or other things which when burned give off an unpleasant pungent odor, and carry them round and round the child. They say that if they do this the spirits cannot bear the foul odor and flee. The matter of carrying things round and round the child is similar to our carrying offerings or the rice of the purchasing mother round and round a child when it is ill. This procedure in Indian is called ārati (ārātarika). The circling candles rite may perhaps be a form of ārati. I will leave this to discuss under the subject of khwǎn rites.

After she has lain near the fire for three days, there are many ways of caring for and performing superstitious rites for the woman lying near the fire and for the child. I will speak first of matters concerning the woman lying near the fire.

Methods of Producing Milk. Normally a woman who has borne a child has milk to feed the child, which when it has passed three days of age is counted as having escaped "the beaks of hawks and crows," which is to say, it has passed one stage without dying. When the child is first born, its mother does not yet have genuine milk. There is only yellowish milk, not white like ordinary milk. This is called yellowish milk and is regarded as poor milk. They have the mother eat boiled leaves of Cardiospermum halicacabum and Ipomsea aquatica, in order first to expel the yellowish milk. When it has all been expelled, the mother's breasts will be firm and will produce milk. If the child does not suck it, the mother will feel pains; sometimes she may even have fever. If the pains continue like this for many days, a boil may arise on the breasts because the milk goes into the wrong tubes. The mid- wife must roll and press the nipples in order to cause the pimple-heads which plug up the milk tubes to come out, and then take many hairs together and poke with them to make a hole; then the milk can come out easily. If after this the milk still does not flow out easily, they must use cupping. An easy method is to burn paper and throw it into a pickled garlic jug or into another bottle or vessel which is hollow and plugged at one end, depending on what can be procured easily, in order to create a vacuum inside. The mother bends over and thrusts the breast into this jug or vessel, and there is suction as in cupping blood. At first the breast hurts very much, but it is necessary to endure the pain. If the cupping method is not used, they can suck with a bamboo tube. Finally, in later times there have been instances of sucking with a lamp chimney. If it is the breast of the mother of a first child of the sort called a "blind breast," that is, without a projecting nipple, usually only one of the breasts is "blind," the other having a nipple, called "monkey breast." If the child sucks only one breast, that is, the breast having a nipple, this will cause only the breast that is sucked to grow large. The other breast which is "blind" will not grow large. This is of the sort called "Lady Monthoo with only one developed breast."[35] This is not beautiful because it is not symmetrical. It is necessary to seek a trick to make the child suck the "blind breast" also. They have a method of correcting this so that the breasts are equally large: they roll the "blind breast" with warm water and then pull the nipple out so that it projects; then they fasten it with a clamp made of bamboo like the clamps for broiling fish but small in size, in order not to allow the nipple to shrink back again. When the child sucks, the clamp is removed; when the child has finished sucking, the clamp is applied as before. If this is done for two or three days, the nipple will continue to project, and the child can suck it in the normal way.

The Womb Enters Its Cradle. In from three to seven days after the child is born, the midwife comes and "restores the belly" every day; that is, she presses on the pubic mound with her hand in order to lift the womb back into its "cradle." I suppose the place where the womb lies is a hollow, and so it is called this. When it has been restored, she presses and rolls the pubic mound. This is called "soothing the womb," to make the mouth of the womb shrink and return to its original position. At this time of "soothing the womb," water with a fishy odor spurts out, making the mother feel comfortable.

Women lying near the fire must enter a tent and have hot applications, and bathe with a salt pot and sit over coals.

Entering the Tent. Before the mother enters the tent, they grind or pound the "golden lady" plant, pressing out only the juice and mixing it with liquor and camphor. This is smeared all over the body of the woman lying near the fire; when she has been smeared, she enters the tent. This tent has a frame made of bamboo like the frame of a mosquito net, or other things which it is easy to lay hands upon, such as a large basket, may be used. This is covered completely with cloth and set up on the porch or other high place. Underneath the place where the tent is set up they set a stove to boil a medicine pot with a sealed lid. Into this they insert a bamboo pipe, leading up into the tent, in order to make the steam from the medicine in the pot which is boiling violently rise through the pipe into the tent. The person entering the tent will receive the vapor from the medicine. In doing this it is necessary to have someone stand watch and see that the proper amount of steam is sent up; or if this is not convenient, they may take up the medicine pot which is boiling violently and put it into the tent. The woman in the tent opens the lid a little at a time and bends her face down to the mouth of the pot, so that the steam may whirl up and bathe her face. The medicine that is boiled includes pomelo rind, leaves of Acacia concinna, sweet flag, lemon grass, Ipomaea aquatica, a kaffir lime cut into four sections, and one pinch of salt. Some of these may be omitted, or others added, depending upon what can be found.

Entering the tent is supposed to improve the complexion and prevent blemishes on the face, prevent the lymph from going bad, and remedy many other conditions. The woman steams herself for about half an hour, or if longer than this then all the better, but usually she is unable to remain long because it is unbearably hot and confined. She is flooded with perspiration as if bathing in water; then she can emerge from the tent. Entering this sort of tent is called "entering a medicine tent." If they are poor people, unable to procure anything easily, they use bricks heated red-hot in a fire. These are taken into the tent in place of the medicine pot. Then they pour salt water over the bricks; there is a sizzling sound and steam swirls up bathing the face and body. This is called "entering a brick tent." Entering the tent is usually done in the morning.

Guesses as to Reasons for Lying near the Fire. This matter of entering a tent as described the Occidentals call "bathing in sweat" (sweat bath). [36] It is said that the natives of North America everywhere like to enter tents, saying that it cleanses them of impurities and perspiration in the body; it is a method of cleansing them of impurities ceremonially as well. [37] One need not doubt that our practice of entering the tent is not merely to improve the complexion and prevent blemishes on the face. It is no doubt a matter of cleansing impurities arising out of childbirth also, for various nationalities regard childbirth as an impurity. If anyone approaches and merely smells the odors of childbirth, he is rendered impure, and if he possesses any magic spells they will lose their efficacy. For example, among the Palaung in the north of Burma, at the time of childbirth a man cannot come within the area for fear that if he has charms tattooed on his body or possesses magic objects, these will lose their efficacy. Therefore they must keep a child posted in front of the house to inform those who do not know, so that they do not wander into the area of childbirth. If anyone happens to enter the area, he must leave at once, and go and bathe in order to wash off the impurities. [38] Some Kha tribes in the Banthat Mountains on the left bank of the Mekhong River, at the time of childbirth, take pieces of bamboo or rattan and fit them together to form a sort of large pentacle, planting this at the head of the path in order to inform all of the prohibition, so that they will not trespass. The practice of the northern and northeastern Thai in calling childbirth jùu kam [39] (I believe the spelling jù· kam[40] would be more correct, because kam means "to hold, to believe") and planting magic pentacles is the same sort of superstition. In India they close off the woman who gives birth, not allowing her to remain in the same room or house, or under the same roof with other people, until she has been ceremonially cleansed completely of impurities; then she may return to the association of other people. This is like our old custom that women who come pregnant from elsewhere, or are pregnant outside the marriage ceremony, may not come and give birth in the house; they must go and give birth elsewhere. At best, if the situation must be accepted, they build a shed or hut for her to give birth at a distance. If it is necessary to give birth in the house, they must perform a ceremony of purification according to their beliefs. Palace custom, according to M.R.W. Pèɛd Theewaathîrâad Maalaakun, has it that if anyone gives birth to a child in the palace, a purification ceremony must be performed. [41]

If one considers the practices and beliefs relating to childbirth that have been described, he feels that both entering the tent and lying near the fire are matters of cleansing the impurities that arise from childbirth more than matters of care and treatment; for the bearing of children occurs in the natural way, and does not require special medicines as in treating diseases. Rather, the original purpose has been forgotten, and so it is assumed that it is a medical treatment. In childbirth there is discharge of blood and filthy

matter; this is regarded as impure, and for removing impurities there are
two methods, namely cleansing with water or with fire. Lying near the fire
is cleansing with fire, in order to dry up the things which are impure. If
water were used to wash and cleanse ordinarily they would not all be removed,
and so they must wash with heat. When the mother emerges from the fire
they must still sprinkle thɔɔráaniisǎan holy water also. Thus they cleanse
with both fire and water. Lying near the fire is a procedure connected with
childbirth belonging to various nationalities in the Indochinese peninsula and
in the Indonesian archipelago. In India they use a brass stove with a charcoal
fire placed under the bed for ten days.[42] This is as much as I have found
given in books. It is impossible to know what nationality was the first to lie
near the fire, other nationalities following their example, because these were
nationalities that originally all believed in spirits and gods and the magic
efficacy of various objects. It was not difficult to imitate one another.
This is the sort of phenomenon that westerners call diffusion of cultures. Perhaps the practice of lying near the fire had its origin among the people of the
Indonesian archipelago, but it is impossible to know. This opinion is a guess
based on what has been related. It all depends upon what the individual pre-
fers to believe.

Hot Applications. These consist in taking the liquid medicine remaining
from entering the tent and pouring it out of the boiling pot, mixing it with
cold water, and then making a ball for massaging. They use Zingiber
casumunar, the "golden lady" plant, Curcuma zedoaria, tamarind leaves,
leaves of Acacia concinna, pounding them and then mixing them with salt;
they wrap them in a cloth and tie them tightly, forming a ball for massaging.
They dip this in the liquid that has been mixed and rub it over the face and
body. In the case of a young mother who has had her first child, they must
use three balls, one for sitting upon and the others for massaging. They
massage the breasts and roll the nipples with the ball also, in order to relieve
the tension and facilitate the flow of milk, because at this time the breasts
contain hard lumps which hurt and cannot bear to be touched; after the
lumps have been massaged with a ball, the pain gradually lessens. Sometimes it takes as long as seven days before they are normal and the pain
disappears. After massaging with the ball, they bathe in the liquid medicine
that remains, and then wash this off with plain warm water. They do this
every day until they emerge from the fire.

Pressing with a Salt Pot. Pressing with a salt pot consists in putting salt into
a sugar pot covered with a lid and putting this onto the fire until it is very
hot. The salt in the pot pops and crackles, but does not jump out because
the lid is closed. They take up the salt pot and lay it down on leaves of the
castor-oil plant or leaves of Crinum asiaticum, depending upon which kind

of leaf is easy to find, and then wrap up the sugar pot, together with the
castor-oil or Crinum asiaticum leaves on which it rests, in a large square
cloth, leaving enough of the ends of the cloth to gather together in a bunch
for carrying. They take this and rub it all over the body, especially rolling
it over the pubic mound, saying that this causes the womb to shrink and return to its original position in its "cradle." Usually they apply the salt pot
once in the afternoon and once again in the very early morning. This is done
every day, if they have the diligence to do it, until they emerge from the
fire. Midwives of Indian nationality use sifted ashes, putting them in a bag
and placing them over a fire till warm for sitting upon, instead of pressing
with a salt pot. After using the bag of ashes and bathing in water, they use
a sheet of raw cotton cloth as long as four to five yards to wrap the abdomen
and below. They do this for three to four days and then stop. Those who
have done this say that it is quite comfortable.

Sitting on Coals. They use the rind of a kaffir lime dried in the sun, sweet
flag, "golden lady" plant, Zingiber casumunar, Curcuma zedoaria, a quid
of betel from which all the juice has been chewed out, the plant chárûud,
powdered turmeric, and camphor leaves. These things are chopped fine and
put in the sun to dry in readiness beforehand. These are sprinkled a handful
at a time into a small stove, so that the smoke swirls up toward the buttocks
of the sitter. They say this has to do with the healing of the wounds arising
from childbirth.

The procedures that have been described are methods of medicinal
treatment. I have included them in order to show what methods of care and
treatment of mothers were used in olden times. It will be seen from this that
the medicines frequently used, such as turmeric, lime, betel leaves, salt,
lemon-grass bulbs, and kaffir limes, are all medicines which are easy to procure; almost all of them are regular household articles or can be found easily.
Even quids of betel from which all the juice has been chewed out can be used
as medicine. If they really have nothing and can obtain nothing, they use
methods of enchanting, such as enchanted lime or enchanted Zingiber
casumunar, and this is regarded as efficacious because it has to do with
psychological beliefs. The addition of certain strange medicines to the group
that can be procured easily is no doubt a later modification, when these
other things became easy to obtain. As for vessels employed, the basic items
are pots and lids. For lids, they use "widowed" lids, that is, lids whose pots
have been broken. If it is not a "widowed" lid, use is forbidden. The reason
for this prohibition is obvious; if they used a lid which has a pot and then
used it to cover the pot when it contained rice or curry, it might cause the
fire or curry in the pot to have an unpleasant odor, or might cause unclean-
ness in cooking. In the south they roast fish on "widowed" lids, forbidding
roasting on the lids of good pots. These utensils show that we common people

formerly were terribly poor, and lacked the convenient equipment that we
have nowadays. There were also no modern doctors to be found; there were
only village doctors, and even these were not easy to find. For the most
part people had to depend upon themselves. They used whatever traditional
methods of treatment had always been used. Even though our ancestors had
hardships and lacked conveniences to this degree, they were yet able to keep
us alive and see us through, according to the intelligence and ability that
they had in those days, with the result that today we have progressed and expanded. This is to be regarded as another item of antiquarian information
worth knowing; one should not simply judge the knowledge and opinions of
those times by the standards of these times. If you had been born in those
times you would necessarily have had the knowledge and opinions of those
times; it would be intrinsically impossible to think like these times. We
think our fathers are stupid and ignorant, and our children have the same
opinion of us: this is the thought of a stanza of poetry by an English poet
named Pope.

Prescribed Number of Days for Lying Near the Fire. These are 7, 9, 11, 13,
15, 17, and 21 days, or sometimes at most 29 days. All of these prescribed
numbers of days for lying near the fire are odd numbers, because there is a
belief that in lying near the fire "an even number of days, children in close
succession; an odd number of days, children at long intervals."[43] I do not
know the reason for this. It is of the same category as the saying about the
number of steps in a flight of stairs: "Even-numbered, a spirit's stairway,
odd-numbered, a stairway for human beings."[44] The belief, however, is
the opposite of that which is held at the time of bouncing on a basket, "Three
days the spirits' child, four days a human child," and in the oath, "May I
die in three days or seven days," which are odd numbers. The number of
days a woman lies near the fire, chosen from the list of prescribed numbers
above, is up to her. The longer she can remain, the better. They say that
if she can remain a long time, when she emerges from the fire her complexion will be clear and lovely. If she is a young woman who has had her
first child, they usually have her remain many days.

When the prescribed number of days for lying near the fire is up, at the
time of emerging from the fire they make an offering of the sort colloquially
called "prawn and fish salad"; that is, whatever small items of food they
have, they put in a small banana-leaf container to offer to the female spirit
of the fireplace. The mother prostrates herself and talks to it, taking her
leave respectfully, and then puts out the fire and bathes in thɔɔrániisǎan holy
water as an act of warding off evil. Thus the lying near the fire is ended, but
in some cases one day before emerging from the fire they have the woman
lie near a chaff fire; that is, they use chaff instead of firewood, laying sea-
holly leaves over the chaff to make it smolder. When she has passed one

night lying near this sort of fire, they sprinkle the fire and the child with thɔɔrâniisǎan holy water, and the mother takes her leave of the fireplace, comes out and bathes in holy water, and so has emerged from the fire, She is forbidden to lift chaff baskets and kapok baskets for about a month. Why she is forbidden, I do not know. It would not seem to be for fear of prolapsis uteri resulting from excessive strain, because chaff baskets and kapok baskets are not so heavy to lift as other things on which there does not appear to be any prohibition.

Furthermore, after emerging from the fire and throughout a period of three months, the woman was forbidden in olden times to sleep with her husband. Sometimes the woman's mother might come and sleep with her to protect her in this matter. The prohibition was due to a belief that if it were disregarded the woman would have children in close succession, her womb not yet being completely dry. How many modern people have feelings about this sort of thing?

Concerning the Child

The Umbilical Cord. During a period of from three days upward after the birth of the child, the portion of the umbilical cord which was tied and bound as described above will come loose from the child's navel. When it has dropped off it is put away in a little box, cup, or any other sort of vessel, and is sprinkled with turmeric. Why it is kept I do not know; they simply do it as a tradition. When it has been kept for a long time it gets tossed about, no one taking any interest in it, and finally it simply disappears; when it disappears no one complains. I have run across information about beliefs of westerners and various other nationalities which allow of some comparisons. They believe that a child's umbilical cord that drops off is an object having magic power, and later on when the child to whom the umbilical cord belongs falls ill he can suck on it to ward off danger. Among people . in the city of Berlin, Germany, the midwife gives this dry umbilical cord to the child's father to preserve with care. So long as he preserves it, the child will grow and be free of sickness. Among the English over a century ago there were often advertisements asking to buy dried umbilical cords. They believed that these were magically powerful to prevent shipwreck and to bring good luck to the owners. If one had one of these objects on his person and fell into the water, he would not drown even if he did not know how to swim. The Burmese believe that if one carries this object with him it will cause everyone to be kindly disposed. Hindus of some localities mix the ground umbilical cord with egg for the child to eat, believing that it causes intelligence. If they sew it onto the clothing of the child, he will be very brave. The Palaung people take good care of the umbilical cord, believing that if it is rubbed on an aching tooth the ache will vanish immediately. The people of Ceram Island and other islands in the South Seas, including Australia, tie the dried umbilical cord around the child's neck as a talisman, believing that it prevents children's diseases, or if the child falls ill they use the umbilical cord as medicine. In addition, the umbilical cord will cause the child to grow fast and learn easily, and it will serve as a talisman to ward off danger when traveling or when going to war.

Consideration of the beliefs of various nationalities as described above leads to the conclusion that the umbilical cord is an important part of the child, because the child lives in the womb by depending upon the umbilical cord as its means of sustenance; it is therefore fitting that it be regarded and preserved as an object of magic efficacy. Having this thought in mind, I made inquiries among some elderly people and obtained the information that the Thai preserve the dried umbilical cord to use with other medicines. When anyone is seriously ill and nothing that is taken relieves him, they grind the dried umbilical cord and mingle it with other medicine, as a magic remedy. Besides this they also use the dried umbilical cord ground up with lime juice to smear on insect stings.

Also, if the umbilical cord is about to drop off but there are still fibers holding it to the navel preventing it from coming completely loose, in the very early morning when the mother of the child awakens, before washing her face and rinsing her mouth she is to spit out her saliva and allow it to drop on the child's navel. This kind of saliva is called "rotten saliva." This name is correct, for it has a rotten odor. This procedure is probably due to a desire that the germs of decay cause the remaining fibers to decay also, so that the umbilical cord will drop off. They dare not use anything to cut it loose. This saliva before rinsing the mouth is regarded as an efficacious substance. For example, when a boil has first appeared they usually touch the finger to this sort of saliva under the tongue and rub it on the boil, which will then go down. Westerners say that the Romans, when they were going to speak well of themselves, had to spit on their own chests, believing that this kept the gods from despising them. When they were going to perform a religious ceremony they had to spit, because saliva was magic and drove away spirits. (To say nothing of spirits fearing it, human beings are afraid of it too, and run away from it.)

When the umbilical cord has come loose, the mother of the child takes three betel leaves and heats them in the smoke of a torch or the smoke of charcoal till they are moderately hot, touching them with the hand to see how hot they are. Then she applies these to the abdomen of the child. The use of three betel leaves is said to be in order to heat them alternately over the fire, and perhaps the number three is also regarded as magic. When the betel leaves have been applied, they heat a kaffir lime in the smoke of a torch, and roll it about on the abdomen in the area surrounding the navel.

152

This is said to make the belly thick like the rind of the kaffir lime, so that
the child will not have stomach ache. Then they take three roasted pepper-
corns, roasted diatomaceous earth, and crystals of Pagostemon cablin, and
grind these things together to sprinkle on the child's navel to knit the wound.
If after sprinkling this medicine it still does not heal, they are to scrape out
the skin from the inside of a coconut shell, grind it together with crystals of
Pagostemon cablin, and sprinkle this on the navel. Then they put ground
assafetida and sweet flag mixed with kaffir lime juice into a potlid and heat
this over a fire to apply to the area surrounding the navel. This is likewise
a medicine to apply to the belly of a child to make it thick. In applying it
they must not allow it to touch the navel, because the child will feel smarting pain. When this is finished they roll assafetida into long bars of small
size, wrap them in thin white cloth, and tie them to both wrists of the child
in the manner of bracelets. When the child happens to raise his arms they
will touch his nose and he will inhale the odor of assafetida; he will thus not
be subject to fainting.

Medicine for Swabbing the Child's Throat. Besides these there are also medicines for swabbing the throats of children when they are ill. They use the
bulbs of lemon grass, grinding them on the bottom of a curry pot that has been
used, because there is soot adhering to it. When a child is already sucking
the breast, they sometimes grind Strychnos roborans, roots of holy basil, and
Vitex glabrata bark to swab. In some localities they use the piece of bamboo
which has been used to hold open the mouth of a fish-condiment jug, burning
it and grinding it to powder and then dissolving this in honey and applying it
to the child's tongue.

Hot Applications for Children. If the child is a boy, they heat betel leaves in
the smoke of a cajeput torch and apply them to the scrotum, pressing upward,
so that when the child is older he will not have scrotal hernia. For girls
there are also applications to give her organ a proper shape. Then they rub
the breasts, squeezing out the milk, because this is regarded as milk existing
from birth; it is transparent milk like lymph, and not good. If it is not
squeezed out it may cause boils to form, because it is in lumps. Besides these
things they pull the nose in order to make it arched and beautiful, because
we do not usually have arched noses.

Infant Menstruation. During the period three to seven days after the day of
birth, some girl babies menstruate. This sort of menstrual discharge is regarded as a good thing.[45] They usually wipe it off with cotton and keep it,
believing that if they have it on the person when they go to gamble they will
not lose. The reason that the menstrual discharge of infants is regarded as a
"good thing" is perhaps that they regard the menstrual discharge as a symbol

of birth, having special power to destroy the efficacy of spells and charms or the power of spirits and gods, or perhaps they have the same belief as the Indians, that a woman's menstrual discharge is pure because it is a symbol of the god Agni.

Capturing a Cold. Young babies are liable to become ill easily, because their bodies are still delicate. For example, they may take cold and have blocked noses so that they cannot breathe easily. If a child has these symptoms they must make a medicinal poultice to apply to the top of its head. They use onions or bulbs of sweet prɔɲ[46] pounded and mixed with turmeric, red lime, and liquor. They dip cotton into this medicine and form it into a flat, round, thin plaster with a hole in the center, and apply this to the child's head. The juice of the pounded onions remaining from making the poultice for the head is used to apply to the bridge of the nose and to the body. This method of applying a poultice to the head and smearing the body of the child until it appears red and blotched all over is called "capturing a cold."

Coated Tongue. About fifteen days after birth, the child's tongue may develop a white coat called "fine powder." If it is left it will become thicker and thicker and turn into pharyngitis, making the tongue stiff so that the child cannot suck the breast. It is necessary to take a diaper which is moist with the child's urine and wipe the white coat off the tongue. Sometimes they use the "gum" of raw bananas to wipe; if they can get the "gum" of "water bananas," then all the better. They cut the raw banana in two and wipe out the "gum" onto a cloth.

Heat Rashes and Hiccups. Sometimes children have heat rashes; that is, they have rashes on the face and body consisting of fairly large transparent white pimples. If these pustules burst, the pus will spread and be messy and malodorous. They are to sprinkle diatomaceous earth and crystals of Pogostemon cablin. If a child has hiccups, they must tear off a corner of a diaper and apply it to the top of the head or the forehead of the child. While applying it they must hold the breath. If they fear that the cloth that is applied might drop off, they are to moisten it with saliva. This is a terribly simple procedure.

The things that have been described are not exhaustive, because small children are given to having a great many diseases. Those which have been mentioned are only the ones which are treated by the methods of the folk, without having to go to the extremities of calling a doctor to treat them. It can be seen that most of the medical remedies are things that can be found easily, just like the medicines that have been described earlier.

Diapers. Also in the matter of diapers there are special rules that must be followed; for example when washing them it is forbidden to wring them out. They are merely to squeeze them enough to make the water run out, believing that if they wring the diapers the child will feel twisted. This is the sort of thing which in English is called homoeopathetic magic, according to the principle that things which are similar produce similar results, or can be contracted one from another (Law of Similarity and Law of Contract or Contagion).[47] When washing diapers it is necessary to be careful not to throw away or discard any; they say that the child will cry without ever stopping. When a child cries incessantly and no reason can be found for its crying, they usually count the diapers to see if any are missing. If it is found that some are missing, someone or other is inevitably scolded with such words as "Do you see? The old saying is not wrong. People disregard it, taking up the beliefs of westerners, and so things have come to this pass!" In the afternoon when the sun sinks low, diapers that have been hung out must be gathered in. If they persist in leaving them out until dark, the cloth will be covered with dew and the child will catch cold, in the manner of a contagious disease. When diapers are soiled they must hurry to wash them; they must not leave them in a heap. This is a good thing. If it is the rainy season sometimes it rains hard all day long, and there is no sunshine to dry the diapers fast enough for use. They build a bonfire on the ground, cover it with a chicken coop,[48] and then lay the diapers on this, in order to dry the wet diapers. When touched by the steam and heat they dry more rapidly. Later on when there were charcoal stoves to use, they used charcoal stoves, but if care is not taken the fire may become very hot and burn the basket and the diapers. This is a question of using new and more convenient things without making suitable adjustments; people think they are like the old things and so this sort of damage results.

Piercing the Ears. When the child has passed three days in age, if it is a girl the midwife usually pierces the ears as part of her job. The method of piercing is to prepare a needle threaded with cotton thread dyed black with Diospyros mollis.[49] At the time of piercing she must roll the outer ear until it is numb and examine the ear so as not to pierce it at a nerve.[50] Then she takes a betel-leaf stem, dips it in lime, and touches it to both sides of the ear to serve as a marker. A tiny slice of the rhizome of Zingiber casumunar or turmeric is placed under the ear as a support, and then the ear is pierced, allowing the thread to remain. After piercing, they apply coconut oil and turmeric to knit the wound, and pull the thread back and forth constantly, continually dropping coconut oil to prevent dryness; or if they can use household oil which is applied to infant's sores and pimples, then all the better. They take shell from the bottom of the coconut, leaves of the neem tree, jasmine leaves, and gummy turmeric, pound these together and then squeeze

out the juice. Then they sprinkle salt on this and place it in the sun until it
dries and turns to oil, and then it can be used. Another method of piercing
causes the child little pain but is slow and time-consuming; they take an
angular piece of lead with both ends bent to form a ring and clamp this to
the ear, gradually pressing it in a little at a time until the ear is perforated.
I have heard complaints that this method is not good, and cannot compare
with the more rapid method of piercing with a needle, but I suspect that the
method of piercing with a needle is a recent method. After the ear is pierced,
it is desired to make the hole large; that is, when the wound heals and the
thread has been pulled out, they enlarge the hole with the stem of a head of
dried garlic or young grass, or use the wood of Sesbania roxburghii or roots
of Sonneratia caseolaris, which expand when touched with water. The hole
can be made as large as is desired; for example, in some localities they
gradually replace this wood that is inserted by pieces of larger and larger
size. This procedure of piercing the ears is done only to ordinary people. It
is known that women of the old upper classes, such as royalty, did not pierce
their ears, because they regarded it as a low thing. The reason that it is
necessary to pierce the ears while the child is still very small is that at this
time the child is not yet very sensitive to pain, because the flesh is still immature, and also the child does not yet know how to pull and tug at the
thread so that it comes out.

Burying the Afterbirth

I beg to drop the subject of the child for the time being and return to
the subject of the afterbirth, which was placed in a sugarpot and set beside
the place for lying near the fire. When a period of seven days after the birth
is past, they may perform the ceremony of burying the afterbirth. Sometimes they wait a whole month or even three months before taking it out and
burying it. Sometimes they bring the pot containing the afterbirth and enter
it into the khwǎn and shaving of the fire hair ceremony when the child
reaches the age of one month. When they take the pot containing the afterbirth out to bury it they have a superstitious way of carrying it, to wit: they
shift it alternately from left hand to right, saying that when the child grows
up it will be ambidextrous. If they carry the pot containing the afterbirth in
only one hand, the child will be handy with only that one hand. When they
return from burying the afterbirth, if the afterbirth is that of a boy, the people who took it out must sing a song or chant in the cadence of preaching.
This shows that this sort of thing was popular in olden days. If it is a girl,
when they return from burying the afterbirth they are to gather edible plants
and firewood; when the child grows up she will be diligent and be a good
housewife.

For burying the afterbirth there are many procedures laid down in textbooks. In the textbook, Phrommácháad, it says: "If the child is born in the fourth, fifth, or sixth lunar month, the afterbirth must be buried to the north," and so on.

In the textbook, Pàthŏmcindaa, it says: "When you are going to bury an afterbirth, you are to take fragant powder, perfumed oil, exploded rice and flowers, powdered aloewood and sandal, incense sticks and candles, and offer them to the gods of the air, and worship the gods of the trees and the gods of the earth, and then you may bury it." Besides this it is specified that the afterbirth in the fourth, fifth, or sixth lunar month is to be buried to the southwest, contradicting what is said in the textbook, Phrommácháad, which says north, saying that the child will be easy to raise. If it is buried to the south, the child will be in danger and will be many other bad things. "If the cord of the afterbirth was wound around the child at the time of birth, you are to roast it over a fire until crisp, and then grind it up in rice and give it to the child to eat." It will never whine or cry at all. It will have good fortune and many other good things. "If the afterbirth is wound around the neck, put the afterbirth in a pot of one thousand (one thousand what, I do not know), and then spear it in the middle with an iron and roast it dry over a fire. Grind it up for the child to eat, and the child will have a beautiful figure," and so on. (Much like the story of European children sucking the dried umbilical cord as already described.)

Another procedure: "If the child was born on Sunday, the purchasing mother is on an anthill. The afterbirth must be buried in an anthill." If it was born on some other day there are also rules about various other places for burial, and so on.

Before burying the afterbirth, they are to place the desired articles with it in the pot, and then take it and bury it in the prescribed direction. It is said that the child will be expert in the three Vedas, will behave like its father and mother, and other things. (See the details in the above-named textbooks.)

According to northeastern custom, they place the afterbirth in a new pot with a lid. If there is no lid, they cover it with cloth and seal the mouth. They take it and bury it under the stairs in front of the house. Then they bring a section of log and light it at the edge of the grave, keeping it burning brightly both day and night until the period of lying near the fire is up, and then they stop. The reasons for this I do not know.

Concerning burying the afterbirth, to judge from the above textbooks, it is necessary to perform many ceremonies, as if the afterbirth were a thing of importance. But so far as I have been able to observe the usual procedure of the peasants, they do not do a great deal, except to take it and bury it at the base of a big tree. Burying it is proper; there does not seem to be any

purpose in keeping it. Burying it at the base of a big tree is said to be a superstition that it is in a cool and shady place, and the child whose afterbirth
it is will live "in coolness and happiness"[51] and will have a long life like a
big tree. Sometimes they do not bury it beneath a big tree, but bury it under
the stairway of the house. According to Indian custom they put a one-pie
coin, turmeric, an areca nut, and a little salt in the pot with the afterbirth,
and then bury the pot underneath the bed for lying near the fire. In some
places they throw it away.

Regarding customs of the south of Siam it has been ascertained that
they have ceremonies requiring the selection of a good direction, a good day,
and a good place, such as an anthill, which is, for example, regarded as
good. They are superstitious about throwing the afterbirth into water; the
child whose afterbirth it is usually comes to harm by falling into water and
drowning. Only this much has been learned.

In burying the afterbirth there is a belief that they must employ a right-
handed person to dig the hole; otherwise the child will be left-handed.
Sometimes after the burial they are to plant a coconut tree. Probably it is
desired that it serve as a marker. In some places there is not only burial of
the afterbirth and planting of a coconut tree, but also sprinkling of the pot
containing the afterbirth and the coconut in advance as well. This is said to
be to cause the "silver and gold coconut" to flourish, and the child to have
happiness and prosperity. It is learned that the "silver and gold coconut" is
an ordinary dried coconut, but it is covered with silver and gold papers which
are supposed to be real silver and gold. This is the same category of thing
as the silver and golden bricks laid down in auspicious moments.

For burying the afterbirth it is necessary to seek persons named "Steadfast Merit," "Enduring Merit," "Abiding Merit," and "Having Merit" to do
the burying.[52] If they cannot find people with these names, they may let it
pass; they may have other people with other names do the burying, but they
must do the burying correctly with respect to direction as determined for
them by the astrologer. These are all matters of superstition. No doubt they
are beliefs of astrologers, and ordinary people probably do not perform them.

Why do they plant only coconut trees? May they not plant other trees?
Or is this a belief belonging to some other place where they are fond of
planting coconuts, and we acquired the belief? Or has the original conception been modified, and not only coconut trees but other trees may be planted
as well? Perhaps this is connected with the matter of titulary trees of children,
for there is a belief that every person born has a personal tree. Thus in the
textbook, Phrommáchâad, it says that the guardian spirit abides in banana
trees and coconut trees. The Semang, a Negrito people in the Malay peninsula, believe that a person is born with a titulary tree. The father selects
this titulary tree beforehand; it is a tree near the place where the child is to
be born. When he has made his choice, he cuts blaze marks in it as a sign;

these marks extend from the base to breast height. This tree is the place where the afterbirth is buried, and it is absolutely forbidden to cut it down. When the child is grown, he is forbidden to damage any tree of the same species, or even to eat the fruit of it. [53]

The textbook, Pàthŏmcindaa, says: "If a child is born in the year of the rat, it is attended by a god and the coconut tree. If born in the year of the ox, it is attended by a male human and the sugar palm." For other years there are other trees; for example, year of the tiger, a male butterfly and the tree Pentacme siamensis. If it is held that the afterbirth must be buried and trees planted as laid down here, there are certain difficulties. In some years, for example in the case of persons born in the year of the tiger, it must be a Pentacme siamensis tree. This would seem to be no easy matter, if it is a locality where Pentacme siamensis does not occur or where it is hard to grow it, as in Bangkok, where it can hardly be made to grow because it is lowland. What is to be done? The answer is that if it cannot be found, then stick a branch of some other tree in the ground instead and pretend that it is Pentacme siamensis, or else write the Thai name for Pentacme siamensis on the tree, in the same way that the name of a dead person is written in the funeral ceremony, or a name is written and cremated in place of a corpse. Perhaps this is what has happened. It would seem likely that it would be possible simply to alter the customs in this way. Some textbooks say that if a Pentacme siamensis tree cannot be found, a breadfruit tree may be used. I do not know why Pentacme siamensis and breadfruit trees may substitute for each other. Furthermore, the breadfruit is easy to find in the south, but is rare or nonexistent in the northeast. The Pentacme siamensis tree is easy to find in the northeast, but rare in the south. No further convenience than this is allowed by the regulations. I should therefore like to guess that the belief has been modified to permit the planting of coconuts, because it is easy to find them to plant and they are more useful than Pentacme siamensis trees. Combined with this the coconut is a tree used in divination; if it grows straight upward it is regarded as a good thing.

According to tradition the coconut is a symbol of fertility and plenty. The people of India call the coconut śrīphala, that is, the tree of Śrī, the goddess of grace and fortune. In various ceremonies of the Indians the coconut cannot be omitted. They offer it to the gods and use it in various auspicious rites. An offering of coconuts is auspicious. In making an offering to the goddess Lakshmi, a coconut may be used as a substitute if they have no image of the goddess. Beliefs about coconuts seem to be Indian, and have been diffused to us. For example, in khwăn ceremonies there must be coconuts, and in offerings there are also coconuts. In Malaya when a child has reached the age to speak but is slow to talk, they perform a ceremony to open its mouth. They split open a young coconut and feed its milk and meat to the child. The person doing the feeding must count from one to seven,

and when she reaches seven she gives the child a bite. The Fijians in the
South Seas, when they bury a child's umbilical cord, must plant a coconut
or breadfruit tree. They believe that this tree that is planted has a connection
with the child to whom the umbilical cord belonged. Whether the child encounters difficulty or good luck in the future depends upon the tree. If the
tree grows and flourishes, the child will do well; if the opposite, then so
also with the child.

Why are there so many beliefs about what must be done in burying the
afterbirth? So far as one can see from what usually happens, once it is buried
no one seems to take any interest in where his own afterbirth is. It is buried,
and that is the end of the matter. Even in the case of the afterbirth of royalty, so far as has been ascertained, there is no ceremony performed, and
there is no special royal term in the textbooks for the afterbirth of princes
and princesses, except to call it phráʔ tràkuun, [54] which, however, is a word
not generally known. Thus it may be seen that the afterbirth is not a thing
of any importance, differing from the prescription as set down in the textbooks,
that it is necessary to select the direction for burying. Or perhaps the original conception has long since been modified, for reading of works on the
subject of the afterbirth of various nations, as set down in western books,
shows that nationalities which are still at a low stage of development believe
that the afterbirth is a part of the soul.

For example, people of the continent of Australia believe that people
have many souls, and one soul resides in the afterbirth (similar to our belief
in the khwǎn; our entering the pot containing the afterbirth in the khwǎn and
shaving the fire-hair ceremony bears some resemblance to this). When they
bury the afterbirth, Australians plant many sticks in the ground and gather
their tops together to form a cone to mark the place of burial. This is probably comparable with our planting coconuts; originally it was probably
planted as a marker of the place where the afterbirth was buried.

The Purchasing Mother

If a child is ill -- for example, its body is hot and it sleeps restlessly --
they believe that the purchasing mother is punishing and haunting it. It is
necessary to perform a ceremony of throwing rice to the purchasing mother.
They are to take cooked rice from the top of the pot (probably it is easy to
scoop up, and it is hot rice and still pure, no one yet having scooped it up
to eat, and it is easier to mould into balls than rice which has cooled; it is
part of the category of first fruits;[55] (see my work on the Sarda festival) and
form it into four balls of four colors, namely, white (which it is already),
yellow (mixed with turmeric), red (mixed with red lime), and black (mixed
with soot). They lay these four balls of rice in a potlid, a dish, or a

banana-leaf container, and then raise them one at a time and carry them three times around the child. Then they speak words to ward off evil:

> Purchasing mother of the city below, purchasing mother of the city above, purchasing mother who treads the air, purchasing mother under the bed, come and accept your child's rice. Let all disease and illness go away!

There are also words to ward off evil which differ from the above, for example:

> Purchasing mother of the city below, purchasing mother of the city above, purchasing mother who treads the air, purchasing mother at the head of the stairs, purchasing mother under the bed, do you come and accept the balls of white, yellow, red, black rice (changing the color of the ball of rice as the words are spoken) of your child. Do not let the rice that it eats be bitter; do not let it vomit the milk it sucks; do not let it start in its sleep. Let it recover from illness.

Another version is:

> Purchasing mother of the city below, purchasing mother of the city above, purchasing mother under the bed, do you come and accept the balls of white rice, red rice, yellow rice, black rice.

Another version is:

> O purchasing mother, O lady! Your child is our child. Do not come pinching or scratching it; do not trouble and torment it; do not cause it distress and illness. We will rear it in happiness and contentment, to live with us until old age.

These versions were obtained from the memory of a number of persons who could remember them, and so they vary from one another.

When they have spoken these words to avert evil, they take the white, yellow, and red balls of rice and throw them over the roof of the house. Any ball may be thrown first; there is no rule. As for the black ball of rice, it is to be thrown under the house or thrown onto the ground anywhere. Then they take water and wash the potlid or dish in which the rice was laid, and toss this water after the riceballs. When they throw the rice they are to shout out "woo" in unison. Some people say that the ceremony of throwing the purchasing mother's rice is to be performed at twilight. There are also instances of using white rice, black rice, and yellow rice, without red rice, a total of three balls, and throwing them over the roof. Some people say they must be thrown from the east toward the west. In some instances they throw across the roof from the front of the house to the back of the house. This is as much on the subject of ceremonies that are performed as I have been able to learn.

This rice of the purchasing mother dyed various colors has the same characteristics as the balls of black rice and red rice put in a ceremonial container of some sort in some regions; and it can be seen that we use things for dyeing which are easily found at home, just as in the case of obtaining medicines as already described.

Who is the purchasing mother? I will first quote the Invocation of the Purchasing Mother for you to read, in order to facilitate discussion of the subject.

Invocation of the Purchasing Mother (inscribed on the walls of a pavilion in the grounds of Wád Phrá? Chêedtùphon):

> Hail to the gracious and auspicious powers! I prostrate myself.
> I will recite an invocation inviting all the great gods. I invite the
> great god Vishnu, and also the god Shiva of majestic power, who
> is the lord of Mount Krailasa. I bow down and do homage to you.
> Also the goddess Uma, whose grace sustains the world. May you
> conquer diseases. I invite the god of the wind and the god of fire,
> the blazing god Kala and the god Brahma. Also Yama and the
> guardian of the four quarters, the god of the sun and the god of the
> moon. Also the Lord Indra who is monarch of the world of the gods
> -- twelve great deities in all. I fold my hands in reverence and
> raise them over my head. I invite you to come and take up your
> positions over my head. I offer you incense, candles, and lamps,
> and white rice and flowers and perfumes; also a ceremonial fence
> with flags of victory. I beg you to bestow your blessing, endowed
> with magic power. Grant wisdom to me. I will invoke the figure
> instead of the human being. Purchasing mother of the city above,
> and purchasing mother of the city below, seven beings of seven
> different kinds, the purchasing mother in the middle of the path,
> bold and harsh, the strong purchasing mothers of the particular days
> having traditional names, to wit: the purchasing mother of Sunday's
> child is named Wícîdtrànaawan; the purchasing mother for Monday
> is named Wádthánaanoŋkhraan; the purchasing mother for Tuesday
> is named the pure giantess (yág bɔɔrísùd); the purchasing mother
> for Wednesday is named Lady Sǎamáláthád; the purchasing mother
> for Thursday is named Lady Koolaathúg; the purchasing mother for
> Friday is named the lovely giantess (yág noŋjaw); the purchasing
> mother for Saturday is named the Lady Eekaalaj. If you hear your
> name, make haste, and bring with you all ghosts and spirits. I
> will reward you to your heart's content. When you have eaten then
> go, do not stay, as I command you.

> Hail to the gracious and auspicious powers! I invite you, O pur-
> chasing mothers. My teacher taught me how to recognize you, the
> purchasing mother of the city above, the purchasing mother in the
> middle of the path, the purchasing mother of the city below, each
> one causing a different kind of harm.

Some purchasing mothers inhabit the entrails, and cause the child
to cry and moan. Some purchasing mothers lie athwart the navel,
causing wind and diarrhea and making the child sob and squirm.
Some purchasing mothers inhabit the head and cause vomiting and
dry voice. Some purchasing mothers hide in the flesh, making the
child toss in its sleep and scream and have nosebleed and turn pale.
Some purchasing mothers inhabit the top of the head, making the
child cry out with fright and causing its feet, hands, and calves to
be chilled. Some purchasing mothers inhabit the veins, making the
child cry and twist its body and its four limbs, and scream till it is
blue in the face. Come, all you purchasing mothers, and abide
here, all twenty-eight of you who are the authors of harm. Do not
be angry; restrain your tempers. Come and partake of meat, fish,
and liquor, and of the cups of water and rice, and of the ornaments.
Crowds of people are gathered all around. We invite you to accept
our offering. Eat your fill, you and all your kinspeople. Come
and admire the figure instead of the child. Be auspicious. Do not
think of harming the little child who has been born among humans.
He is not of your kind, living in the great trees that grow in the
forest, or in caves or among cliffs and marshes, or in woods and
thickets beside streams and caverns and mountains, or on rocky
shores, or in forests and meadows or among tall trees, or beside the
paths that humans walk, or beside monasteries and pavilions. When
you have eaten, go where you like. Be not slow. Do not tease
and fondle and play with the child that has been born. Let the
child flourish. We invite you to be kind to the child, to protect it.
We offer you rice, water, crab, and fish. May the child support
and maintain religion and not be idle. If it is a boy let him become a monk; if it is a girl let her become a nun. Let the child
obey the precepts and be gentle in heart. Let the child dedicate
half its merit to its mother for having reared it. We beg to purchase
this child for a price of thirty-three cowries. For three days it is
the spirits' child; after the fourth day it is a human child. It is
not your child; do not yearn after it. We give you a figure in its
place. Take the figure in this vessel away and admire it. We have
paid you with these offerings. Do not linger here. When the child
grows we will send merit to you to assist you to escape grief and
attain Nirvana. Make haste. Be enamored of our offering that we
make to you. Make a promise, as if it were a sealed contract,
that you will not after this day cause harm to the child. We ask
to keep the child and care for it. We will grind turmeric and mix
it with chalk to make golden powder like moon-rain to anoint the
child, and also rice made golden with turmeric. We will blend

these together and enchant them and put them on the forehead of the child to guard and protect it. Do not tarry to admire the child. Hurry and begone, and take with you all illness and disease, coated tongue and bloated stomach and sore throat; let none of these remain behind. Purchasing mothers of all seven days, make all these things vanish, leaving the four elements and the three sources in full measure. Let none of these vanish or be in danger. Let the child be easy to raise, so that it may support and foster the religion of the Buddhas -- of Kukkusandha, and Dasabalakonagamana, of Gotama, of Kassapa, and of Ariyamaitri, all five of the Buddhas, to whom we dedicate a share of the merit in all that has been said.

This invocation is called the Small Sarateja rite for driving out the evil caused by the purchasing mothers. Three days after a child has been born from the womb of its mother, let a doctor do all the foregoing. This must be done after three days, and then the child will flourish. This concludes it.

Discussion of the Subject of the Purchasing Mother

When one has read the material quoted above he learns that the purchasing mothers are spirits which come to molest and abide in the body of newborn children. There are seven purchasing mothers assigned to the birthday of the child. Besides these there are the purchasing mother of the city above (that is, the city of the sky), the purchasing mother in the middle of the "path" ("path" means "way"; it probably lies in the middle of the air?), and the purchasing mother of the city below (that is, upon the earth). Then there are purchasing mothers inhabiting the entrails, the navel, the flesh, the top of the head, and other places in the child's body, making a total of twenty-eight. But in this invocation there is no mention of the purchasing mother under the bed; probably she is included in the twenty-eight.

The purchasing mothers usually trouble children and cause them various illnesses. Probably they want to carry the children off because they love them, and so it is said, "tease and fondle and play with the child," and so it is necessary to play a trick and ask to buy the child from the purchasing mother; that is, haunt the ghost in turn. The price is thirty-three cowries. Three days after a child's birth, they are to make an offering and mould a figure of the child for the purchasing mothers to carry off and admire in place of the child. The child will remain here and have comfort and happiness, when the purchasing mother has eaten the offerings, which are like a bribe or reward. "When you have eaten then go, do not stay, as I command you." This is an act of chasing away the purchasing-mother spirit, like the Chinese making offerings to spirits and then lighting firecrackers to drive them away.

It has been related at the point where the child was born that when the umbilical cord has been cut and the child placed on the basket, the midwife bounces the basket and says, "Three days the spirits' child, four days a human child." This is probably derived from this matter of asking to purchase the child from the purchasing mother. Probably the midwife is assumed to represent the purchasing mother, but the ceremony that we perform does not coincide too well with the original ceremony set forth in the Invocation of the Purchasing Mother. Our performance has lost the part requiring thirty-three cowries, and the bouncing must be done after three days have elapsed, not on the day of birth. Also, in the bouncing ceremony it is necessary to make an offering, moulding a figure of the child and placing it with the food offerings; this has also been lost from our performance. If one examines the subject as set forth in the textbooks on medicine, in the part dealing with characteristics of purchasing-mother illnesses, it appears that they make an offering and mould a figure of the child and put it in every time that they perform anything relating to the purchasing mother. For example:

"Siddhikāriya. I will describe the purchasing-mother illnesses of children born on Sunday. If it is born in the waxing phase of the moon, the illness is localized above the navel; if in the waning phase, it is localized below the navel. The purchasing mother named Wicldtrânaawan abides in the cradle. If the child falls ill it will have various symptoms; it will feel pain in its body, and will not be able to take rice or milk. Let doctors know the following:

"If you would cure it, take earth from the two banks of a river and mould it into a figure of a mother holding a child in her arms. Then make offerings to it with white flowers, five incense sticks and five candles, and all sorts of fragrant things. Then exorcize the illness with the following mantra three times:

" 'Om namo bhagavampati danikāmukkham dharaṇikhibalimapakādabalā buñcayyah savāha om ṛddhi. Begone! Savāhaḥ.'

(Many mantras used in Tibet end "Savāhah. Begone!" Probably there is a common origin in the Tantric Buddhism of India.) "When the mantra has been recited, place the figure in a begging bowl and place it toward the east. If this is done for three days the child should recover. If it does not recover, make up the following prescription for an inhalant to drive out the poison:

"For the medicine use the seeds of chard plants, gum from sŏn fruit, hairs from a cat, hairs from a human, sàdaw leaves, and beef tallow, in equal parts. Heat this as an inhalant for the child; it is very good." (This agrees with the Indian belief that if you want to drive spirits out of a child's body you must use medicines that are swallowed, inhaled, and applied externally.)

This matter of taking earth from the two banks of a river and moulding it into a figure of a mother holding a child in her arms is strange. An elderly person told me, "This is startling, for I have seen enameled dolls in the form of a mother holding a child in her arms as described here. There are some at the enamel kilns of the city of Sukhothai, and some at the museum in the island of Bali in Java. I do not know whether they were used as dolls in rites or not."

Why must we perform a ceremony of bouncing a baby and asking to purchase it, saying, "Three days the spirits' child, four days a human child?" This is probably derived from the belief that when human beings are born spirits form them to be born. "Spirit" [phĭi] is here an old Thai word, referring to those having power over human beings, invisible to human beings unless they cause themselves to be seen. Later on we called aristocratic spirits "gods" [using Sanskrit-Pali devatā, "divinity"], and called bad spirits "evil spirits" or simply "spirits." When spirits are going to form human beings they take earth and model a figure, as is related in the verses teaching children to read words ending in -d in Muunlábŏd Banphákìd:[56] "The spirits who mould children straightway affixed the nose and eyes," or in the story of Khŭn Chá̌aŋ Khŭn Phĕɛn:

> I will sing verses on the birth of all the characters. When they first entered the womb, it is said, a most evil spirit on a treetop in the nighttime moulded a figure, giggling and pinching and squeezing it shapelessly. He moulded and moulded, snickering all the while, taking a little of this a little of that and squeezing and adding them until complete.

> One night the spirit was moulding on the treetop. There was a creature in hell, enduring severest sufferings. When he had expiated his demerits he was freed from torment and was delivered from the status of creature of hell. He scurried about running in search of happiness. He could not go to heaven, for he had not yet escaped sorrow. The spirit moulded him and tucked him into the womb.

So we humans are born because spirits or gods create or mould us. What business is it of gods or spirits that they should constantly create human beings? Because spirits want to carry human beings off. If a child that is born has an attractive figure, the spirits like it and would like to take it and rear it, or, to speak frankly, cause it to die. This coincides with the belief of westerners that "those whom the gods love die young." If the spirits don't like the child, they leave it for human beings to rear. Because of this belief, it is necessary to find various methods of protection against spirits, for example, by asking to purchase the child. It is forbidden to admire a child directly with the word "lovable." They must speak the reverse, saying that the child is "detestable." When the spirit hears this he will believe that it is true and will not take the child away. Sometimes they even give children the names Pig, Dog, Frog, Treetoad. This is to deceive spirits, because spirits are usually more stupid than people.

The belief that it is the spirits that shape human beings that are born is also held by the Australians. They believe that spirits form earth into the shape of a human being, and then take the soul which inhabits the buried afterbirth and put it into the human figure. Then they put it into a woman's womb. The custom of admiring children but having to speak the reverse also exists among many peoples. Among some nationalities, for example Europeans and the people of Uganda in Africa, they even spit on the children. [57] The ancient belief of various nationalities that spirits will come and carry off newborn children is due to the fact that newborn babies are very delicate and may easily die in three days or seven days. (We swear with the words, "May I die in three days or seven days." This comes from this matter of children.) In those times medical care of children was not sufficiently advanced, and whatever happened to children was all blamed on spirits. If a child cried a great deal, they said that the purchasing mother teased it. If it had a stomach ache, they said that the purchasing mother had entered and was disturbing its intestines. Or if its umbilical wound hurt, they said that the purchasing mother was lying athwart the navel. Therefore it is probable that in olden times children often died in the first three days after birth, and hence the saying, "Three days the spirits' child." When the three-day limit was past they were somewhat relieved, and hence the saying, "Four days a human child." The Indians believe that a newborn child may die very easily because the spirits will carry it off, and the child is called for the first three to seven days not a human being but a creature, because they do not have confidence that it will survive. Europeans also believe that spirits may carry off a newborn child, and so a protective ceremony must be performed to cleanse it of sin. In English a small child is referred to as "it," showing that at this time it is not fully human.

This assumption that the midwife represents the purchasing mother is also strange. It looks as if the midwife were a spirit, and the word "witch" which is used together with the word "doctor" also would seem to be a matter of spirit doctors. [58] Moreover, nowadays the word "witch" is also used in connection with spirit possession; this suggests that medical treatment in former times was a matter connected with spirits. The Shans call the midwife mɛ̂ɛ kɛ̀b [literally, "gathering mother" or "collecting mother"] and call other children which one brings in and rears lûug kɛ̀b [literally, "gathered child" or "collected child"]. The word kɛ̀b here perhaps means that the midwife gathers or collects children that are born, and so they must be purchased. The Vietnamese call both midwives and spirits that come to disturb children bàa mùu or màa mùu; apparently one is to understand that the midwife and the purchasing mother are the same person. Perhaps it is also because of this notion that people detest the word "midwife."

There is a matter that I still do not understand. Why is the word "purchasing mother" reversed in meaning? The midwife who bounces the child should be the "selling mother"; she is the person who sells the child for other people to purchase and take away for a price of thirty-three cowries. Or perhaps the word "purchase" [Thai, sýy] was not originally the same word as the ordinary Thai word, sýy, meaning to purchase. But the things that are done include purchasing, and so it is difficult to try to interpret it in some other way.

In the Invocation of the Purchasing Mother the names of all seven purchasing mothers assigned to the days are mentioned, but the other twenty-eight have no names. The names of the seven purchasing mothers assigned to the days are strange; each rhymes with the name of the day immediately following, as follows:

Sunday [Thai, ʔaathíd], name wícídtrànaawan, rhymes with
Monday [Thai, can], name wannánoŋkhraan, rhymes with
Tuesday [Thai, ʔaŋkhaan], name jâg bɔɔrísùd, rhymes with
Wednesday [Thai, phúd], name sǎamonláthâd, rhymes with
Thursday [Thai, phárýhàdsàbɔɔdii], name kaaloothúg, rhymes with
Friday [Thai, sùg], name yág noŋjaw, rhymes with
Saturday [Thai, sǎw], name ʔeekaalaj, rhymes with
Sunday, see above.

These names were probably not obtained from India, because some of the names are not words from Indic languages. Phra Theewaa Phínímíd (Chaaj Theewaaphínímíd) has kindly noted down the names of the seven purchasing mothers for me, together with the shape of the purchasing mothers and the weapons that they carry. Some of the names that he gives differ from the above.

1. Sunday, name Lady cídtraawan; head and face of a lion, vermillion in color; left hand carries a bow, right hand carries a fan.

2. Monday, name Lady (man)thánaa noŋkhraan; head and face of a horse, white in color; right hand carries a sword, left hand carries a fan.

3. Tuesday, name Lady jâg bɔɔrísùd; head and face of an albino buffalo; right hand carries a sword, left hand carries a fan.

4. Wednesday, name Lady sàmùdthácháad; head and face of an elephant, orange in color; right hand carries a sword, left hand carries a fan.

5. Thursday, name Lady lôogkàwágkháthùg; head and face of a deer, light yellow in color; right hand carries a spear, left hand carries a fan.

6. Friday, name Lady jâg noŋjaw; head and face of an ox, yellow in color; left hand carries a bow, right hand carries a fan.

7. Saturday, name Lady ʔèegkhàmaalaj; head and face of a tiger, black in color; right hand carries a long-handled trident, left hand carries a fan.

If one considers the forms of the purchasing mothers he will see that their bodies are those of women, but the heads change according to the animals which the gods of the seven planets ride. I am puzzled as to why each one carries a fan, for it is precisely because each one carries a fan that the purchasing mothers are called mɛ̂ɛ wâaj mɛ̂ɛ wii [wii is an old Thai word for "fan"]. On the back of the sheet of cloth with the figure of the god tháaw

wêedsàwan that is hung over the cradle they draw a figure of the purchasing
mother having the body of a woman and the face of a horse. This would
logically mean that the child lying in the cradle was born on Monday, but
the artists who copy old pictures make it always a horse's head. No matter
what day the child was born, they draw a horse's head, not changing the face
according to the animals which the gods of the seven planets ride. From
this it can be seen that astrologers have invented something new; it is not
the original thing. As to what the faces of the other twenty-eight purchasing
mothers are like, I have found no mention. The figure of a woman and face
of a horse are strange. I have tried investigating the figures of gods and
spirits of various nationalities and have found many that have human bodies
and horse's heads, but they are all male gods and male spirits, not agreeing
with the matter of the purchasing mother with a horse's face. There is a
similarity to the graha spirits of India, whom they worship and ask to protect
children, but their faces are rather those of goats.

In the Yajurveda of India it is said that the spirits which come to molest children are collectively called graha (which probably means "to drag
off"; it is the name of evil spirits which cause children to be ill and die).
It says that there are nine, four males and five females, which have a special
name pūtanā (the name of a giantess, daughter of King Balī). In one text
it says that there are twelve spirits attending upon a child, all of them female spirits, called mātṛkā. These spirits usually come and pounce upon
children, or cause children to be ill. There is yet another spirit which the
Hindus reverence a great deal, called Sasthī (meaning "the sixth"). Six days
after a child's birth they must perform a ceremony of worshiping Sasthī,
which is a god or spirit attending the child's person. (In the Brahmavaivarta-
purāṇa it says that Sasthī is the favorite wife of Khandhakumāra.) The ceremony that is performed consists of taking four lumps of rice, one lump white,
one lump mixed with turmeric to make it yellow, one lump mixed with red
lime to make it red, and one lump mixed with ashes of chaff to make it
black. (Indians do not use earthenware pots, regarding them as unclean.
They must use metal pots for cooking and must polish them clean. Therefore they must use ashes of chaff instead of soot from the bottom of an earthenware pot.) These four lumps of rice are laid in a vessel and the ceremony
of worshiping is performed. During the worshiping they tell stories about
Sasthī, and then call the child to come and eat. [59]

The matter of the purchasing mother's rice and the story of Sasthī seem
to be similar to something found in a western book, that children six days old
often die of lockjaw (which has the symptoms of a stiff chin and twitching
muscles, similar to the disease called in Thai làq, which is caused by poison
from the navel when the umbilical cord is not cut properly and disease germs
arise). The people of India are very much afraid of this sixth day. They believe that Sasthī will change herself into a black cat (the cat is the mount of

Sasthī) or into a chicken or a dog and come to chew up the skull and heart of the child. They must stand watch and keep lights burning all night on this sixth day, to prevent cats or other animals from coming near. The Orāon people (a Dravidian group) are afraid of black cats. They believe that black cats are the spirits of women who died in childbirth; they will transform themselves and come to do harm to a woman who has given birth or to the newborn child, and so they must stand guard all night.[60] It is perfectly proper that they should be afraid of cats that might come to do harm to a newborn child, but it is stretching it a little too far to think that if a cat crosses a corpse the corpse will rise up.

To summarize what has been said, the purchasing mothers are evil spirits. It is fitting that their bodies and faces be made detestable and frightful, for example, like those of giants (jág), but the astrologers have gone astray in decreeing that their faces are those of the animals ridden by the gods of the seven planets. There is another strange point, that the spirits of children's illnesses and of epidemics are all female spirits.

Why must they mould four lumps of rice, of four colors, as in our throwing of the purchasing mother's rice? I have inquired of Hindus and obtained no information. The Tamil have a ceremony called dṛṣṭiparihāra which employs lumps of rice of various colors. Brahman P.S. Sastri has related to me the following: "I have seen this performed only once at a wedding ceremony. I recall that there were lumps of black, red, white, and yellow rice. A woman performed the ceremony, and she let no one know what she spoke when she performed the ceremony, or where she threw away the lumps of rice. In the case of a child they perform the dṛṣṭiparihāra ceremony only in abbreviated form: they use rice of only one color; it is usually a lump of rice floating in water in which turmeric and white lime are dissolved. If they use lumps of white rice, they hold them in both hands and encircle the child three times, the right hand circling to the right and the left hand circling to the left. Then I believe they throw the rice over the roof. I have never heard Tamil people speak of purchasing mothers." What is described here seems to be the same as the throwing of the rice of the purchasing mother.

The Vietnamese also have a custom of moulding lumps of colored rice. When the child has reached the age of one month, they shave the fire hair, which they perform as a ceremony with glutinous rice moulded into three lumps, one lump dyed red and one lump dyed yellow, and there is also a cup of pulse boiled with sugar, to offer to the bâa mùu, that is, the spirit connected with children. This matter is very close to the throwing of the purchasing mother's rice. As regards the colors, according to Indian belief yellow, red, and black are detested by spirits. The color red is good to use in chasing away spirits for it is the color of fire and of the god of flames.[61]

The Palaung people have a belief that when they build a new house it is very bad if a dove flies into it; they must perform a ceremony to remedy matters. They make five balls of rice and color them green, red, black, yellow, and white. Then they cut up paper of various colors and make flags which they fix in the balls of rice so that the colors match. A little curry and tobacco is mixed with the rice. They find a bowl of water, and then place all of these things at the door or window. They recite a magic spell and then throw out the balls of rice, following them with the water. If a dog eats this rice that is thrown out, it is regarded as a good omen. [62]

This is a ceremony similar to our throwing the rice of the purchasing mother. According to northeastern custom, when they perform the ceremony of averting evil they also throw white, black, red, and yellow rice.

Why are four lumps of purchasing mother's rice used? Perhaps this means that they are for the purchasing mother of the city above, the purchasing mother who treads the path, the purchasing mother of the city below, and the purchasing mother under the bed, for the number is just right, and also only three lumps are thrown, the other lump, black, being tossed under the house. Probably this refers to the purchasing mother under the bed. Or the throwing of four lumps of rice may be an offering to the spirits of the four directions, like offerings to spirits in other ceremonies in which offerings are placed on banana leaves and laid out in the four directions. But in this case they do not throw them in various directions, so I do not know the reason for doing it.

The encircling of the child with rice is comparable to the āratī ceremony of India, already described. It would seem that the encircling of the child is due to a desire that the disease or spirit come out, as with the people of some settlements in the western part of the island of Borneo. If anyone is suddenly and violently ill, they believe that a spirit has possessed him. The doctors are mostly old women. The doctor takes a stick of wood and whittles it into the shape of a human being. She touches this seven times to the head of the patient, saying, "O disease, this figure will substitute for the patient. Enter this figure!" Then she puts white rice, salt, and tobacco into a small basket together with the figure, and lays this down in a place that is believed to have been the dwelling-place of the spirit. She sets the figure upright and then says, "O spirit, this is the figure that substitutes for the patient. Release the soul of the patient and then enter into this figure, for it is truly more beautiful and fine than the patient." This is a matter of using figures and food to entice the spirit or disease out. In the Invocation of the Purchasing Mother it says, "Do you go and admire the figure in the offering," and our ceremony of propitiation would seem similar in the purpose for which it is performed. Therefore the lumps of rice of the purchasing mother are perhaps food to entice the purchasing mother to come out. Why do spirits like to eat rice, and not fresh, raw things as is generally understood? Probably we acquired the idea of rice offerings from India, but their rice offerings are made to the spirits of deceased ancestors, and are a symbol that the dead ancestors still come and share the meals with the family and are not cut off. Or perhaps the performance has been modified from the offerings to the purchasing mother mentioned in the Invocation of the Purchasing Mother, which we know are still sometimes made.

Perhaps the throwing of the rice of the purchasing mother is like the Chinese throwing of liquor to offer to spirits because they do not know how to send it to the spirits except by throwing it out. In India there is a custom of taking balls of rice and small offerings and throwing them up into the air behind the house. In the Laws of Manu it is said in two places (chapter 3, sections 83 and 90) that when one has finished making an offering he is to toss the sacrificial rice in four directions, beginning with the east and circling to the right, i.e., to the east, south, west, and north, in order to dedicate it to the gods Indra, Yama, Varuna, and Soma together with their attendants. Perhaps we acquired the rite of throwing rice from this ceremony.

The Khwăn and Shaving of the Fire-Hair Ceremonies

Three days after the child's birth it is regarded as having passed one stage of danger of being a spirit child. The parents are glad of this and arrange a khwăn ceremony. [63] This khwăn ceremony is not done showily; they probably perform only an abbreviated ceremony among the family, not informing many people. The reason for doing it quietly is probably that they have not yet lost their fear that the spirits will come and carry the child away. Only when the child is a full month old do they perform the big fire-hair-shaving and khwăn ceremonies. They have probably lost their fear and believe that the child will survive, and therefore the big khwăn ceremony is performed when the child is a full month old.

In the third-day khwăn ceremony they arrange a baaj sĭi in a dish and offerings to sacrifice to the spirit of the place, including an Ophicephalus fish made into soup, a young coconut, a bunch of water bananas, boiled red pudding and boiled white pudding and other sweets as may be appropriate, and flowers, incense sticks, and candles. The equipment used in the khwăn ceremony includes scented powder, scented oil, or perfumed flour to anoint the white rice placed in the metal bowl in which three candleholders are set. [64] Then they bring the magic thread of cotton and enchant it, tying it to both wrists of the child; this is called "tying" the khwăn. Then they bestow blessings in the customary way. At this point they may transfer the child from the flat basket to its cloth cradle, but in some cases they have it continue to sleep in the basket.

Also, on the third day parents whose children usually do not survive or are as they say hard to raise customarily invite a person who raises children successfully to come and tie the khwăn for the child. In the days when there

were fýaŋ and sàlÿŋ coins, the object that was tied was one of these coins
which they were to purchase from a widow or they made the purchased coin
into a "spirit-fetter" bracelet, that is, a smooth bracelet which could be adjusted in size. The person invited to come and perform the khwǎn ceremony
was usually the person who purchased the fýaŋ or sàlÿŋ coin from a widow or
the person who made it into a bracelet. The parents of the child must pay
the person tying the khwǎn an amount of money equal to the price of the silver tied on. In tying the khwǎn they used raw cotton thread tied on the
wrists; it must be tied with a square knot. Sometimes a small lock was also
strung on it, with the idea of having tied the khwǎn and locked it. This lock
was a little odd in that it was made from the wood from a support under the
monks' water closet, cutting off only a little and carving it into the form of
a Thai lock. An elderly person has told me that this Thai lock was a brass
lock like a Chinese lock, except that in the center there was a sharp pro-
jection like a girl's cache-sexe, in which a hole was bored for inserting the
key to unlock it. The key was like that of a European lock; after turning it
they squeezed the lock, causing the bolt to slide to the side. But it may be
that this kind of lock is Malayan, and we received it from them.

If they do not tie on a lock, they may substitute the bone of a frog's
leg, which is like a Chinese lock in shape, or may tie on a vulture's bone
made into a cylindrical talisman. This is probably the oldest of all. Sometimes they tie on little bells. Things that are tied on in place of a lock are
understandable as meaning that the khwǎn is tied on to remain with the body,
but why are little bells tied on? It might be said that it is good to tie them
so that when the child wanders off we will know from the sound of the bells,
but that would be for bigger children who can come and go, whereas in what
is described the child is still small, and there is no need for knowing where
the child has gone from the sound of the bell. I have obtained a clue from
the beliefs of the people of the part of Africa called the Slave Coast, that
when a child is ill and thin it is believed that it is inhabited by a spirit. They
must tie iron hoops and little bells to the child's ankles, and place a great
many iron hoops around its neck. They say that the sound of the iron and
bells knocking together will frighten the spirit away.

Customs concerning tying the khwǎn for children resemble other customs concerning birth; the methods depend upon the locality and the time
and the popular beliefs thereof. In times and places that are not yet advanced, they do these things simply. Later their practices may change and
become more elaborate, but a clue as to their origins remain. You can see
this in my critique on khwǎn ceremonies, which have been already treated in
detail separately.

Shaving the Fire-Hair. When a child reaches the age of one month and one
day (probably they wish to make sure that it is a full month, and so they add

another day), it is past danger from illnesses which are understood to be in-
flicted by spirits. They arrange a big fire-hair-shaving and khwăn ceremony.
Sometimes they also name the child at this time; this is a matter of receiving the newborn child into the register of membership in the family.

In shaving the fire hair they must make an offering for the spirit of the
place according to custom. When they shave the hair they leave a clump at
the top of the head, saying that it protects the top of the head which is still
thin. The hair that is shaved off is placed in a banana-leaf container with a
Caladium or lotus leaf laid in the bottom; sometimes flowers are mixed in.
In cases where things are done well, the whole is placed in turn on a stand.
Then it is taken and floated on the water at low water, or is thrown away,
whichever is convenient. The person who takes it and floats it must say,
"We ask for a life of coolness and happiness like the sacred Ganges," or some -
thing else of this sort. In the Grhyasūtra text of India it is prescribed that the
hair that is cut or shaved is to be hidden in a cowshed or in a pool or in a
place near water. Our floating the hair on the water is probably derived from
this last Indian custom; it was probably inconvenient for us to put the hair in
a cowshed as in the first custom. Then the relatives perform a ceremony of
tying the khwăn cotton thread around the child's wrists and ankles, and give
a blessing according to custom; or if things are done well there are also gifts
for the child. What has been described is the ceremony which ordinary people may perform. In the case of wealthy or prominent people the ceremony
may be as large as their resources, ability, and birth permit. That is, they
must have an astrologer name the auspicious day for the khwăn ceremony;
there must be Brahman and astrologer's ceremonial things (the astrologer goes
and speaks in a low tone beside the eye-level shrine on which offerings are
laid; what he says I do not know, but if you ask an astrologer he can no
doubt tell you); there are various offerings;[65] there must be a baaj sĭi;[66]
there is a person to perform the khwăn ceremony, called the child's purchasing mother; there is encircling with candles; and there are monks to give
Buddhist chants in this ceremony. Sometimes the pot containing the afterbirth which has been saved is also entered in this ceremony, together with
the silver and gold coconuts for planting when the afterbirth is buried. What
has been described briefly is not always performed exactly like this. There
are sometimes additions or deletions. It is rather a matter which depends on
one's teacher.

In the evening the monks recite their Buddhist chants. Next morning
the holy water that they have blessed by their chants is placed in a big metal
bowl and set in the ceremonial circle. The child is placed with its face
turned in the direction prescribed by the astrologer. When the auspicious
moment arrives the elderly person who is presiding is invited to pour holy
water from a conch shell over the head of the child, and then he cuts the
hair with scissors. At that moment the monks give the victory chant. If

there are Brahmans they blow conch shells and rattle their ceremonial drums, and the astrologer worships the auspices. The orchestra plays a piece of victory and blessing. When the ceremony is finished, the child is turned over to others to shave the fire hair. They put the shaved hair in a banana-leaf container with a Caladium or lotus leaf, set this in turn on a stand, and then take the banana-leaf container and float it on the water. This is a brief account of the fire-hair-shaving ceremony according to mingled Buddhism and Hinduism. This is chiefly an affair of wealthy city dwellers. There are a great many ceremonial details, too many to relate; even if I were to describe them there might be omissions or misunderstandings, for my knowledge is not sufficient for me to give a detailed description. I have asked persons who have this sort of knowledge, but they usually guard their textbooks closely, not allowing one to borrow or examine them. It is impossible to criticize them, for this is their way of making a living; if they alone know, no one can say whether they perform correctly or incorrectly. I speak in this way because it applies to myself. On second thought, I wonder if it is possible that there are no written textbooks, and so they say simply that they cannot lend them, for in olden times in Thailand there were few writers of textbooks; what there were, were only on things that could not be remembered, such as medical books. Even if the owner of a textbook died he could not take the textbook with him; the textbooks would have had to survive for us to see.

The leaving of a clump of hair in the middle of the top of the head in shaving the fire hair, and then leaving this hair to grow long, is in order to leave a topknot and perform a topknot-shaving ceremony when the child grows up and is almost to reach the period of young manhood or young womanhood. I have seen Chinese children with a clump of hair on the top of the head and the rest shaved smooth. Sometimes there is a patch of hair toward the side, or sometimes two such patches. This makes one wonder, if it is to protect the thin top of the head, why patches are left on the side also. Sometimes a clump of hair is left forward, beyond the center of the head. Sometimes the clump is precisely at the whorl in the hair. One is reminded of some groups of people in Java and Malaya who, when they shave a child's head, leave a clump of hair. They believe that this is to provide a dwelling place for the khwǎn, and that if no hair is left the khwǎn will have no place to stay and so will flee elsewhere, causing the child to fall ill or even to die. Even if there are head lice and it is necessary to shave off the hair, they refuse to shave it all off; they must leave a clump so that the khwǎn will have a place to stay.

Leaving hair in the center of the head is probably the same sort of belief, because the top of a child's head is thin and can be seen to pulsate, as if the khwǎn or life were right there. In India they call this thin spot at the top of the skull the brahmarandhara because they believe that the soul of a person enters and leaves at that point. When a Yogi dies they usually break the skull at that point to assist the soul to leave the body easily. This is the same sort of belief. Later they substituted a dried coconut shell, which we also took over; that is, we break a coconut before cremating a corpse.

Ceremony of Entering the Cradle. When the khwǎn and shaving-the-fire-hair ceremony is finished, they perform a ceremony of placing the child in the cradle. They are to procure a white gourd (washing it clean and then smearing it with flour), a medicine-pounding mortar and pestle, and a tomcat. They must tidy up the cat first. Besides these things there are small cloth bags, one filled with paddy, one with pulse, one with sesame, and one with cottonseed; there may also be other things depending on cases. (These are like the things prepared for the ceremony of making a bridal bed and the ceremony of entering a new house.) These things are laid in the cradle. If the child to enter the cradle is a boy, there are to be a notebook and pencil; if it is a girl, there are to be a thread and needle laid in the cradle also (if this was not already done at the time of bouncing on a basket, already described). Besides these there may also be a baaj sǐi in a dish and encircling with candles. In some places they also make an offering to the cradle. When the objects named above have been placed in the cradle they begin at once to swing it because the cat does not like this and if there is any delay it will jump out of the cradle. When they have swung it three times they take the cat out of the cradle and carry the child in the arms and put it in the cradle in place of the cat. They swing it three times in the same way, pronouncing a blessing upon the child according to custom, as they swing it. Thus the ceremony is finished. If the child is also to be named at this time, some teachers write the child's name on a paper and lay it in the cradle also.

Of the various things, including the cat, that are placed in the cradle, the rice and vegetable products probably refer to prosperity and fertility, while the gourd, pestle, and cat probably refer to the proverbial blessing, "May you be cool as a gourd and heavy as a pumpkin; may you stay at home like the stones of the fireplace, and guard the house like a tomcat." This is a blessing given by old people not only to children; when they bless a bridal couple they use the same words. It is probably a very old blessing, for the words are simple and ordinary, unlike the blessings that are pronounced today, which contain terribly few old Thai words. The "pestle" in the blessing is "stones of a fireplace." Probably the stones of the fireplace were earlier, and were changed to a medicine pestle later. The change is a good thing, for stones of a fireplace are terribly dirty and unpleasant. As for the tomcat it is a large male cat, an adult cat with whiskers. If compared to a human being, it is like a person who has attained legal age, and so it is a cat that does not abandon its home. Its superstitious use can be understood. Tidying up the cat before putting it in the cradle is a good thing, as protection against dirt resulting from its fondness for sleeping on the stove.

Rearing Children

When a child is about three months old and has become stronger, it can roll over on its belly. The first time that it rolls over on its belly, they usually lay a metal bowl of cold water on its back. They explain that they do this because when a child turns over on its belly its face will drop down; it does not yet know how to bend its head backward, and might turn on its belly, stick its face in the pillow, and be unable to breathe, which might be dangerous. They place the bowl of water on the child's back and it no doubt feels that there is something heavy and cold, and so it is automatically startled and throws back its head. Later if it turns over on its belly it may be able to raise its head of itself because of the experience. If an adult helps to hold the child's head up when it turns over on its belly, no one has ever seen it. The child might not learn to help itself, even though it has the physical ability. It is probably for this reason that in olden times they forbade helping a child directly when it practiced turning over on its belly or walking; they preferred to have the child learn to help itself. This means that they knew the correct methods of teaching.

At the age of three months, the child may be allowed to eat some rice mashed up with nám wáa bananas; that is, mix cooked rice with a little salt and pound it up with the bananas till a paste is formed, or the bananas may be first cooked. Only the flesh of the bananas is to be used; the hard core is not used, because it is said to be hard to digest. For bananas to feed to children, select the kind that have white or light yellow cores. Bananas with pink cores are not popular because they are sour and not good to eat. These bananas with pink cores are called by a special name, kàlîa ฉจ๊ฎ bananas, sometimes distorted to mãlîa. For a utensil to mash up the rice and bananas use a coconut-shell spoon; that is, cut and scrape a coconut-shell to make it the shape of a spoon, and then rub and polish it till it is smooth and lovely. Take this coconut-shell spoon and mash up the rice and bananas in a vessel such as a bowl until they are seen to be fine and well mixed. Then take up the mashed rice with the hands and form it into small lumps of appropriate size and feed these to the child. If it ate rice alone this might stick in its throat, and so water must be dropped as well. Dip all five fingers into a vessel containing cold water and then draw the fingers together to hold a little bit of water, and let this drip into the mouth of the child in order to moisten its mouth and facilitate swallowing. In some cases this mashed rice is put in a vessel and set on the fire to cook the rice, unless the bananas have already been cooked.

From what has been described it may be seen how short of things our ancestors were; for vessels they had only coconut shells, which are natural products. We call thick, poor quality, enameled dishes "coconut-shell" dishes. This is probably a name surviving from the times when coconut-shell

dishes were used instead of china dishes. There are still vessels made of coconut shell, including water dippers, ladles, curry spoons, and rice-measuring
vessels. A coconut-shell water bowl can also be used instead of a mirror;
there is still a saying surviving to this day, when one would criticize a person for not having taken a good look at himself: "You did not dip up water
and put it in a coconut-shell bowl and bend over to look at your reflection."
Today we have progressed and can have better, more beautiful, and more
convenient utensils, but in some rural localities they still like to use vessels
made of coconut-shell, because they are convenient and easily found, not
requiring unnecessary expense to buy these things. Actually coconut shells
are produced on an elevated place, but we usually turn them into various
kinds of vessels for low use, for example for washing the feet or buttocks.
This has given the coconut shell a low status. Even if it is polished and
smoothed beautifully, we never get away from the notion that it is a low and
poor thing. The use of the fingers to dip up water and drip it into the child's
mouth is also more due to the lack of small-sized spoons to use than anything
else. What has been said applies only to poor people. Even wealthy people
sometimes do the same, following easy and effortless methods. Some people
use spoons made of clamshells, called clamshell spoons, for dipping up water
to drip into the child's mouth instead of using the fingers. Nowadays we also call china spoons "clamshell spoons." People who still use coconut-shell
spoons to mash rice for children to eat, not using better spoons even though
they have them, explain that they deceive spirits that the child that they are
feeding is a child of no consequence, and so they use a poor coconut-shell
spoon to feed it. Some people say that if they use vessels made of china the
china may break and chip into the rice. This is probably a question of always having done one thing and so continuing to do it. Even though it is
seen to be inappropriate, they still do it, and so must find various rationali-
zations, for customs are slow to die.

There is another method of feeding rice to children. They chew the
rice up fine, sometimes with banana also, and then take it out of the mouth
and feed it to the child, at the same time dipping the fingers in water and
dripping it into the child's mouth. The Shans call this sort of rice khâaw
màm. Feeding rice to children in this way is certainly not good. It is probably a custom surviving from very long ago. No doubt many nationalities
did this when they were still at a low stage of advancement. Perhaps it is believed that the saliva of the chewer also helps to digest the rice for the child.
Formerly I frequently saw khâaw màm. Usually those seen to do this were
low-class Chinese women. It is a practice of uneducated people, not a general thing.

I forgot to describe the ceremony of opening the mother's breasts,
which is performed the first time they let the child suck the breast. The
ceremony of opening the breasts is more frequently performed among

aristocrats than among common people. They invite a woman who raises children successfully -- if it is an aristocratic woman of prominence, all the better -- to come and suck the breasts as an auspicious first event. They believe that if they do this the child will grow big and not be ill.

When the child reaches the age of seven months, it will be able to rise up and assume a squatting position, or in some cases will be able actually to sit up. When another month has passed, it is able to crawl. Some do not crawl; they inch or shove themselves along on the buttocks. Next, at an age of approximately nine months, the period is reached for the teeth to appear, called "flowers arising." They forbid referring to these as "teeth"; for what reason, I do not know; or perhaps they believe that such words as "tooth" [which is homonymous with a verb meaning "to slash, cut"] are not auspicious words. (In old people whose teeth are all lost, if new teeth appear they call them faaŋ, not "teeth" (fan); actually fan and faaŋ are probably the same word.) Next the child will practice standing, called "setting up an egg"; then it practices walking. The time periods that have been mentioned are only approximations, because there are also some children who are faster or slower to learn than this. The Chinese texts fix these periods as follows: "Seven sit, eight crawl, nine teeth arise." The Thai have it: "Three lift (probably meaning to lift the head), six sit."

During the period that the child is learning to sit and crawl, its teeth appear, and it practices standing, the child usually has symptoms of fever, choking, and diarrhea at each stage; some children have none of these, and some have some of the symptoms at some of the stages. This is all probably due to changes and growth of the organs, causing abnormal symptoms at every stage. These symptoms are regarded as an ordinary thing; they say that if they are disregarded for three or four days they disappear of themselves. It is merely forbidden to speak of them. It is believed that if [these symptoms] are mentioned, the child will have diarrhea as many times as one speaks. If it is observed that three or four days have passed and the child has not yet recovered, this is suspicious, and they summon a doctor. They set up a metal bowl filled with rice, which in former times contained money for the fee for treatment in the amount of one and one half bàat. If the child has fever they usually perform a rite of throwing the purchasing mother's rice. In some cases they swab the throat, using lemongrass bulbs and a little salt, ground up on the bottom of a pot or in the lid, as medicine for swabbing. The medicine that is left over from swabbing the child's throat they smear on its forehead; this is the same sort of thing as anointing. They believe that it prevents recognition by the spirits, for the illness of the child shows that spirits would come and take it away. This is the way they treat the child; if it still does not recover they go and see a doctor.

At the time when the "flowers arise," in some places they take gold, which may be a ring or anything which is gold, and rub the child's teeth gently, believing that the child will have a mouth of silver and gold. Or there may also be other reasons; I have not been able to ascertain clearly. Probably this is the sort of thing which in English is called "sympathetic magic." In some cases at this stage they mash up rice mixed with gold and have the child eat it, believing this will cause its voice to be euphonious and its complexion to be like gold. [67]

When the child is able to stand up for the first time they call it "setting up the egg," because it still cannot stand up straight for a long time; it is like an egg placed on end, and so it is called thus. At this time the child will try to take steps. The ancients forbade helping the child walk, because this would keep the child from learning to help itself. They therefore have a method of teaching walking: they have the child stand against the wall, with its back and arms braced against the wall. Then it tries to take a step. An adult stands in front of the child at a short distance, making a gesture with the arms of receiving the child. The child will stagger forward toward the adult. The first time it will be able to take only one or two steps before falling. The adult in front of the child must take care to catch it, not allowing it to fall. Then it tries to take a step again. At the time when the child can hardly hold itself up straight, the adult sings out, "Set up an egg; if the egg falls, boil it and eat it. If the egg falls to the ground, I'll eat it up."[68] This singing is to amuse and distract the child, so that it will learn to stand up and take steps. After a child has sufficient skill in taking steps, some people make a circle of wood for the child to cling to and walk and turn itself around, to make it stronger and more agile.

When a child is able to prattle, but not yet in language, it is called "playing with saliva." Soon afterward it will practice speaking. If it speaks early it is called "light-mouthed." If it speaks late, perhaps only after one year, it is called "heavy-mouthed." If the child is heavy-mouthed to an abnormal degree, it may be a mute. One should observe by clapping one's hands to call the child behind its back; if the child turns to look, the child is not a mute, because mute children are usually deaf also. When one carries the child in one's arms and it points and cries "ʔɯ̌ɯ ʔá̂a," it can be observed that it is not a mute, but merely heavy-mouthed. If one calls or jests with the child behind its back and it does not hear, or if when it is carried it merely points and opens its mouth and cries "ʔɛ̌ɛ," and acts like this every time, the child is certainly a mute.

For children of wealthy aristocrats they have a mouth-opening ceremony. They invite a woman of good lineage who raises children successfully to come and speak auspicious words, teaching the child to speak politely and nicely. Sometimes they also give the name at this time. They usually seek out someone with knowledge of astrology to give the name, selecting the name according to the rules laid down in textbooks of astrology. (There are already books on the subject of giving names. They are not very hard to find;

it is therefore unnecessary to speak of this.) Some people have the mouth-opening ceremony on the next day after birth, but I regard this as inconvenient; one should not perform it at this stage.

On the subject of naming the child, probably no invariable time can be set down. In some cases, when they have shaved the fire hair they give the name at the same time. In some cases they wait until the child is big; when they go to turn it over to a monk to be his disciple, the monk who is its teacher names it. If one notices the names which were given in former times, they are seen to be Thai words, but at present names which are Thai words are very few indeed. Now names are mostly Pali and Sanskrit words. Probably people imitate the aristocracy, in order to avoid the names of ordinary peasants. In ancient times the giving of the name was probably a temporary matter. They called children according to sex and relative order, for example, ɋâaj, ĵîi, sǎam, and sîi. This sort of naming is also found among the Shans and among the Indonesians, that is, Javanese and Malays. Perhaps it also occurs among other nationalities. This sort of name is changed when the child goes to the monastery to study, or else when it reaches the age of three or four years; then a name is given in accordance with the rules that they believe in. If the child is often ill, or they think that the original name was not auspicious, they may rename the child, in order to make the spirits think it is a different person; they will not molest it and cause it to be ill often, this being a sign that the spirits would carry it off. Old-time names, such as Pig, Dog, Frog, Tree-toad, Worm, are probably names given to deceive the spirits that these are not people, but only pigs and dogs; the spirits will be convinced and will not carry them off. This is a phenomenon which in English is called "cacophemism," which occurs in old customs of all nations. Some names, such as Tiger and Elephant, are given according to dreams or events that occur. There are also names given according to the figure, face, and other characteristics of the child, such as Fat, Pudgy, Squat, Little, Topknot, Pigtails. These are probably names that people call the child, not real names that are given to it, and these names stick to the child and are not changed. Sometimes names are also given according to color, such as White, Red, Purple. There are also names given which are names of things of value, such as Silver, Gold, Jewel, Ring; or characteristics of wealth and prosperity, such as Much, Wealthy, Possessor. There are also names implying admirability; names of this sort are very numerous, such as Refreshing, Cheering, Graceful, Admirable. There are also many names of plants, such as Cinnamon, Sandal, Pinflower, Pandanus. There are also names which have no meaning, for example sěem, cɔɔn, cûj, lǎm. Probably some of this last group are shortened forms of words of many syllables, and probably some are distorted forms of words from other languages.

When a child is learning to sit, if it is often ill, besides renaming it, they usually also let patches of its hair grow. This is probably derived from the belief in the khwăn; they fear that the khwăn will flee, and so they leave locks of hair for the khwăn to reside in, as has already been described. Also if a child is fat, it is forbidden to speak of this or admire it as fat or lovable; one must speak the opposite, that it is detestable. This is a trick to deceive the spirits into not carrying the child away.

If a child's mother becomes pregnant again before it is weaned, the child usually is not strong; it is inclined to be ill and fretful. This is called "losing out to the younger sibling," for the mother's milk for feeding the child has less value than before she became pregnant; it is impure milk, and insufficient to give the child normal nourishment. The child must eat other things to help, some of which are difficult for a child to digest, and it eats irregularly, not at fixed times. Finally its digestion goes bad and its body gradually weakens. This may turn into the disease of bloated belly. If a child has symptoms of "losing out to the younger sibling," they employ the method of having the child's mother, when she bathes, take the child between her legs, her thighs holding the child so that its head projects and comes even with the upper edge of the lower garment. When she dips up water and bathes, part of the water flows off the edge of the cloth and falls directly onto the head of the child. This is done only enough to serve as a matter of form, until the child's head is wet, and then they stop. I do not know why they do this. I cannot think how this might cure the disease of "losing out to the younger sibling."

There are miscellaneous rites relating to the rearing of children which are performed by some people in some localities. For example, when they are going to take a child out of the house to spend the night elsewhere for the first time, they must first smear the child's face with soot, and then it may be taken out of the house. This is probably a matter of deceiving the spirits, as usual. Another one: if the parents have necessary business requiring them to go away overnight, they are to rip a cloth or cloth remnant which is part of the parents' clothing and tie or wind it around the child, saying, "Do not cry out for father and mother." When one considers this custom, it is moving, for it is a matter of love and concern for the child. They have nothing to fasten it with, so they use instead a part of their own clothing to tie it, for the garments are regarded as like oneself, as has been described in my book on the khwăn ceremony. According to a belief of the Palaungs, when a child is frequently sick they must smear its face with soot in order to make it unattractive to the spirits so that they will not carry it off. This is comparable to the practice of smearing with soot described above.

In the south they have a ceremony of the child treading on the ground. It is performed at the time when the mother of the child has emerged from the fire. They are to carry the child in the arms, holding a parasol over it, and arrange a stand on which are laid the clothing of the child, which a person carries after the child. The person carrying the child takes it down out

of the house to the ground, and then touches the child's foot to the ground;
or they may merely make a gesture, the foot of the child not actually touching the ground. This ceremony is similar to the earth-treading ceremony in
the northeast, but there they perform it on the day of birth, when the cord of
the afterbirth has been cut. In the ancient royal ceremonies such a rite also
occurs, called the royal ceremony celebrating the touching of the earth by
the king's children. This royal ceremony has long been abolished. [69]

When the child reaches the age of one year, if it is a boy there is usually something tied to its waist, such as a phallic talisman, a clamshell, or
cowries strung on a cord and called "paying-the-vow cowries." They tie
these on if the child is often ill; sometimes they tie them on [even] if it is
not ill. Sometimes they tie them at the neck, saying that they protect the
teeth. Sometimes they make silver and gold into the shapes of peppers or
other shapes; this belongs to the period when people had become wealthy.
Besides these, I cannot remember whether there are other things that they tie
on. If it is a girl, they usually tie a cache-sexe and figures of turtles around
the waist. I have read an account of customs of Ceylon concerning the tying
on of the cache-sexe, written by a westerner. He explains that it is not to
hide shame, but is to ward off spirits and protect [the child] from what westerners call the "evil eye." This is striking, for little children have no reason
to be ashamed or to hide anything; they are still in the age of innocence.
The belief that the cache-sexe is tied on to hide shame is perhaps an opinion
which arose later. The cache-sexe (càbpı̂ŋ) is also sometimes called càpı̂ŋ
and tàpı̂ŋ; it is a word derived from a Portuguese word referring to a metal
plate of small size for covering various holes and openings, as keyholes or in
boats. Then it came to be used with children. We probably got this custom
from the Malays, because formerly Malay girls also wore these cache-sexe
and called them by the same name. To speak only of our own country, the
cache-sexe most often seen in use is of silver. If it is better than that, it is
a cache-sexe of a copper-gold alloy. There are also cache-sexe of gold,
not merely of gold but also inlaid with green and red jewels. They say that
these golden cache-sexe are worn also even by some persons who are not children, but I have never seen this and so I can say nothing. If it is true, then
considered from the modern point of view it is terribly stupid. Poor people
sometimes make the cache-sexe out of coconut shell, and I have sometimes
seen these edged with silver. In later times the cache-sexe that has been
described came to take the form of a silver or golden mesh, like the cord
around the waist and a piece hanging down in front in ancient India, which
was called a girdle. Today these are no longer used because children have
to wear lower garments, lest the westerners criticize them as savages, and so
the cache-sexe is gone. The feeling of embarrassment of the child increases
because of wearing a lower garment. There is a matter I forgot to relate:
formerly girls wore anklets made of silver, copper-gold alloy, or gold,

depending upon the station. They wore them until puberty or later, if they had not yet established a household of their own, showing that formerly one could tell by looking at the ankles; if a girl wore anklets she was still unmarried and had no home of her own. Today anklets are worn only on the stage. Nevertheless they sometimes change from gold anklets to anklets made of cloth embroidered with gold.

Also, in the case of a child that is frequently ill and hardly likely to survive, if it is a boy, the parents usually take the child to "cast cloth in the forest,"[70] that is, to offer it to a monk. The monk who receives it takes cotton thread and ties it around the child's wrists. If it is a girl, the monk gives the cotton thread to them, for them to tie it themselves at home. The reason that the child is often ill is that spirits deliberately cause it to be ill; spirits hate adults, and can do nothing to adults, and so they work on children. If the child is not ours, but belongs to a monk, the spirits will not dare to continue to afflict it, for spirits fear monks. (Whether true or not, I do not know.) So the child recovers from illness. If a child falls accidentally and then afterward has symptoms of fever, the adults usually take a metal bowl with rice covered with a cloth and carry it together with a big spoon to the point where the child had the fall. They call out to the khwǎn, which they understand was left deserted from the moment of alarm. Then they dip up air as if dipping up the khwǎn, put it in the metal bowl, and return home. Then they have a khwǎn rite for the child that had the fall.[71]

While the child is lying in the cradle, besides singing lullabies and swinging it to sleep, there is also a fish or a waterskipper for the child to look at, hanging over the cradle toward the head, but not too high, for the child will roll its eyes upward to look at it. When a child rolls its eyes upward like this, they believe that this is a time when the purchasing mother comes to molest it. These fish are tied and woven of nipa palm leaves in the form of a fish of fairly large size, and painted green, red, and yellow. Then there are many small fish which are supposed to be its young, hanging from it. Even now these are sometimes seen for sale. As for the waterskipper, originally it was made of bamboo woven in the form of a waterskipper of the kind that has the body of a spider and swims on the top of the water. Later when there had been progress they took various remnants of colored or figured cloth and sewed them together, stuffing them with kapok like a square cushion with bulging center. At the corners were small triangular cushions, supposed to be its young, hanging down in a row, seven to each corner, arranged in descending sizes, but these young were not called waterskippers; they were given another name, that of "water chestnuts," because they were triangular in shape, resembling water chestnuts that are eaten. The sound of lullabies sung to children which one used to hear, a melancholy, tranquil, rhythmic sound, is not often heard now in Bangkok, because it has been replaced by the sound of cars, the sound of automobile horns, and other sounds.

The sound of lullabies can be heard only at a distance from crowded centers, and it is more frequent in huts and old houses than in brick buildings or modern houses. This is a matter of changing tastes. Formerly there were many lullabies; today so few can remember them all the way through that the melodies are becoming shorter and shorter. Finally they will probably become antiques existing only in the museum. There is also the matter of amusing children, as by spreading out the hand and turning it back and forth in front of the child's face while crying, "They are bringing Granny in a procession; when they reach the pavilion they set Granny down." These may also disappear in the same way. (Fortunately H.R.H. Prince Damrong Rajanubhab ordered the Royal Institute to collect these verses in all localities, lullabies, teasing verses, and children's playing verses. If they vanish from memory, they will then survive only in the National Library.)

There remains another matter, namely, the dolls and toys of children. One that I have seen ever since childhood is the Brahman doll. A good kind is the palace-dweller doll, modeled of clay and then fired and painted. It is a small figure of a palace lady, wearing a figured lower garment and a diagonally draped stole, in a sitting position resting on an arm. This is a girl's doll. If it is for a boy, there are tumbling dolls made of straw paper and then painted, hollow inside, usually in the form of a child with a topknot. At the buttocks there is a clay weight to make it heavy. When it is pushed over, it automatically rights itself. Then there are also figures of very fat children painted bright yellow, likewise made of paper and hollow inside. There are also masks and other sorts of things which I cannot remember. I recall only small leather drums and small cymbals, which are Chinese things, not Thai. Drums which children make themselves for fun are sugarpot drums. They stretch rags over the mouth of a sugarpot, and then fasten them tight at the sides with clay, beating the sides of the sugarpot with a stick to make the cloth tight. Then they mix mud with water and smear it on the cloth, and beat it with a stick to make a noise that deafens the neighbors. However great their strength, they put it all into the beating, until the sugarpot drum can stand no more and breaks to pieces, and then they make a new one. Besides these, they model oxen and buffaloes of clay. I have never seen them model elephants and horses, probably because they are harder to model. Then they also model cups with the thinnest possible bottoms, to cast face down with full force on the ground, to make a loud explosion which breaks the thin bottom of the cup open into a large or small hole, depending upon the case. The other children in the game must pay up an amount of clay equal to that lost in the explosion. They take turns playing in this way until they are bored, and then they stop. I believe that games involving modeling of clay probably existed before others. As the period of progress was reached and better dolls and children's toys were imported from abroad, the old things vanished. Wherever progress is retarded, some of these old things still remain.

The change is gradual, following in the wake of national progress. It makes one feel he would like to get an old-fashioned doll to have to look at, to serve as a memento of the days when one was a child. But no one makes them for sale as they did so generally in the old days, because if they made them no one would buy them. There is nothing beautiful about them; why make them? There are still some, only of the hollow paper doll kind. These are figures of elephants and horses and actors which they make to offer to spirits and to the guardian spirit of the land. Even so, the figures of actors are cut out of paper rather than modeled of clay. This means people are more clever, but this is cleverness mixed with cheating. They assume that the spirits do not object, and so they make them worse, and the spirits can do nothing. There are also Brahman dolls offered. These are probably offered for the spirit to take and use as servants. There are still corpses of more than ten Brahman dolls at a spirit house right here in Phuttan Gardens.

Footnotes to <u>Customs Connected with Birth and the Rearing of Children</u>

1. <u>Tamjɛɛ</u>, "nettle."

2. "<u>Tamjɛɛ</u> doctors."

3. Crooke, William, <u>Religion</u> and <u>Folklore of Northern</u> India (London, A. Constable, 1896), p. 203. <u>A.R.</u>

4. See my <u>Customs Connected with Death</u>. <u>A.R.</u>

5. Meaning "assorted or miscellaneous." We call all wood, with the exception of teak and a few other kinds, "five species." <u>A.R.</u>

6. Pronounced in Thai, <u>námoo phúdthátàdsàʔ</u>.

7. "Cut" in Thai is <u>tàd</u>.

8. The word for grandchild in Thai also includes nephews and nieces.

9. Glowworms.

10. Bull's-eye lanterns. <u>A.R.</u>

11. Enlightened one.

12. The Thai word for "east" is "the sun comes out," and the word for "south" is the same as the word for "down."

13. "Stitches" translates an anatomical term referring to the tissues at the rear of the female organ.

14. Literally, "woman who receives."

15. Prolapsis uteri.

16. Hemorrhoids.

17. A Thai term for the female organ.

18. Thai euphemism for the male organ.

19. A slipknot with two loops like a rabbit ear and the two ends of the string spreading outward. A.R.

20. A thornless bamboo.

21. A high rank, usually a child of the king.

22. Literally, the "mother" or "woman" who "raises" or "lifts."

23. Cf. p. 126, footnote 14.

24. See the subject of camphor leaves in my Customs Connected with Death. A.R.

25. Le May, Reginald Stuart, An Asian Arcady: The Land and Peoples of Northern Siam (Cambridge, W. Heffer & Sons, 1926), p. 191. A.R.

26. See my work on ceremonial fences. A.R.

27. See the subject of thɔɔráaniisǎan holy water in my Customs Connected with Death. A.R.

28. "Rafters" or "rafter bones" are the pelvic bones on either side of the vagina.

29. Used as face powder.

30. See the section on the color red in my book on Customs Connected with House Building. A.R.

31. The cabalistic design trínisímhe will be discussed in a separate section. A.R.

32. Buddhist protective stanzas.

33. In Thai, sǎaj sǐn is the name for the magic thread.

34. "Eight or nine houses" is a Thai idiom which means "far away" and reflects the people's mode of living in the old days. A.R.

35. Lady Monthoo, wife of Thódsàkan, king of the giants in the Thai Rama epic, is known to all Thai young and old as "Lady Monthoo with only one developed breast."

36. Original parenthesis in English.

37. Encyclopaedia of Religion and Ethics, Vol. 10, p. 465. A.R.

38. Milne, Mrs. Leslie, The Home of an Eastern Clan (Oxford, 1924), p. 279. A.R.

39. Literally, "to be in karma."

40. With kam spelled simply kam, not karma.

41. Probably taken from the little book, Customs of the Palace and Royalty, by the named author, better known as Phájaa Theewaa, the Lord Chancellor.

42. Stevenson, Margaret, The Rites of the Twice-Born (London, Oxford, 1920). A.R.

43. The original is a neat, pithy rhyme.

44. The original is a rhyme similar to the above.

45. The Thai phrase "good thing" is often used to mean "something having magic power," and the author probably intended some of this meaning to be suggested here.

46. An aromatic sedge.

47. Original parenthesis in English.

48. A simple round basket which is inverted over chickens.

49. The best black cotton cloth in Thailand is that dyed with this substance, because the color is unusually fast.

50. The Thai term could also mean blood vessel or tendon.

51. A Thai idiom for happiness, since coolness rather than warmth is desirable in Thailand.

52. These are very common Thai names.

53. Skeat, Walter W. and Charles O. Blagden, Pagan Races of the Malay Peninsula (London, Macmillan, 1906). A.R.

54. Literally, "royal lineage."

55. "First fruits" is given in both Thai and English in the original.

56. A famous reading primer dating from the reign of King Chulalongkorn.

57. Encyclopaedia of Religion and Ethics, Vol. 2, p. 639. A.R.

58. In Thai, "doctor" is mɔ̌ɔ; "midwife" is mɔ̌ɔ tamjɛɛ; and "witch" is mɛ̂ɛ mód. Often a single word is expanded by adding another, many times meaningless word. The word mɔ̌ɔ (doctor) takes the expander mód, giving the phrase mód mɔ̌ɔ, also meaning "doctor."

59. Noted down as Swami Satyanandapuri told me. A.R.

60. Encyclopaedia of Religion and Ethics, Vol. 9, p. 504. A.R.

61. See my book Customs Connected with House Building. A.R.

62. Milne, Mary Lewis, Home of an Eastern Clan: A Study of the Palaungs of the Shan States (Oxford, Clarendon Press, 1924), p. 184. A.R.

63. The khwǎn is an individual's soul, spirit, morale, or life-force. At times of crisis the khwǎn is believed to leave, and must be called back. In many Thai idioms the word khwǎn is best translated as "morale." The same word is used for the whorl in the hair, and some children have two khwǎn in this material sense.

64. Candleholders here are flat, leaf-shaped objects of metal, with handles to grasp, against the side of which the candles are fixed.

65. See my work on offerings. A.R.

66. See the subject of the baaj sǐi in my work on the khwǎn. A.R.

67. A glowing golden skin is a Thai ideal. Turmeric is used to achieve and enhance this; monks are admired for their golden skin, caused by the dye in their yellow robes.

68. The original is a neat verse, like a nursery rhyme.

69. See the critique on Hindu customs of the twelve months in Collected Miscellaneous Writings by H.R.H. Prince Damrong Rajanubhab. A.R.

70. The idiom "cast cloth in the forest" refers to a custom of giving robes, etc. to monks without specifying a particular recipient, by putting them on a tree where they are supposed to be found accidentally by a monk. Here the process is not described but apparently the child is "given" to a monk.

71. See my work on the khwǎn rites. A.R.